PREVAIL

PREVAIL

365 DAYS OF ENDURING STRENGTH
FROM GOD'S WORD

SUSIE LARSON

BETHANYHOUSE
a division of Baker Publishing Group
Minneapolis, Minnesota

Published by Bethany House Publishers
11400 Hampshire Avenue South
Minneapolis, Minnesota 55438
www.bethanyhouse.com

Bethany House Publishers is a division of
Baker Publishing Group, Grand Rapids, Michigan

Printed in the United States of America

Library of Congress Cataloging-in-Publication Data is on file at the Library of Congress, Washington, DC.

ISBN 978-0-7642-3393-7

Unless otherwise indicated, Scripture quotations are from the Holy Bible, New Living Translation, copyright © 1996, 2004, 2015 by Tyndale House Foundation. Used by permission of Tyndale House Publishers, Inc., Carol Stream, Illinois 60188. All rights reserved.

Scripture quotations identified ESV are from The Holy Bible, English Standard Version® (ESV®), copyright © 2001 by Crossway, a publishing ministry of Good News Publishers. Used by permission. All rights reserved. ESV Text Edition: 2016

Scripture quotations identified MSG are taken from THE MESSAGE, copyright © 1993, 2002, 2018 by Eugene H. Peterson. Used by permission of NavPress. All rights reserved. Represented by Tyndale House Publishers, Inc.

Scripture quotations labeled NIV are from THE HOLY BIBLE, NEW INTERNATIONAL VERSION®, NIV® Copyright © 1973, 1978, 1984, 2011 by Biblica, Inc.® Used by permission. All rights reserved worldwide.

Scripture quotations identified NKJV are from the New King James Version®. Copyright © 1982 by Thomas Nelson. Used by permission. All rights reserved.

Scripture quotations identified VOICE are from The Voice Bible Copyright © 2012 Thomas Nelson, Inc. The Voice™ translation © 2012 Ecclesia Bible Society All rights reserved.

Cover design by Kathleen Lynch/Black Kat Design
Cover art and interior art on pages 13, 42–3, 72–3, 102–3, 132–3, 162–3, 192–3, 222–3, 252–3, 282–3, 312-3, 342–3, and 372–3 by Joyce Klassen; "Acrylic Pour." Remaining interior art by Paul Higdon. Interior design by William Overbeeke

Author represented by The Steve Laube Agency

Baker Publishing Group publications use paper produced from sustainable forestry practices and post-consumer waste whenever possible.

21 22 23 24 25 26 27   10 9 8 7 6 5 4

To Jesus . . .
The more I know You, the more I love You;
I cannot wait to see You face to face

To my husband, Kev . . .
Your patient persistence and humble strength
make God's love absolutely tangible to me

And to you, my dear reader . . .
I pray that each day's reading for you is divinely timed.
I pray God's Word comes alive and fans the flame
within you. And I pray Jesus grants you a fresh revelation
of His love, His power, and His divine purpose for you

Table of Contents
by Subject

Introduction

God is on a rescue mission. We could never jump high enough or perform well enough to save ourselves, so Love came down to rescue us. He made a way where there was otherwise no way to secure our eternity, no way to begin the miracle work of inner transformation within us. If you are in Christ, *Christ is in you!*

God is profoundly committed to us. We're prone to wander. He is utterly faithful to His promises; we tend to forget those promises. His mercies are new every morning and His compassions never fail. We're the ones who turn on ourselves. God sees the big picture while noticing every nuance of our story. Our gaze either drops to our feet and we forget about faith, or we stare off into an imaginary world where the enemy reigns and God has seemingly forgotten us because we've forgotten all about love. Yet in it all, Jesus beckons us to follow Him and, in the process, we become more like Him.

Jesus came to destroy the work of the devil. When we're perfected in love, fear no longer has the last say in our lives. When we remember who we are, the enemy doesn't get away with as much as he used to. The whole arc of Scripture is God's love letter to the ones He created. Everything He does, He does for love. Everything He asks of us is for our good and for His glory. I want everything He has for me. Don't you?

God wants us to *prevail*—to prove we're more powerful than our enemy. He wants us to overcome every battle with increasing courage and strength.

I've learned that whenever I ask for more from God, He asks for more from me.

As you align your life—every part of it—with His Word and His ways, you *will* find freedom, wholeness, and redemption you never dreamed possible. Use this book in a way that best suits you. Read chronologically from Genesis to Revelation, or read only by topic. I'm praying for you as you work your way through these pages. I'm so very honored to get to spend this time with you.

Affectionately His,

Susie Larson

Build an Altar

Then the LORD appeared to Abram and said, "I will give this land to your descendants." And Abram built an altar there and dedicated it to the LORD, who had appeared to him.

Genesis 12:7

*W*e have to let go of the old to lay hold of the new. We have to leave what's comfortable if we want to experience God as our provider, our defender, and our way-maker. God called Abram away from everything he knew to a land God had not yet revealed. But God's promise to Abram far outweighed his need to know every detail about the journey ahead. It's the same for you and me. We are pilgrims, traveling to a most holy city. And God's promise over us far outweighs our need to control every twist and turn. We're on a need-to-know basis, and when we need to know, God will let us know! But this we do know: The land ahead is a good land. And our good God will ensure we make it to our new home safely. Will you pause today and build an altar of remembrance? Before you take another step, remember His faithfulness. Remember His goodness. It'll strengthen you for the road ahead.

LEARN Read Genesis 12:1–9.

FLOURISH As pilgrims, we're always on our way to a next place of promise. Take some time today and "build an altar." Make note of this sacred place where you now stand. God is in this place. How would you describe the holy ground beneath your feet? What treasures will you take with you to your next place?

PRAY

You are here with me. I pause today to remember Your presence in my life. Thank You, Lord.

Release and Trust

"The whole countryside is open to you. Take your choice of any section of the land you want, and we will separate. If you want the land to the left, then I'll take the land on the right. If you prefer the land on the right, then I'll go to the left."

Genesis 13:9

*W*e can go through life one of two ways: We can posture for position, constantly trying to maintain control, or we can live wholly submitted to God, trusting Him with every step. But did you know that God will never bless faithless posturing? He won't pour provision into a clenched fist. Both Abram and Lot acquired great wealth. Soon the herdsmen began to bicker, and the two men needed to part ways. Abram gave Lot first choice of the land. Though Lot had benefited greatly from Abram's constant generosity, he still grabbed for himself the best share of land, even though it meant he'd live among the ungodly. His story didn't end well. Scarcity and abundance both reveal the condition of our hearts in different ways. If we'll grab for ourselves in difficult times, we'll grab for ourselves when there's more than enough to go around. As Christ-followers, it's always a good idea to refuse selfishness, to open our hands and receive and release. We can trust God.

LEARN Read Genesis 13.

FLOURISH No matter which season you find yourself in at the moment, determine to release your grip on anything you're holding too tight. Breathe in faith. Exhale fear. And know that God does His best work through His surrendered saints.

PRAY

You come to me with open-handed provision, so I come to You with open-handed trust. You've always provided, so I have nothing to fear. I trust You, Lord. Amen.

Deal with the Disconnect

Then Abraham bowed down to the ground, but he laughed to himself in disbelief. "How could I become a father at the age of 100?" he thought. "And how can Sarah have a baby when she is ninety years old?"

Genesis 17:17

God promised Abraham that the generations would come through Abraham and Sarah. His response? He bowed low. *But he laughed on the inside.* How often do we do the same? We sing about God's faithfulness, but do we really believe He'll do the *impossible* in our situation? When the gap widens between what our outward "Christian" actions reflect and what our inward beliefs reveal, we must make note of it (but without condemnation). We often arrive here because we're weary in the waiting or tired from battle. But we must not allow the gap to linger within us for very long. Reengage your faith today. Remember, God can do in a moment what takes us a lifetime to accomplish. And when faith awakens your heart *and* inspires your actions? Well, that's the stuff of miracles.

LEARN Read Genesis 17:15–17.

FLOURISH It's time to deal with the disconnect. God is better than we know and He's kinder than we can fathom! Remind your soul today that NOTHING is impossible with Him! Wrestle with God and contend for His promises until you believe them again. Your faith is so very precious to Him.

PRAY

Precious Lord,
*   You are a faithful God! Show me the gap that exists between what I do and what I truly believe, and then fill in those empty spaces with more of You. Awaken my heart and I will engage my faith. Do the impossible in my life. In Your name, I pray. Amen.*

When Our Unbelief Speaks

So Abraham said to God, "May Ishmael live under your special blessing!"
Genesis 17:18

Out of the heart, the mouth speaks. When we've waited long to see a breakthrough or a fulfillment of a promise, our hearts grow faint. Unless we regularly take the time to strengthen ourselves in the Lord and remind ourselves of His faithfulness, unbelief and even offense will settle into our souls. In due time our own words, which reflect the condition of our hearts, will diminish our own faith. Abraham and Sarah had waited long for their promise. When the time of fulfillment was upon them, they laughed in unbelief and Abram tried to edit God's promise by telling God where the blessing would land! Pay attention to how you talk about the longings of your heart. What do they reveal? Your faith is precious to Him. There are no time constraints on God's ability to do what He will do. If He's making you wait, it's because He's making you ready. May God bless you with a fresh and hopeful expectancy today. May your words inspire hope and reflect your actively engaged faith!

LEARN Read Genesis 18:1–14.

FLOURISH Has unbelief or offense settled into your soul? Today's a good day to remember and rehearse the things God has promised you. Talk about them. Sing about them. Remember them.

PRAY

Lord, I believe; help my unbelief! Help me remember the promises You've made to me. I've got to remember in the darkness what You told me in the light. I know Your voice. I know what I heard. I know what Your Word says. Fan the flame of faith within me today. I choose to trust You. Amen.

God's Wisdom and Revelation

"Should I hide my plan from Abraham?" the LORD asked. "For Abraham will certainly become a great and mighty nation, and all the nations of the earth will be blessed through him."

Genesis 18:17–18

*W*as God talking to himself here? Wondering out loud? We know this: God knows the end from the beginning. Our days are established before Him. He knows the plans He has for us and they are good plans. He also knows what troubles lie ahead for us and He intends to be intimately near during such times. In and through His wisdom, God reveals what we need to know. Scripture also tells us that He confides in (tells secrets to) those who fear Him. Eventually God told Abraham about His plan. Interestingly, that occurred just after Abraham radically trusted God with his future. Could there be a connection between our obedient faith steps and God's revelation in our lives? Absolutely. As we walk intimately with Him, He reveals His heart and His ways to us. Upward and onward we go.

LEARN Read Genesis 22:1–18.

FLOURISH God has some great plans and good gifts up His sovereign sleeve, and they're assigned to you! He wants to give you insight into your story and your future. He wants to fill you with hope. He wants you to persevere. Do you believe Him enough to trust Him? What would reverence and obedience look like for you today? Don't delay. Trust and obey.

PRAY

Nobody modeled trust, obedience, and faith like You. And Your life was marked by wisdom, power, and revelation. Give me a heart to do Your will. Please reveal Your heart and Your ways to me. In Jesus' name I pray. Amen.

How to Lose Your Credibility

So Lot rushed out to tell his daughters' fiancés, "Quick, get out of the city! The LORD is about to destroy it." But the young men thought he was only joking.

Genesis 19:14

*A*braham interceded for the city of Sodom because God was about to destroy it. (His nephew lived there, and Abraham hoped to influence God's decision.) He begged God to promise not to destroy the city if He could find even a small remnant of righteous people still there—perhaps fifty people, or forty, or even ten. But Sodom's sins had piled so high, there weren't even *ten* individuals who feared God within its borders. Imagine! God sent angels to warn Lot about the coming destruction. But when Lot tried to warn his family, they thought he was joking. They didn't take him seriously. Lot had camped among the ungodly for so long, he lost his credibility. Lot didn't live a set-apart life, so his words didn't carry much weight. Most compromise happens subtly. A fallen pastor once explained it to me this way: "I kept changing the rules, a little at a time." We are drifters by nature, and the drift happens subtly. May God recapture your heart today.

LEARN Read Genesis 19.

FLOURISH Ask God to show you if you've blended with society in a way that's affected your testimony. Get with God and make things right again. Repent, reset your course, and ask God to fill you afresh with the convicting and assuring work of the Holy Spirit.

PRAY

Show me how my little compromises have affected my relationship with You. Show me how my justifications have diminished Your life-giving power in my life. Call me up higher with You. In Your name, I pray. Amen.

Your Birthright
for a Bowl of Soup

"Look, I'm dying of starvation!" said Esau. "What good is my birthright to me now?"

Genesis 25:32

When we let ourselves get overtired, overextended, and over-committed, nothing good comes of it. God never asks us to grind our gears to the point of exhaustion. Such a life not only wears us out, it also makes us vulnerable.* We tend to take shortcuts when we're tired. And worse yet, we lose sight of the life to which our souls are heir. Esau was so wrapped up in his immediate need for comfort that he lost sight of his inheritance. We must not go through life reacting to our immediate cravings at the expense of the greater story God is writing in our lives. Though God graciously gives us all good things to enjoy, not everything is profitable for us. If you've overdone it with your indulgences, now would be a great time for a sacred fast, a time to seek God and reset your ways. Whenever we say yes, we say no. And what we say yes and no to today will impact the lives of many tomorrow. Our story matters that much.

LEARN   Read Genesis 25:27–34.

FLOURISH   Maybe it's time to loosen up your calendar, adjust your task list, and give yourself some time and space to be restored so you can think and see clearly again. Your choices today deeply impact your tomorrows.

PRAY

I'm so quick to forget who I am and Whose I am. Forgive me from digging my own wells and for being surprised when they don't satisfy. I want more of You in me, Lord! Awaken fresh life in me! Amen.

*I write all about this in my book *Your Sacred Yes*.

No Hindrance, No Harm

You know how hard I have worked for your father, but he has cheated me, changing my wages ten times. But God has not allowed him to do me any harm.

Genesis 31:6–7

*L*aban was a manipulative, passive-aggressive man. He changed Jacob's wages ten times. He tricked him and cheated him, seemingly bent on controlling Jacob's future. But God observed everything, and He refused to let Laban stand in the way of His promise to Jacob. Laban was in a position of power and authority, yet ultimately, he'd have no power to actually hinder Jacob or keep him from prospering. Let Jacob's story encourage you today. You may have people in your life who are impossible to deal with. They may seem to slow your progress. But when you're in Christ, there's no enemy scheme or man-made manipulation that can keep you from all God has for you. Christians experience only *temporary* setbacks. God's purposes will ultimately prevail. Take some time today to reset your perspective if necessary. Scripture tells us that the powerful aren't what they appear to be.* Nobody has more power to establish you than God himself. He will use difficult people to chisel your rough edges and to make you more like Christ.

LEARN Read Genesis 31:1–16.

FLOURISH Rejoice today that no man can hinder what God has appointed. Praise!

PRAY

You are all that I need. Forgive me for giving people power that belongs to You alone. Give me savvy wisdom to navigate difficult relationships. Grant me the calm assurance to know in the face of frustration that all will be well because You are with me. I trust You, Lord. Amen.

*See Psalm 62:9.

Perspective before the Breakthrough

When Joseph saw them the next morning, he noticed that they both looked upset. "Why do you look so worried today?" he asked them.

Genesis 40:6–7

When Joseph was a young man, God put a dream in his heart. Yet the journey getting there involved painful betrayal, injustice, and false accusation. God used heartbreak to prepare Joseph for greatness. And at every turn, Joseph rose to the top of his game in attitude, performance, and perspective. One day he noticed two prisoners who looked distressed. In so many words, Joseph asked, "Why the long face?" What? Why *wouldn't* you be distressed if you were unjustly thrown into prison? Yet Joseph had found such joy and perspective that he could minister to others while he waited for his own breakthrough. My pastor used to say, "You're not free to go until you're free to stay." May you wrestle for a right perspective. May you see those who need what you possess. And may you believe, with all of your heart, that God will move you on when the time is right.

LEARN Read Genesis 40.

FLOURISH You may not be where you want to be, but God has you here for a reason. Find the high place of joy today. Look for those God has given you to encourage. Forgive your offenders and believe with all of your heart that no man, no scheme, and no devil can thwart God's purposes for you!

PRAY

Father, show me my heart so I can find You here. Whom do I need to forgive? How should I pray? Help me to steward my life in this place while I wait for You to move me to my next place. I trust You, Lord. Amen.

May God Remind Them, and You

Finally, the king's chief cup-bearer spoke up. "Today I have been reminded of my failure," he told Pharaoh.

Genesis 41:9

Joseph honored God and guarded his heart through every painful, unjust circumstance he endured. One day while in prison, God used Joseph to interpret dreams for the cupbearer and the baker. Interesting how the man with a dream helped others to interpret their dreams. Joseph asked the cupbearer to remember him when God restored him to his position. But he forgot all about Joseph until a later time. You've no doubt crossed paths with those who've witnessed and confirmed God's gifts in you. Maybe they promised they'd help you and open doors for you. Yet you've heard nothing. Pray for those people today. Ask God to remind them of their words to you. And trust God's perfect time and grace in your life. He is faithful. Though man sometimes forgets, He never will. Remember too that Jesus consistently called greatness out of others. He saw them not for where they'd been but for who they could be if they followed Him. May you do the same for others. You have a position of influence.

LEARN Read Genesis 41:8–13.

FLOURISH Who can you encourage today? Help someone succeed today. Move them forward in their God-given calling. And trust that God will remind your cupbearers of your God-given gifts at just the right time.

PRAY

I seem to fall into one of two extremes: I either forget to dream because I'm consumed by my problems, or I'm so consumed with my dreams, I forget to help others achieve theirs. Use me to help others. And remind others to remember me when the time is right. Thank You, Lord. Amen.

You Sold Me; God Sent Me*

But don't be upset, and don't be angry with yourselves for selling me to this place. It was God who sent me here ahead of you to preserve your lives.

Genesis 45:5

*H*ow do you endure betrayal and injustice with such honor that you actually feel compassion for your enemies, even to the point that you don't *want* them to blame themselves? How do you get to a place where you trust God so much that you know that man's sins against you can never interrupt His purposes for you? Joseph stewarded his perspective so faithfully that when God called him from the prison to the palace, he was ready for it. How do we know he was ready? By looking at his heart for those who hurt him most. The work of forgiveness is painful and messy, and it calls so much out of us. But as Christ-followers, it's our only option. Not that we automatically trust again. But if we truly believe that God can redeem any situation, we will trust Him with those who've hurt us most. A heart like Joseph's is renewed over time, not overnight. Do you believe that God is ultimately in control and that He cares about your story? Then do the work of forgiveness, fight for a redeemed perspective, and put your trust in the Lord once again. God rewards your faith, and your vindication comes from Him.

LEARN ▶ Read Genesis 45:1–15.

FLOURISH ▶ It's for our good and for His glory to forgive as we've been forgiven. God is up to something good.

PRAY ▶

> *Father,*
> *Refresh my perspective. Help me to see my "enemies" the way that You do. You are ultimately in control, so no scheme of man can ever interrupt Your ultimate plan. Yours is to establish me; mine is to trust You with my whole heart. Lift my eyes above my problems to the greater purpose You have for me. Amen.*

*This line came from pastor and author Steven Furtick.

It's About Who He Is

> But Moses protested to God, "Who am I to appear before Pharaoh? Who am I
> to lead the people of Israel out of Egypt?" God answered, "I will be with you."
> Exodus 3:11–12

God had prepared Moses throughout his whole life for his purpose and destiny. But when the Lord finally called Moses, the task was still too big for him. Moses asked, "But who am I?" Notice that God doesn't affirm Moses' giftedness; nor is He bothered by Moses' weaknesses. God simply said, "I will be with you." *God's nearness* was all the assurance Moses needed. When the Lord calls you to attempt something that's far beyond you, your instinct (and your enemy) will compel you to count your weaknesses. But the Lord God Almighty charges you to rely on His strength. Most of the angst in our souls comes from our circumstances and our own limitations. Yet neither of these things is an issue or an obstacle for God. The truth is, if God is for us, who can stand against us? If His promises are true, what problem will overcome us? The God who calls you is the same God who moves the mountains and parts the waters. He uses the willing, available, humble heart. You are tethered to a good and strong God.

LEARN ▸ Read Exodus 3:1–15.

FLOURISH ▸ May you take time today to remember that more rests on God's shoulders than on yours. It'll do wonders for your soul.

PRAY ▸

Nothing is too difficult for You! Strengthen my heart today! Lead me to a rock that is higher than I! I am strong in You, secure in You, and forever established in You. Do the impossible in and through me. Lead me onward, dear Lord. Amen.

Not the Shortest Route, the Best Route

> When Pharaoh finally let the people go, God did not lead them along the main road . . . even though that was the shortest route to the Promised Land. God said, "If the people are faced with a battle, they might change their minds and return to Egypt."
>
> Exodus 13:17–18

Though Christ paid a full ransom for our freedom, it sometimes takes a while to get captivity out of us. On our way to our promised land, God will lead us on a long and winding path that doesn't always make sense. Our feet will get tired, our patience will be tried, and our attitude will be tested. Why? Because when we hit our limits, we learn to seek our limitless God. Our desires are always far inferior to God's desires for us. We want comfort. God wants to conform us to His image. We want convenience. God loves to provide in a way that completely alters our history, which takes time. We want immediate relief. God wants total redemption of our story. Replace grumbling with gratitude. Cast aside entitlement and impatience. Re-embrace a heart of humility and wonder. You follow the star-breathing God. His way might take longer, but it's the best way for you. Go with God. He's most certainly with you.

LEARN Read Exodus 13:17–22.

FLOURISH Smile and laugh hard every day. It's healthy for your brain, good for your soul, and wonderful for your spirit. You can flourish here. So flourish here.

PRAY

Forgive me for being so shortsighted at times. You are faithfully leading me in the way that I should go. Transform me from the inside out. Make me promotable. Write a beautiful story with my life. Amen.

What's Better?

"Didn't we tell you this would happen while we were still in Egypt? We said, 'Leave us alone! Let us be slaves to the Egyptians. It's better to be a slave in Egypt than a corpse in the wilderness!'"

Exodus 14:12

*T*he Israelites predicted their failure before they ever started on the journey because captivity was embedded in the core of who they were. If God promised to deliver them, wouldn't He? Is it really *better* to be held captive than to face your fears of the unknown? My friend once said to me, "The devil can't attack a corpse. Die to your fears and you'll walk free." Lots of things need to die in the wilderness: our love of control, our performance-based identity, our fears, our impatience and sense of entitlement. Is it *better* to stay captive than to have your flesh challenged? No. It's better to follow Jesus through your wilderness, trusting wholeheartedly that He brought you here not to dismiss you but to deliver you. Remind yourself of those promises. Say them, pray them, and then march forward unafraid. Some things will die in this wilderness, but you're not one of them. God will purify and preserve you. He's set His affection upon you.

LEARN   Read Exodus 14:10–14.

FLOURISH   Today's a good day to let go of your agenda, lay down your fears, and look up to God. He's made promises to you that He intends to keep.

PRAY

Father,

I place my hand in Yours and I trust You with my life. Cleanse me from hidden faults. Keep me back from presumptuous sins; may they never have dominion over me! I want to walk purely and blamelessly before You. Make me ready for my next place of promise. Amen.

He's the Way-Maker

But the people of Israel had walked through the middle of the sea on dry ground, as the water stood up like a wall on both sides.

Exodus 14:29

*L*et's push pause and then watch this scene unfold in slow motion. The people of Israel—who identified more with their captivity than with their Maker—walked through the middle of the sea, on dry ground. And the deep waters stood up like walls on both sides. This happened! *This* is the God we serve. He takes feeble, weak-kneed saints and reveals His power and goodness to them time and again. What's your Red Sea—the do-or-die thing that threatens to swallow you whole? Will God part your waters because you are good, or because He is? Dare to believe that though the odds may be against you, they're really irrelevant when God comes on the scene. Today, remember the great things God has done with seemingly no effort: He spoke, and the heavens came to be. He put the stars in their place and calls them each by name. And He knows and loves *you*. He'll intervene at the right time because He is God and He is good. It's time to believe for your miracle.

LEARN Read Exodus 14:21–29.

FLOURISH Ponder His greatness and His nearness today. Doing so will add strength and hope to your heart. He *will* make a way for you.

PRAY

I invite You into my impossible situation. You are the God who parted the Red Sea, and You will make a way for me! I declare Your goodness over every area of my life. I refuse to be defined by my troubles. I'm already claimed by heaven! Thank You, Lord. Amen.

Finding Fault, Finding Favor

Then Moses added, "The LORD will give you meat to eat in the evening and bread to satisfy you in the morning, for he has heard all your complaints against him. What have we done? Yes, your complaints are against the LORD, not against us."

Exodus 16:8

One of the great temptations of the wilderness is to complain, finger-point, and blame. We don't like our circumstance and so we look for someone to pin it on. Sometimes we do suffer because of someone else's sin. That's a painful proposition we must sort through. But every trial is ultimately a test of our hearts and a challenge to our belief systems. Is God good? And can we trust Him? Our circumstances won't hinder us as much as we think they will, but our attitudes will. An earthbound heart is always looking for someone to blame. A heaven-bound heart knows that we're passing through our valleys to a better place. In Christ Jesus we are surrounded by the favor and the provision of God. May we believe it, receive it, and walk in it today. Lift your eyes to the Lord and remind your soul that ultimately, He's in control. What He allows, He will redeem. Look *above* your circumstances and remember that He is God.

LEARN Read Exodus 16:2–18.

FLOURISH Thank Him for His provision today. He's been good to you and He'll be good again. Keep walking.

PRAY

Lord,
Forgive me for giving too much power to people and circumstances. I have every reason for hope because I have You! I lift my eyes heavenward and I raise my hands. You will surely guide, provide, correct, and direct as I need it. I'm in divine hands. Thank You, Lord.

Your Part in the Epic Story

As long as Moses held up the staff in his hand, the Israelites had the advantage. But whenever he dropped his hand, the Amalekites gained the advantage. Moses' arms soon became so tired he could no longer hold them up. So Aaron and Hur found a stone for him to sit on. Then they stood on each side of Moses, holding up his hands. So his hands held steady until sunset.

Exodus 17:11–12

*W*hy did God insist that Moses keep his arms in the air? Could He have established a victory without Moses? Absolutely. He was able to. He just didn't want to. God loves to involve His children when He intervenes on the earth. Even when we're tired? When it's a battle? Yes and yes. Without faith, how would we change? If we don't persevere, how will we grow? Joshua led the troops into battle and needed Moses to stand in that place of intercession. Moses needed Aaron and Hur to hold up his arms when he lost strength. Together, they won the battle. The victory belonged to all of them! What does faith look like for you today? Who are you helping? Who's helping you? You're part of a grander story than you can imagine.

LEARN   Read Exodus 17:8–15.

FLOURISH   Ask for a fresh perspective on the importance of your calling. Let your tribe know how eternally grateful you are for them. And don't forget to celebrate your victories.

PRAY

Father,
Open my eyes to the height of my calling. Give me faith to believe You for the great things You want to do in and through me. Show me those You've given me to stand with. Help me to add strength to my tribe. Make me a kingdom woman.

Face to Face, As with a Friend

Inside the Tent of Meeting, the LORD would speak to Moses face to face, as one speaks to a friend.

Exodus 33:11

Once Moses entered the Tent of Meeting, a pillar of cloud hovered over the entrance. Imagine. The people stood back and watched, amazed. God's nearness to Moses caused the Israelites to bow down in front of their own tents. Notice Moses' humble yet bold appeal to God. And God dialogued with him! God distances himself from the proud, but He draws near to the humble. And He loves faith. Jesus is all-powerful and intimately near. Jesus invites each of us into such an intimate, thriving relationship with Him. He longs for us to know Him, not just as a star-breathing God, not just as a Savior (though salvation is everything), but also as a trusted and faithful friend. What if your interactions with God were so sweet that your very relationship with Him compelled others to bow before their Maker? When was the last time you enjoyed that kind of fellowship with the Most High God? Know this: He speaks tenderly to His friends. He guards, He guides, He protects, and He provides, all with a heart of love and strength. Today's a great day to enjoy His presence.

LEARN   Read Exodus 33:11–18.

FLOURISH   The Maker of the universe knows your name and wants to do life with you. Draw near. Pray big. Listen well.

PRAY

Jesus,

You've granted me access to Your presence, and You're glad to see me every single time I meet with You! Thank You for Your goodness to me. Give me faith to believe for the impossible. Speak to me as a dear and precious friend. My soul waits for You, Lord. Amen.

The Power of Intercession

> Moses immediately threw himself to the ground and worshiped. And he said, "O Lord, if it is true that I have found favor with you, then please travel with us. Yes, this is a stubborn and rebellious people, but please forgive our iniquity and our sins. Claim us as your own special possession."
>
> Exodus 34:8–9

D r. Warren Wiersbe writes, "The people of Israel had no idea what Moses had experienced on that mountain and how close they had come to being rejected by God and destroyed. Never underestimate the spiritual power of a dedicated man or woman who knows how to intercede with God. One of our greatest needs today is for intercessors who can lay hold of God's promises and trust God to work in mighty power."* Moses stepped between God and a people in rebellion and prayed, "Forgive *us* for *our* sins." Even if it doesn't feel natural to you, become an intercessor. Stand in the gap for politicians you don't like, for leaders whose personalities irk you, and for neighbors who leave you flummoxed. What would happen in our day if Christians humbly stood in the gap, bowed low, and asked for God's mercy? A revival might break out.

LEARN Read Exodus 34:1–11.

FLOURISH Do for others what Jesus does for you each and every day.

PRAY

Lord,
Break my heart for what breaks Yours! Forgive me for missing Your heart for Your wayward children. Teach me to pray. Help me to see Your image in the ones I struggle most to love. Give me a glimpse into their story so that Your compassion rises up within me. Make me a praying saint, O Lord. Amen.

*Dr. Warren Wiersbe, *The Wiersbe Bible Commentary* (Colorado Springs: David C. Cook, 2007), 203.

Rest as a Gift

"Keep my Sabbath days of rest and show reverence toward my sanctuary. I am the LORD."

Leviticus 19:30

*M*essages often get lost in translation when we misunderstand or don't fully know the messenger. Yes, the call to honor the Sabbath was a law, but God instituted it as a gift to a people who possessed very real limits, people who needed regular reminders that the world was not on their shoulders. Yet what did the religious zealots do with this law? They used it to parade their "holiness" for all to see, and to absolve themselves from helping someone in need because their rigid religion forbade it. Then Jesus came. He offered rest to the weary, understanding to the disillusioned, and compassion to the weak. He restored the Sabbath to its rightful place. We still need the Sabbath. Our hearts need mending, our souls need healing, and our bodies need rest. Even more so, we need *regular* reminders that God carries the weight of the world, so we don't have to. God created us for fellowship with Him. We're our best selves when our hearts learn to rest in His provision and rely on His love.

LEARN Read Leviticus 19:1–30.

FLOURISH Ask the Lord how He'd like you to institute a true Sabbath in your life. How will you approach that day differently from the others? What stresses will you set aside? What will you do that nourishes your soul?

PRAY

Father,
Thank You for such a gift. Forgive me for so often refusing Your gift of rest because of my own earthbound mindset. I want to tap in to heaven's provision and perspective. Show me what a true Sabbath could look like in this season of my life. I'm following You, Lord. Amen.

Honor Your Elders

"Stand up in the presence of the elderly and show respect for the aged. Fear your God. I am the LORD."

Leviticus 19:32

I love this command. I've been saying it for years: Honor those who've gone before you. If there's a silver-haired saint in your midst who still has a twinkle in her eye and humility in her heart, know that it's not because she's never endured anything hard. On the contrary, she has weathered the storms of life with her faith intact and her love for Jesus evident. Celebrate her! Stand when she enters the room! Oh, that such honor would make a comeback, especially toward those who've served so faithfully through the years. It's no small thing to finish strong. We live in a day when elders are dismissed and youth are idolized. Yet we need to acknowledge every generation for the Body of Christ to function in a healthy way. Honor the unborn. Pour into the youth. And glean from those who've gone before you. Their hard-fought wisdom is worth more than gold. Find a wise sage to honor today! Honor is the equity of the kingdom. Honor means something to God. When you give honor, you actually reveal the honor within you.

LEARN Read Leviticus 19:31–37.

FLOURISH Thank the Lord for the seasoned saints in your circle. They impact you more than you probably realize.

PRAY

Dear Lord,
Thank You for being so honor-worthy! You are mighty and kind, coura-geous and true. You love justice and mercy and faithfulness. You call me to honor my leaders and my elders. Raise up a new standard within me. May the way that I honor others, greatly honor You. Amen.

Pay Attention

As long as the land lies in ruins, it will enjoy the rest you never allowed it to take every seventh year while you lived in it.

Leviticus 26:35

*T*his is a sobering passage. God warned His people that if they refused to acknowledge Him by honoring the Sabbath, they would endure unimaginable hardship and suffer great loss. We're not the only ones who pay when we grind our gears to the point of exhaustion. Our families pay. Our relationships are strained. Our resources are drained. We're not meant to live this way. God issues a warning to us, but if we blow right past it, He will allow us to suffer the consequences. One way or another, He will get our attention. Think about a time when you paid a price for living on overdrive. Did your relationship with God take a backseat? Is there any area of your life currently begging for your attention? You'll do your best when you put Him first. He's more concerned with the condition of our souls and the perspective of our hearts than He is with our temporary uncomfortable consequences. Pay attention to the warning signals God places in your life. God knows what's best for you, and His plans for you are good.

LEARN ▶ Read Leviticus 26:18–20, 33–35.

FLOURISH ▶ Take some time if necessary, examine your activity level, and reset your course and your heart today.

PRAY

I humble myself before You, Lord, and acknowledge my tendency to forget Your Word and Your ways. Forgive me, Lord. Show me the areas in my life that have fallen out of balance. Open my eyes to the ways I've stopped honoring You. You are my God and I will follow You forever. Amen.

Humility and the Lord's Favor

But Moses replied, "Are you jealous for my sake? I wish that all the LORD's people were prophets and that the LORD would put his Spirit upon them all!"

Numbers 11:29

*M*oses was so humbly confident in God that nobody could steal his thunder (because he had no thunder to steal). He reveled in a rich and personal relationship with God. They were good friends. They talked intimately and often. Clearly, the favor on Moses' public life came as a result of his faithful private life. Something beautiful happens when we're secure in God's love and assured of our place in the kingdom story. We cease to be threatened by the giftedness of others. In fact, we celebrate how God works in and through His people! And we continually remember that God's story is always bigger than ours. This reality inspires holy confidence and humble dependence. The Lord Jesus offers the precious gift of intimacy and assurance to each and every one of us. Never has there been a better invitation. Consider the places in your life where you're prone to jealousy, insecurity, and territorialism. Imagine these areas of your life as plots of land. Picture yourself kneeling down on the land and offering it back up to the Lord.

LEARN Read Numbers 11:16–29.

FLOURISH See yourself as part of the bigger story. No one can steal your thunder. It's God's thunder that ignites and empowers you!

PRAY

> Lord,
>
> Fill me afresh with the knowledge of Your love. Assure me once again of my place in the greater kingdom story. May there be no shred of cattiness or insecurity in me! I'm made for bigger things. Do a mighty work in me. Amen.

Humility and the Fear of the Lord

They said, "Has the LORD spoken only through Moses? Hasn't he spoken through us, too?" But the LORD heard them. (Now Moses was very humble—more humble than any other person on earth.)

Numbers 12:2–3

*T*he devil uses a common tactic on believers to sow doubt in their hearts. It usually starts this way: *"Did God really say . . . ?"* When we question God's character, we fall down in battle. The enemy uses the same tactic to get weaker Christians to attack seasoned leaders. He tempts them to question the character of their leader. Their jealousy compels them to look for fault (and they usually find it). And before you know it, they're out of rank and in full rebellion all while thinking they represent God's heart in the situation! Someone once said that there's enough flesh in every one of us to singlehandedly destroy any thriving work of God. That should put the fear of God in us. If you want to avoid being used by the enemy in this way, stay humble, pray for your leaders, and if you aspire to leadership, learn from those in front of you.

LEARN Read Numbers 12:1–8.

FLOURISH Pray for the leaders and influencers that you're tempted to criticize. You don't know what their call costs them. The measure that you use will be used on you. Sow grace, faith, encouragement, and support, and you'll reap those things.

PRAY

Lord,
Forgive me for my tendency to have flippant, jealous, or judgmental opinions about others, especially leaders. Help me to remember that You hear every word and every thought. I long to live with honor. I will pray for those ahead of me, knowing You will promote me at exactly the right time. Thank You, Lord. Amen.

Obstacles and Opposition

> This was their report to Moses: "We entered the land you sent us to explore, and it is indeed a bountiful country—a land flowing with milk and honey. Here is the kind of fruit it produces. But the people living there are powerful, and their towns are large and fortified."
>
> Numbers 13:27–28

God told Moses to send out men to explore the land that He had designated for them. This would be a land flowing with provision. Moses sent out twelve men to get a look at the land God commanded them to possess. The land was just as God described and better than they'd imagined. Yet they would encounter obstacles, enemies, and battles up ahead. Ten of the men lost their nerve because for them, the threat of battle eclipsed the promise of blessing, even though God promised this land to them. Over and over again the Lord has whispered in my ear, *I'm not going to let you lose, but I have to let you fight.* Every place of promise God calls us to possess will come with opposition. But the blessing will always far outweigh the battle.

LEARN Read Numbers 13:1–30.

FLOURISH Do you shy away from battle when your promised land depends upon it? If so, you simply need a fresh revelation of God's love for and promise to you. You'll have the heart for the fight when you remember God has equipped you for battle.

PRAY

God of angel armies,
Open my eyes to see the promised land ahead of me! Help me not to shrink back in fear or to posture in self-preservation. I belong to You. Give me faith for every step until I'm standing on the land You promised me. In Your mighty name, I pray. Amen.

Look above It

> But Caleb tried to quiet the people as they stood before Moses. "Let's go at once to take the land," he said. "We can certainly conquer it!"
>
> Numbers 13:30

God called the spies to scope out the land so they'd better understand the journey before them. Yet ten of the twelve spies lost heart once they glimpsed the challenges on the road ahead. Perhaps this is why God in His wisdom reveals only so much to us even though we constantly beg Him for more information! Yet Joshua and Caleb saw what God wanted them to see. They saw possibility, potential, and the reality of God's promise coming to pass in their lives. The ten other spies were so vocal about their doubts that unbelief spread through the camp like a plague. Think of your words and perspective not only as critical food for your own soul, but as fuel for others' faith (or doubt). If the devil can convince you to look down, he'll get you to turn back. Maybe today is a good day to look above your troubles to the One who promised to empower you every step of the way.

LEARN ▸ Read Numbers 13:30–33.

FLOURISH ▸ Dare to look above your obstacles and declare your faith in God today.

PRAY

Precious Lord,
Open the eyes of my heart today! Tilt my chin upward today until I see You—and only You. Fill my heart with a fresh perspective and my mouth with words of faith. And then use me to fuel the faith in others. You deserve our trust and our praise.

Rebellious Fears

"Why is the LORD taking us to this country only to have us die in battle? . . . Wouldn't it be better for us to return to Egypt?" Then they plotted among themselves, "Let's choose a new leader and go back to Egypt!"

Numbers 14:3–4

Our fears skew our perspective. They make us miss what God is saying to us in the moment. And our fears almost always cause division in the camp. Look around at the culture today and see the masses reacting to their fears in the most ungodly ways. God brings peace to our hearts and promises to deliver us from all of our fears. He aches for us when we're afraid. But scholars describe the Israelites' fears as downright rebellious. They coddled their fears more than they clung to the promise of God, to the point that they refused to trust Him, and they defied the godly, humble leader He provided for them. Learn from their error. God's promises are greater than you can imagine, and His intentions for you can never be shaken. Determine not to rebel against the Lord because of your fears. Yes, you'll need courage and grit to walk out His purposes for you. But your faith is a treasure to Him and He's highly protective of you.

LEARN ▸ Read Numbers 14:1–9.

FLOURISH ▸ Fear God, not your fears. Only then will you walk free.

PRAY

Dear Jesus,
Thank You for Your patience with me! I repent of and renounce the fears that have held me back up until now. I refuse to allow the enemy to bully me into rebellion. Instead, I submit my will to You. I will obey You. I will trust You. Show me what to do, my eyes are on You. Amen.

Faith Possesses Its Share

> But my servant Caleb has a different attitude than the others have. He has remained loyal to me, so I will bring him into the land he explored. His descendants will possess their full share of that land.
>
> Numbers 14:24

*T*hough the Israelites traveled en masse, God knew who had faith and who didn't. The lines weren't blurry to Him. We, who've been given access to the Most High God, who've been promised His presence and His provision, we His people, have a decision to make. Will we trust Him, or won't we? Will He love us either way? Absolutely. But it's faith that possesses the promise. Our faith shows God that we trust Him, and He so deserves our trust. We don't have to do it perfectly; in fact, we never will. But He does ask us to put feet to our faith, to follow in obedience if we believe His promises are true. Look at this story in Numbers again and note that some never made it to their promised place, even though God had offered it to them. How many good gifts has God offered His people that have been left untouched because of unbelief? Make no mistake about it. Your faith is irresistible to God. Respond to Him in a way that shows you believe in His promises.

LEARN   Read Numbers 14:10–25.

FLOURISH   Spend some time with God today and get a vision for your next place of promise. Ask God what your next faith steps should be. He will surely answer your prayers.

PRAY

Father in heaven,
I want to possess all You have for me! Awaken fresh faith in my heart. Show me where unbelief hides in me. Remove every hindrance to my faith. I want all You've promised me. Amen.

How to Deal with Criticism

When Moses heard what they were saying, he fell face down on the ground.

Numbers 16:4

*W*hat do you do when people talk bad about you? Most of us instinctively rise to our own defense. But not Moses. He fell facedown to the ground. When he sought God for direction, he bowed low. When he interceded for ungrateful, sinful people, he bowed low. And when those very people rose up against him, he went facedown again before the Lord. But then he rose up and in so many words said, "Let's stand before God and see who He defends." When you walk in humble reverence before the Lord and you follow Him wholeheartedly, you can always count on Him to defend and deliver you. It's no small thing to God when someone comes against one of His very own. Keep your heart pure and watch Him defend you. If you find yourself rehearsing your defense in your mind, lay it down. Pick up one of His promises and rehearse that instead. Remember His goodness. Rely on His love. Recall His history with His people. It's precious and powerful. Remember, God will leave no loose ends in your story. He knows what's true and what's false. He cares about justice and will make every crooked way straight again. He's meticulous and miraculous. He'll deal with your accusers and will heal and restore your soul.

LEARN Read Numbers 16:1–7.

FLOURISH Count on God's delivering power to work on your behalf.

PRAY

Father,
You are the God who defends and delivers me! I entrust myself once again to You. Deal with my accusers. Vindicate me at the proper time, and protect me when I'm vulnerable. I'm counting on You to save me. Thank You, Lord. Amen.

Embrace and Own Your Territory

Then Moses spoke again to Korah: "Now listen, you Levites! Does it seem insignificant to you that the God of Israel has chosen you from among all the community of Israel to be near him so you can serve in the LORD's Tabernacle and stand before the people to minister to them?"

Numbers 16:8–9

*W*hen we minimize the importance of our call and sphere of influence because we're jealous of someone else, we set ourselves up for a fall. Our sphere is our place of stewardship. It's where we're trained, where we're called, and where we experience the provision and intervention of the Lord. God is all about promotion but never until we're ready. Our delays allow what's in our hearts to surface. The blessings of others reveal what really motivates us. "Korah had significant, worthwhile abilities and responsibilities of his own. In the end, however, his ambition for more caused him to lose everything. *Inappropriate ambition is greed in disguise.* Concentrate on finding the special purpose God has for you instead of wishing you were in someone else's shoes."* Holy ambition calls for humility, teachability, patience, and trust. Selfish ambition will always produce jealousy, greed, and disobedience.

LEARN Read Numbers 16:8–11.

FLOURISH If there's even a hint of selfish ambition in you, don't wait; repent and renounce it this minute. Then humble yourself before God Almighty and ask Him to use you in miraculous ways.

PRAY

> *Father, I can be such a pile of contradictions. Forgive me for ungodly ambition. I renounce it from my life. But fill me afresh with faith and holy ambition that I might accomplish great things for Your name's sake! Amen.*

Life Application Study Bible (Carol Stream, IL: Tyndale, 2007), 302, emphasis mine.

Is It Time to Move On?

When we were at Mount Sinai, the LORD our God said to us, "You have stayed at this mountain long enough. It is time to break camp and move on."

Deuteronomy 1:6–7

*T*here's a time to pause before the Lord, to seek His face, and to wait for His timing and direction. And then there's a time to get moving. How do you know what obedience looks like for you in this particular season? Should you wait and hold your ground, or should you pull up your tent stakes and move on, even if you don't have all of the answers? Ask yourself these two questions: *Where is the peace of God leading me?* And, *Which scenario requires more faith from me?* Oftentimes, we want to go so we can feel relief. And we want to stay so we can remain comfortable. But God's highest ways defy our selfish whims. He will always lead us on the best path for us if we will trust Him. You may not have all the answers—He may not offer a full road map to your destination—but He promises His presence. Search for His peace. Go in faith. God will faithfully lead you, one step at a time.

LEARN   Read Deuteronomy 1:6–8.

FLOURISH   When you consider your next steps, what does your flesh want to do: seek comfort, save face, make a hasty change? Pause, open your hands, and listen for His still, small voice. What is He saying to you?

PRAY

Father in heaven,
I bow before Your throne once again. You are all I need. I know Your will for me is my best-case scenario. Let me hear Your voice. Give me courage to do what You say. In Your great name, I pray. Amen.

Here's Where
You Trust Him

"And you saw how the LORD your God cared for you all along the way as you traveled through the wilderness, just as a father cares for his child. Now he has brought you to this place."

Deuteronomy 1:31

I wonder if, while Moses recounted the Israelites' journey—the miracles, the provision, the divine direction—the Israelites winced over how often they rebelled against God and doubted His care for them. At this point in Moses' message, he reminded the people of their accusations against God. They spouted things like, "The Lord must hate us!" Have mercy! How often do we blame God for our own self-induced misery? And yet, through all of it, the Lord remains steady and faithful. No matter how many times you've fallen down when it comes to trusting God, today is a good day to rise up and trust Him fully. He goes before you. What He did for the Israelites, He'll do for you: He goes before you. He will fight for you. He will care for you. And like the good Father He is, He will lead you safely to your promised land. Honor Him and trust Him today.

LEARN Read Deuteronomy 1:19–33.

FLOURISH Without any condemnation, take inventory of any entitled attitudes that surfaced this week. Impatience? Grumbling? Ingratitude? Defiant unbelief? Spend some time acknowledging and repenting of these things. Then ask God to bring times of refreshing to your soul.*

PRAY

Dear Jesus,
You deserve my highest praise, a grateful heart, and my loudest song. You've been so, so good to me. You deserve my trust. I will remember Your goodness. I will remember Your Word. And I will trust You on a deeper level, starting today. Amen.

*See Acts 3:19.

Faith for Your Children

I will give the land to your little ones—your innocent children. You were afraid they would be captured, but they will be the ones who occupy it.

Deuteronomy 1:39

My sons are grown now. Some of my greatest regrets as a parent are the times I allowed fear to drive my perspective and my decisions. I didn't cower in constant, gripping fear, but doubts and worry certainly impacted my parenting at times. I've since apologized to my sons. Thankfully, they responded with forgiveness and graciousness. The Israelites were deeply motivated by fear as well as by their love of comfort and convenience. Can you see how these motivations will sabotage the great things God wants to do in and through us? The most pampered and coddled children tend to have the least amount of substance in their character. May God put faith in your heart where there's fear. May He give you the courage to train your children in the way they should go. May they inherit—and embrace—the land that your fears may have kept you out of. And may He restore to you a childlike faith and inspire you to dare to dream again.

LEARN Read Deuteronomy 1:32–45.

FLOURISH Delayed obedience is disobedience. Has God asked something of you that you're putting off for another time? You (and your children) are safest in the center of God's will. Where He guides, He will provide. Obey quickly and trust Him fully.

PRAY

Lord,
Forgive me for the countless times I've let fear (and my love of comfort) dictate my decisions. I want childlike faith! I want to take risks, enjoy the journey, and occupy the land You have for me. Lead me on, Good Shepherd. Lead me on. Amen.

Pay for It

If you need food to eat or water to drink, pay them for it. For the LORD your God has blessed you in everything you have done.

Deuteronomy 2:6–7

God places a high value (no pun intended) on stewardship. If you read through the parables, you'll see how often Jesus speaks of our managing well all He's entrusted to us. But sometimes we take this idea to an extreme. Our penny pinching resembles an orphan spirit or a poverty mindset. And the person on the other side of our transactions doesn't see a generous, joyful spirit, but rather a miser who cares more about the bottom line than the person in front of them. A guest on my radio show once shared his dad's oft-repeated phrase, "Don't go out to eat unless you can afford a big tip." I love that. Christians should be the biggest tippers, the most generous givers, and the ones least likely to take advantage of another. We show the love of Christ when we act this way. Leave a big tip this week. Treat those who serve you with honor and respect. Look them in the eye and ask God to give you a word of encouragement for them. Hasn't God been faithful in the past? Won't He be faithful again? Yes, He will. Ask a generous person. God won't be outdone. He always replenishes the storehouses of the generous.

LEARN Read Luke 6:38.

FLOURISH Reflect God's kindness and generosity. Leave a big tip this week.

PRAY

Father,
You've been so good to me. I lack nothing. Help me to remember that the next time I have an opportunity to offer more than is required of me. In Your mighty name, I pray. Amen.

Remember Not to Forget

"But watch out! Be careful never to forget what you yourself have seen. Do not let these memories escape from your mind as long as you live! And be sure to pass them on to your children and grandchildren."

Deuteronomy 4:9

*T*hough the Israelites seemed to have short-term memory issues (they consistently forgot the ways God loved and cared for them), God instructed them to work on their long-term memory—to remember what they'd seen and to keep those experiences in the forefront of their minds. *Why do we forget some of our most important experiences with God?* Because we so often do what the Israelites did: We zero in on our current lack, inconvenience, hardship, or discomfort. Yet we are made for more. We can endure setbacks, hardships, and even lack because the Lord Almighty is with us. He gives us strategies to navigate difficult seasons, but He never wants us to embrace a scarcity mindset. He is a breakthrough God, and when the time is right, He will come through for us. Remember God's faithfulness today. It'll strengthen your heart. And your history with God reminds you that you also have a future with Him.

LEARN Read Deuteronomy 4:1–10.

FLOURISH Lift your eyes and speak to your circumstances. Remind them (and your soul) that God has come through in the past, and He will surely come through for you again. Tell someone a God-story today. Active faith will strengthen your soul.

PRAY

Dear Lord,

I pause today and remember Your kindness to me. Thank You for all You've provided, all You've prevented, and all You've empowered me to do. Remind me of the times You've come through for me. Give me boldness to pass on these stories to the next generation. Amen.

The First Thing

And now, Israel, what does the Lord your God require of you? He requires only that you fear the Lord your God, and live in a way that pleases him, and love him and serve him with all your heart and soul.

Deuteronomy 10:12

*J*ohn Ortberg joined me on my radio show to talk about what it means to truly follow Christ. He said, "What if, on my wedding night, I had asked Nancy this question: 'What's the least I must do for you in order to stay married to you?' If I dared to ask such a ridiculous question, I'd probably be without a wife today." And yet, we sometimes reduce salvation to a similar mindset. We want to secure our eternity, but we're not always as willing to reorient our whole lives toward God. Why does He ask such a thing of us? John Calvin once said that our hearts are idol-making factories. We bend toward idolatry, which destroys our hearts and dishonors God. Our hearts are most full, healed, and whole when they're set on the One who made them. God asks for our whole lives because He created us, He's worthy of the honor He's asking for, and our soul finds its deepest rest in Him.

LEARN   Read Deuteronomy 10:12–22.

FLOURISH   Ask Jesus to show you if you've wandered or drifted in any way. Smash your idols and live wholeheartedly for the One who made you.

PRAY

Lord Jesus,
I humble myself before You. Search my heart; show me what I need to see. Though You love me whether I wander or not, I'm my best self when I'm found in You. You deserve my highest honor and praise. Draw me near, O God. Amen.

Find Strength and Courage

This is my command—be strong and courageous! Do not be afraid or discouraged. For the LORD your God is with you wherever you go.

Joshua 1:9

*F*ear weakens us. Discouragement derails us. Yet our fears are real. And in certain seasons of perpetual difficulty, it seems we're constantly just moments away from careening into the ditch of discouragement. Maybe that's why God's voice thunders when He charges us to be strong and full of courage. Our feet tend to follow our gaze, and when our perspective is skewed, we lose our way. Yet Jesus' voice continually beckons us back to the path of faith. The reason Jesus charges us not to fear or to let discouragement win the day is because He knows what it'll do to our soul, to our heart. And what He asks of us, He also entrusts to us. When He asks us to be brave, He also gives us courage. Amazingly, He offers us faith and is at the same time pleased by our faith. He has entrusted to us every blessing, every promise, complete access to His presence, abundant wisdom for every hour. You can do this, friend. Just take another step.

LEARN   Read Joshua 1:6–9.

FLOURISH   Have you loosened your grip or lost a bit of your fight? Rise up, brave one, and claim the promises that are yours for the taking! Let the weak say, "*I am strong in the strength of the Lord!*"

PRAY

Precious Lord,
Thank You for not leaving me as an orphan. You've made me an heir. You've provided for my every need and equipped me for every battle. You've never left me alone and never will. Rise up within me once again, Lord. I am strong in You! Amen.

The Living God Is with You

Come and listen to what the LORD your God says. Today you will know that the living God is among you.

Joshua 3:9–10

*J*oshua was about to lead this new generation of Israelites into the Promised Land. They'd need two very important things in order to successfully make this trip: *ears to hear* and *a heart to know* God's mighty power and ability to intervene. We need these too. Pause here for a moment and consider the rogue thoughts and the daily stresses cluttering your brain right now. Set those aside for a moment. Turn off the TV. Put on some worship music and then set your phone aside. Take a few deep breaths. Ponder God's nearness. Lean in and listen to what the Lord your God is saying to you. Listen for His whisper. Do you hear Him? Linger with Him awhile. Though He sometimes seems slow to intervene, do you still believe that His power is matchless and His strength endless? Do you believe He's able to rearrange circumstances and intervene in ways that defy the gravity of your situation? Your presence with Him matters. He has things to say to you. He intends to display His power in your life. The Almighty God is *with you.*

LEARN Read Joshua 3:1–17

FLOURISH Don't rush through this day. Scoot close and listen for His voice. Know that the living God is in your midst. Write down what He says to you. Add the date so you'll remember it later.

PRAY

Mighty God of heaven,
You are all that I need. Forgive me for racing through my days feeling more stressed than blessed. I want to flourish in my soul. I want to trust You more. I'm listening, Lord. Speak to me. Amen.

On the Lord's Side

> When Joshua was near the town of Jericho, he looked up and saw a man standing in front of him with sword in hand. Joshua went up to him and demanded, "Are you friend or foe?"
>
> "Neither one," he replied. "I am the commander of the LORD's army."
>
> Joshua 5:13–14

God had just told Joshua to be strong and courageous, not to fear or fret. Why? Because the Lord was on Joshua's side! If God is for you, who can stand against you? So why didn't this commander also tell Joshua, "I'm a friend. I'm on your side"? It's one thing to put your unwavering trust in the Lord; it's another to presume upon God. Though Joshua's heart was all in, the Israelites still had wandering hearts. The angel reminded Joshua that though God is with us, *we're the ones on God's side.* He sets the terms, He guides our way, and He gets the say. When we fail, He loves us still. When we're unfaithful, He remains faithful. But sometimes we need a spiritual reset—a reminder of just who it is that we serve. He is the God of Angel Armies and we should take Him seriously.

LEARN Read Joshua 5:13–15; 7:1–13.

FLOURISH Are you hiding any idols in your tent? Justifying things you know you shouldn't? Come clean before Almighty God and receive the grace and mercy He's so willing to lavish upon you. Nothing compares.

PRAY

Precious Lord,
Sometimes I get so used to hearing that You are for me that I forget to check my heart, to see if I'm still for You. Give me a heart to love and honor You all of my days! Fill me afresh with the wonder of Your love. Amen.

Humility Precedes Honor

Joshua fell with his face to the ground in reverence. "I am at your command," Joshua said. "What do you want your servant to do?"

The commander of the LORD's army replied, "Take off your sandals, for the place where you are standing is holy." And Joshua did as he was told.

Joshua 5:14–15

God had charged Joshua to lead His chosen people into the Promised Land. He exhorted Joshua not to fear or get discouraged. Then He sent an angel to remind Joshua of God's majesty and honor. Before Joshua could rise up in victory, he first had to bow low in humility. Can you see the progression of events here? The Lord guards and guides our steps in much the same way. He knows what you need in order to face the battles up ahead. He knows what victories He's assigned to you. He knows when you need a word of encouragement and when it's time for you to bow low in reverence. All of these are for your good and for His glory. God never humiliates those who fear Him, but He does humble us. And He meets us intimately in that sacred place and shows us things we'd never otherwise know.

LEARN ▶ Read Joshua 5:13–15; 6:1–5.

FLOURISH ▶ Try praying and reading Scripture on your knees. Bow your face to the ground and tell God how wonderful He is. Ask God to show you His heart for you. Give Him your will and ask for His.

PRAY ▶

Precious Lord,
You modeled humility in the most beautiful way. I will follow Your lead. Open my eyes to see what I cannot see. Grant me a fresh revelation of Your love and majesty. It's in Your matchless name I pray. Amen.

Put the Enemy to Flight

Each one of you will put to flight a thousand of the enemy, for the LORD your God fights for you, just as he has promised.

Joshua 23:10

*W*hen we give God His rightful place in our lives, the enemy will be defeated, his evil schemes against us will eventually fall apart, and his attempts to derail our destiny will end up working in our favor. Whenever they were out of step with God, the Israelites got into trouble and were soundly defeated by their enemies. Whenever they griped and grumbled, lived entitled, disobeyed God's direct commands, and underestimated their enemy, they fell flat on their faces. However, when they walked in the fear of the Lord and trusted Him wholeheartedly, they saw the miraculous unfold before their very eyes. Oh, that we could learn from their mistakes! He's the same God today. He deserves our reverence, our trust, and our swift obedience. And He will intervene in ways we never dreamed as we take our stand and watch what He will do. On your own, you're no match for that enemy of yours. But with God—through your obedience and faith-filled prayers—you can change the world.

LEARN   Read Joshua 23:1–10.

FLOURISH   Dream a little for a moment. If you could live a miraculous life, what would that look like for you?

PRAY

Father,

Teach me to walk in Your way! Do the miraculous, the impossible through me! I don't want the enemy to put me to flight; I want to put him to flight! Show me how to stand in battle so my enemy flees and You win the victory through me. Change the world through me. Amen.

All In

> "So fear the LORD and serve him wholeheartedly. Put away forever the idols your ancestors worshiped. . . . Serve the LORD alone. . . . Choose today whom you will serve. . . . But as for me and my family, we will serve the LORD."
>
> Joshua 24:14–15

*I*t's been said that part-time Christians are some of the most miserable people on the planet. With one foot in and one foot out, they have no sense of belonging, no sense of purpose, and a constant, plaguing sense that they're missing out in both worlds. And they are. Yet what joy awaits us when we trust completely in Him! His will for us is our best-case scenario! Nothing the world offers compares to the power, the presence, and the very personal love the Savior has for us. Are you all in? If not, what's holding you back? Do you dare ask God to show you a fresh revelation of His heart for you? And if you'd say you're all in, I'd say, go deeper still. Plumb the depths of His love, stand more firmly on His promises, and linger longer in His presence. May the generations that come after you benefit greatly from your faithfulness. May they walk in an accumulative spiritual wealth because of the path you forged for them.

LEARN Read Joshua 24:11–24.

FLOURISH What kind of path do you want to forge? Ask the Lord to show you the importance of your promised land, not just for you, but for those who will come after you.

PRAY

Lord,
Too often I get so wrapped up in living for me that I forget about the greater impact of my story. Live Your powerful life in and through me! Give me a heart to be all in. Give me a vision for my promised land. Amen.

Rise Up and Take Your Place!

There were few people left in the villages of Israel—
until Deborah arose as a mother for Israel.

Judges 5:7

*T*hroughout the ages, Christianity has either expanded or contracted throughout the world based on the *influence* of the Christ-followers in those particular times and places. Where there's been a void of Christian influence, there's been a vacuum for the enemy to fill. National women leaders weren't exactly commonplace at the time of the judges, yet God called Deborah to rise up, to lead, and to help care for His people. Where's the need in your midst? What stirs up passion in your soul? How might God use you in this day to impact your world because of what Christ has done in you? Don't wait for someone else to lead—rise up! God has a place of influence for you, He has gifts He's called you to steward, and He has people He's appointed you to touch. May the passion and the purposes of God upstage every lesser voice, every inferior desire, and every earthly distraction. Rise up, dear one.

LEARN Read Judges 4:4–23; 5:6–7.

FLOURISH Set aside your default distractions and seek the face of God. Ask Him what your calling looks like in this particular season of life. Run hard after Jesus. Work hard and steward your gifts. Flourish in life.

PRAY

King Jesus,
I bow before You. I'll never have authority until I'm under authority. You've created me for influence. Show me my place in the greater kingdom story. Where and how shall I rise up in this day for the sake of Your name? Speak, Lord. Amen.

Mighty Hero, the Lord Is with You!

The angel of the LORD appeared to him and said, "Mighty hero, the LORD is with you!"

Judges 6:12

*E*ver feel outnumbered, outmatched, or in over your head? Imagine how Gideon must have felt when he was first called by God to rise up and defeat God's enemies. He saw himself as a nobody—the least of his tribe, which was the least of their clan. And if that weren't challenge enough, God then required him to thin his troops, putting him at an even greater disadvantage. What would that look like in your life? Maybe the Lord gave you a yes for a certain task or commitment, so you followed His lead, only to experience a setback or loss after the fact. Maybe you lost your job, you're battling insomnia, or your dishwasher flooded your kitchen. God *told* Gideon to thin the troops, but sometimes He allows the enemy to do the thinning for us—but only because He's setting us up for victory, and Him for great glory. If you've responded to God's invitation only to suddenly feel overwhelmed, you're in good company. Don't lose heart. Go in the strength you have. It's impossible for Him to fail you. *Mighty hero, the Lord is with you!*

LEARN Read Judges 6; 7:1–7.

FLOURISH Though we live by faith, not by sight, God is kind and patient and knows how to encourage us when we need it. If you need encouragement, ask for it.

PRAY

Precious Lord,
I'm in over my head. Show me a sign of Your favor and goodness, O Lord. Intervene in a way that encourages my soul. I need You every hour. Upward and onward I go. Thank You, Lord. Amen.

Glimpses of Glory

When Gideon heard the dream and its interpretation, he bowed in worship before the LORD. Then he returned to the Israelite camp and shouted, "Get up! For the LORD has given you victory over the Midianite hordes!"

Judges 7:15

God is so good to grant us glimpses of glory when we need them most. Gideon faced impossible odds. He knew without a doubt God had called him, yet he was still unsure of what the battle might cost him or how the story would play out. If you've walked with the Lord awhile, you know that just because God calls us to do something doesn't mean it'll be easy, without cost, and will turn out exactly as we've pictured it. But He calls us forward in faith with full assurance that if He calls us out, He'll hold us up. His ways are higher, His insights run deeper, and His desires for us *far exceed* our small earthbound desires for ourselves. God knows when we've got the inner fortitude to move ahead, and when we just need a glimpse of His goodness to encourage us onward. If you need a peek into His grand plan for you, just ask Him. May a newfound strength rise up within you today! May you be assured of the victory that awaits you on the other side of this battle.

LEARN ▶ Read Judges 7:9–20.

FLOURISH ▶ What do you need from the Lord today? Go ahead and ask Him.

PRAY ▶

Father,
Grant me a higher perspective on my circumstances. Give me a glimpse into Your perfect plan for me so I will march forward, unafraid and full of faith. I know it's impossible for You to fail me. Help me to know it on a deeper level. Amen.

Focused, Grateful, Humble

> One day when Samson was in Timnah, one of the Philistine women caught his eye. When he returned home, he told his father and mother, "A young Philistine woman in Timnah caught my eye. I want to marry her. Get her for me."
>
> Judges 14:1–2

*T*he Spirit of the Lord rested upon Samson, and yet our first glimpse into his character reveals a heart bent on his appetites. Samson's eyes wandered to things that dishonored God. He spouted demands to his father with a thankless, entitled attitude. Unfocused. Ungrateful. Arrogant. These attributes are the antithesis of God's heart for and through His people. How did Samson get like this? One unfocused, ungrateful, arrogant step at a time. Did his parents spoil him because he was called by God? It seems so. Samson's father didn't *have* to give in to Samson's selfish whim. But he did.* Samson's life is a tragic picture of what it looks like when someone who is anointed, gifted, and clearly called by God refuses to humbly submit *to* God.

LEARN ▶ Read Judges 14:1–9.

FLOURISH ▶ How can you live focused, humbly, and grateful today? Ask God to give you laser-like focus for what He's called you to do. Humble yourself when you're tempted to exalt yourself. And look around and thank God for everything you'd miss tomorrow if you woke up without it.

PRAY ▶

Father,
*   I'm prone to wander, I feel it! Help me to feel that inner wince when I exalt myself instead of You. And Lord, here are the things I'm so very grateful for today . . .*

---

*Verse 4 reveals that God worked through Samson's demands to set up His greater purposes, but it doesn't validate Samson's defiant, wandering appetite. God works all things together for the good (Romans 8:28).

When Pain Speaks

"Things are far more bitter for me than for you, because the Lord himself has raised his fist against me."

Ruth 1:13

*N*aomi had reason to grieve, to lament, and to even wonder where God was in it all. She'd lost her husband and then her two sons. She not only grieved as a widow and as a mother, but as a woman who was now at the mercy of the culture, the elements, and the times. Or so she thought. Truth was, she wasn't at anyone's mercy; she was *in* the mercies of God. She just didn't know it yet. Even though Elimelech, Naomi's husband, led his family outside the will of God to a land of idol-worshipers, God never left Naomi's side. He'd made a plan to redeem her story long before she ever knew she needed one. God's always in the process of bringing redemption to our stories. He knows about every enemy scheme, every unfortunate event, and every mess we find ourselves in. Yes, we need to process our pain. Lament is healing to the soul. But consider carefully the great difference between blaming God and crying out to Him. Check your heart today. Your redemption story is already in motion.

LEARN   Read Ruth 1:1–13.

FLOURISH   Ask the Lord if you have any unresolved grief hidden in your soul. Search your heart. Have you allowed hardness to settle in because of the length or intensity of your battle? Ask God to soften, restore, and heal you.

PRAY

Precious Jesus,
    With open hands and a humble heart, I ask You to redeem me from the things I've suffered. Help me sort through my losses in a way that draws me closer to You and heals me from the inside out. Amen.

When Conviction Speaks

But Ruth replied, "Don't ask me to leave you and turn back. Wherever you go, I will go; wherever you live, I will live. Your people will be my people, and your God will be my God."

Ruth 1:16

Naomi's faith must have impacted Ruth over the years because Ruth—a Moabite—saw through her painful loss and embraced the bigger story God was writing with her life. No one would have blamed her if she'd gone back to her small town and small 'g' gods. Most probably expected it. But to everyone's surprise, Ruth pulled up her tent stakes to follow God. She knew the travel would be treacherous; she was well aware of what happens to women who don't have men to protect them. She was smart enough to know that even if she made it to Bethlehem, she'd likely be rejected and excluded by the Israelite women because of where she came from. But none of that mattered to Ruth. She was willing to leave what she knew to follow a God she could not see. We know how her story turned out, but at this particular moment in biblical history, Ruth had no idea that we'd still be talking about her today. Do you believe that your faith matters *just as much*? And that your risks are noted in heaven? Don't choose ease over eternity. Rise up and follow where He leads.

LEARN Read Ruth 1:14–22.

FLOURISH What kind of faith risk is before you? What are you waiting for? Just keep taking the next step. God will do the rest.

PRAY

Lord Jesus,
Give me the courage and conviction to live boldly for You! Forgive me for my tendency to self-preserve and choose comfort over conviction. You deserve my whole heart. Amen.

As It Happened

So Ruth went out to gather grain behind the harvesters. And as it happened, she found herself working in a field that belonged to Boaz, the relative of her father-in-law, Elimelech.

Ruth 2:3

*R*uth was a foreigner—and new in town. However, she was so committed to her grieving mother-in-law that she boldly took initiative and went out among strangers to gather grain. And, *as it happened*, she ended up working in a field owned by a relative of her father-in-law, Boaz. Boaz noticed Ruth right away. It takes honor to notice honor in another. He looked past Ruth's ethnicity and social class and saw what God saw: honor, humility, courage, and conviction. Boaz stepped up and made sure Ruth would be protected and provided for. Ruth took initiative; God took it from there. Isn't it amazing that when we take faith risks to follow God wholeheartedly, He leads us even when we're unaware? He guards and He guides; He protects and provides. One day we'll get to heaven and absolutely marvel at God's intervention in our lives. But for now, we must rest assured that when our hearts are fully set on the Lord, He will be our Good Shepherd every step of the way.

LEARN Read Ruth 2:1–9.

FLOURISH Lean in, and follow Jesus wholeheartedly. Take initiative when it's yours to do so. Believe down to your toes that God will determine your steps. Live with the expectancy. He's already gone ahead of you!

PRAY

Father,
I trust You. I cannot fathom how many circumstances You've already orchestrated for my good and for Your glory. Open my eyes to see what You're up to all around me. Help me to embrace the adventure of following You. Thank you, Lord. Amen.

Refuge and Reward

> May the LORD, the God of Israel, under whose wings you have come to take refuge, reward you fully for what you have done.
>
> Ruth 2:12

*F*aith compels us to do what our flesh would rather not. Faith calls us out when we'd rather stay back. Faith charges us to wait when we'd rather run. Ruth's faith compelled her to action. She couldn't know all of the good things God had planned for her. She had faith in a God who was even better than she believed Him to be. *You* have faith in a God who is far better than you know Him to be. Boaz spoke a blessing over Ruth that's meant for you today as well. May God reward you fully for the times you loved when it didn't suit you, for the times you served when no one saw you, for the ways you followed Jesus when it cost you. May the Lord Almighty bless you for finding refuge under His wings. You trusted Him. May you find Him more faithful and kinder than you ever dreamed.

LEARN Read Ruth 2:10–23.

FLOURISH Take some time to rest today—rest in God's grace, rest in His love, and rest in the fact that He doesn't miss a thing. He sees you. He will reward you. So today, let Him refresh you.

PRAY

Precious Lord,

Thank You for Your kindness to me. You've invited me to take shelter under Your wing. You've put faith in my heart. You've invited me to trust and obey. And then You reward me for doing the very thing I was made to do—follow You. I honor You this day. I know You are good and kind and true. And I am grateful. Amen.

From Famine to Flourishing

Then the elders and all the people standing in the gate replied, "We are witnesses! May the LORD make this woman who is coming into your home like Rachel and Leah, from whom all the nation of Israel descended! May you prosper in Ephrathah and be famous in Bethlehem."

Ruth 4:11

Widows in Ruth's day had little hope for a flourishing future. Yet somehow God orchestrated events so that this Moabite woman of God would marry one of the most honorable men in town. The elders stood at the gate and prophesied a blessing that would surely come to pass. Ruth was no longer a widow; she was a wife. She no longer had to scrape out a living; she was well cared for and provided for. She and Naomi were no longer destitute; they were destined to live out God's sovereign plan for their lives. You may find yourself in the not-yet part of your story. You're still waiting for the breakthrough. I pray Ruth's faith inspires your own. He's the same God yesterday, today, and forever. He loves you as much as He loved Ruth. Don't give up hope. Your story has a wonderful ending. Like my friend Jodi once said to me, "If your story's not good yet, it's because God's not done yet."

LEARN Read Ruth 3; 4:1–11.

FLOURISH What parts of your story aren't good yet? Ask God to intervene. Do what He tells you to. And believe that He's up to something good. He is, you know.

PRAY

Lord, I don't want to feel like a have-not. Forgive me for believing I'm somehow less important to You than Your other children. I know You love me. Show me how to trust You with my whole story. Amen.

Total Redemption

So Boaz took Ruth into his home, and she became his wife. When he slept with her, the LORD enabled her to become pregnant, and she gave birth to a son.

Ruth 4:13

*R*uth—a Moabite widow—married Boaz, son of Rahab, the prostitute. Together, they had a baby boy named Obed, who became the father of Jesse, who became the father of King David. These two unlikely yet beautiful people were grafted into the lineage of Christ! A Moabite woman and a son of a prostitute. Aren't the grace and the mercy of God just breathtaking? This is why we must not allow man with all of his skewed perspectives to derail us from what God has promised us. Like Ruth and Boaz, we've been grafted into the family line! Because of Jesus, we have His royal blood flowing through our veins! It doesn't matter what we've come from or what we've done in our past. What matters is our faith in the One who redeemed us. Boaz was Ruth's kinsman redeemer. Jesus is ours. No one and nothing can separate us from His love. Jesus has not only covered our past with mercy and forgiveness, He's *completely* secured our future. Your story is and will be *completely* redeemed.

LEARN Read Ruth 4:13–22.

FLOURISH Take some significant time today and ponder your secure place in the heart of Christ. Smile at the thought of it. Sing and worship too. You're more blessed than you know.

PRAY

Jesus,
What You accomplished for me, I cannot fathom, but I thank You just the same. I'm secure in You! I'm established in You! I possess all the riches of heaven, because of You. Thank You, Jesus. Thank You. Amen.

Rightly Placed Honor

So Peninnah would taunt Hannah and make fun of her because the LORD had kept her from having children.

1 Samuel 1:6

*H*annah was blessed because she was loved, yet she felt cursed because she was barren. Peninnah pridefully took credit for her own fertility and judged Hannah for her unexplained barrenness. Both misinterpreted their situations. Things are rarely as they appear. Peninnah honored—and elevated— herself when she should have humbly honored God. There's a moment in the film *Gladiator* when the evil king reveled in and bragged about the wickedness he inflicted upon Maximus's family. Maximus stood with his jaw set (and his heart broken) and said, "The time for honoring yourself will soon be at an end." The same is true for every person who insists on honoring him- or herself above God. Neither Hannah nor Peninnah could know that God had actually kept Hannah from having children because He was waiting for the right time to draw a whole nation back to Him. Her future son would become one of the greatest prophets of all time. Don't let the taunters get to you. Their day of discipline is coming. Honor God. He will—in due time—bless you before a watching world.

LEARN Read 1 Samuel 1:1–7.

FLOURISH Even if no one is taunting you right now, ask God if you've misread any situation that's caused you grief. Ask Him to show you what's really true.

PRAY

Lord of heaven's armies,
You are with me. You are for me. Forgive me for putting more weight on my flawed perspective than I do on Your perfect promises. My story fits me perfectly. I trust You. Fill me with faith and perspective this hour. Amen.

Pain Filters
and Passionate Prayers

> As she was praying to the LORD, Eli watched her. Seeing her lips moving but hearing no sound, he thought she had been drinking. "Must you come here drunk?" he demanded. "Throw away your wine!"
>
> 1 Samuel 1:12–14

*W*ould this dear woman never catch a break? Hannah takes her brokenhearted self to the temple to cry out to God, just as she should. She bows low, humbles herself before Almighty God, and asks Him to look upon the sorrow in her heart, only to have the high priest say to her, "Wait . . . are you drunk?" Have mercy! But if you scoot in closer to this story, you'll see that Eli's own sons were the ones drinking in the temple. Eli viewed Hannah's heartbreak through his own pain filter. Hurt people hurt people. Thankfully, Hannah was humble enough to respond with truth—but talk about adding insult to injury! Her husband's extra wife taunted her, and the temple priest accused her. Did she make a mistake, running to the temple? Absolutely not. Did Eli misread the situation? Absolutely. Did God redeem her story? One hundred percent, yes! Life on earth can be so very messy. But you'll never go wrong running to the arms of your Savior.

LEARN Read 1 Samuel 1:9–18.

FLOURISH Don't allow the hurts you've endured from men keep you from running into the presence of God. And may we all be a bit more gracious when it comes to assessing the suffering of another. We don't know what we don't know.

PRAY

Jesus,
Sometimes I allow my wounds and offenses to pull me away from You. But today I take every hurt and every heartbreak, and I bring them before You. People and pain will not have the last say in my life! Amen.

The Lord Has Made Me Strong!

> "My heart rejoices in the LORD! The LORD has made me strong.
> Now I have an answer for my enemies; I rejoice because you rescued me."
>
> 1 Samuel 2:1

*T*he believer's story is one of setbacks and divine setups. The enemy opposes us and God defends us. We lose heart and God strengthens our hearts. We break down and God breaks through. We forget about His goodness and He reminds us once again that He is constantly and continually good. How many nights do you suppose Hannah cried herself to sleep, wondering if she'd done something to chase away God's blessing on her life? How many times did the enemy leverage that opportunity to shoot discouragement right into the depths of her soul? Though Hannah struggled through her heartbreak (understandably so), we never get the sense it developed an offense against God. She stayed humble and teachable, and God not only defended her, He also vindicated her beyond her wildest dreams. Your story has its twists and turns. You have your days of ups and downs, and God will be with you every step of the way. But remember this: He cannot strengthen a hard heart, only a humble one. Stay tender and trust Him. He will make you strong and you *will* have an answer for your enemies.

LEARN Read 1 Samuel 2:1–11.

FLOURISH Discern where you are on the journey today. Trust that God is in the process of delivering and defending you. Stay tender and teachable. Watch what He does for you.

PRAY

Jesus,
This is my story, and I trust You with it. Intervene where I cannot. Defend and deliver me. Make me strong and steadfast. May Your favor upon my life silence my critics. Amen.

Up or Down?

Eli's sons wouldn't listen to their father, for the LORD was already planning to put them to death. Meanwhile, the boy Samuel grew taller and grew in favor with the LORD and with the people.

1 Samuel 2:25–26

*T*hat which is not growing is dying. Life is not static; it's moving in one way or another. From the outside looking in, both of Eli's sons as well as Samuel held places of privilege in the temple. But God sees past our positions, our titles, and our social status; He looks right into the depths of our hearts. It's been said that over time, our most consistent choices either expose us or promote us. In other words, what we've been doing in private in due time shows up in a public way. We cannot rest on past laurels, or even our past steps of obedience. The question at hand is this: In which direction are my feet pointing? Where are my most consistent choices taking me? Am I drawing nearer to the Lord, or am I walking away from Him for the sake of momentary pleasure? As I often say, God's will for you is your best-case scenario. He intends to take you from strength to strength, glory to glory, shining ever brighter until the full light of day.

LEARN ▶ Read 1 Samuel 2:12–26.

FLOURISH ▶ Take an honest inventory of your default comforts. Are you taking more liberties than you ought? Trust Him more than you trust yourself. Reset your course today.

PRAY ▶

Father,
I am prone to wander; Lord, I feel it! Keep my heart deeply connected to Yours. Show me where I'm weakest and help me to shore up my life. I want to grow in favor and stature before You, Lord. Draw me closer still. Amen.

Holy Reinforcement

So the Philistines were subdued and didn't invade Israel again for some time. And throughout Samuel's lifetime, the Lord's powerful hand was raised against the Philistines.

1 Samuel 7:13

*N*o one can fathom the power of one life solely dedicated to the Lord Most High. Before Samuel was even born, Hannah dedicated him to the Lord. Samuel lived in the Lord's presence and honored him continually. Because Samuel lived among God's people, their enemies were held at bay. What if we approached our walk of faith in much the same way? When we take seriously our lives before the Lord, He takes very seriously the prayers that come out of our mouth. Imagine, because of your very presence on the earth today, evil plans come to nothing, enemy schemes break down, and God's people are protected in ways they'll never realize this side of heaven. All because you walked closely with the Lord. God has placed you on this earth for such a time as this. History has proven time and time again that one life—wholly dedicated to the Lord—has the power to change the world.

LEARN Read 1 Samuel 3:7–14.

FLOURISH What injustices break your heart? What evil schemes stir you up? What if, while others shake their fists at the darkness, you commit yourself more firmly to the Lord? You can pray like there's a God in heaven who hears you when you pray, because there is, and He does!

PRAY

Strong and mighty God,
Hear my prayer! Foil the plans of the wicked and establish the plans of the righteous! Cut off the strength of the wicked and increase the power of the godly! Break my heart for what breaks Yours. I want my prayers to change the world! Amen.

Insecurity Is Not Humility

Saul replied, "But I'm only from the tribe of Benjamin, the smallest tribe in Israel, and my family is the least important of all the families of that tribe! Why are you talking like this to me?"

1 Samuel 9:21

*S*aul's question sounds an awful lot like Gideon's, wouldn't you say? But if you watch how their lives play out, you realize that while Gideon may have felt a bit insecure, his weightier attribute was humility, whereas Saul was fueled by his chronic self-sins. Read this powerful study note from my Bible: "Although Saul had been called by God and had a mission in life, he struggled constantly with jealousy, insecurity, arrogance, impulsiveness, and deceit. He did not decide to be wholeheartedly committed to God. *Because Saul would not let God's love give rest to his heart, he never became God's man.*"* When rejection, insecurity, and inferiority remain unchallenged within us, we will repeatedly sabotage our own destiny. We've got to be ruthless with thoughts of insecurity. You and I are called to freedom—humble, bold, courageous freedom. It's the only way we'll live out the amazing call on our lives.

LEARN Read 1 Samuel 9:15–21.

FLOURISH This takes grit but I dare you to do it anyway. Ruthlessly eliminate *any hint* of insecurity from your thoughts and your speech. Live and walk like you are loved. You are an heir of God and you bear His image. Soldier on, mighty one!

PRAY

> *Father,*
> *Forgive me for coddling my insecurities more than I cling to Your promises. I will stand in faith and believe what You say about me. I am called and I am loved. Lead me on, Lord! Amen.*

Life Application Study Bible (Carol Stream, IL: Tyndale, 2004), 563, emphasis mine.

Are You Not?

And Samuel told him, "Although you may think little of yourself, are you not the leader of the tribes of Israel? The LORD has anointed you king of Israel."

1 Samuel 15:17

*W*hen my sons were teenagers, my mentor wisely said, "While discipline matters, it's destiny that will speak to and motivate your sons." Though it was important to stay consistent with our convictions, we learned that rules and consequences weren't enough to motivate our boys to be all they could be through Christ. We needed to cast a vision for what was possible for the one who stays humble, teachable, and faithful. Saul had a clear call on his life. God confirmed it again and again. Yet Saul was bent on doing things his own way. Then he made excuses, blamed others, and even spiritualized his disobedience in order to justify his actions. Saul never fully grasped what God would have accomplished through him, if only he'd dared to trust Him. Learn from Saul's losses. Ask God to help you see yourself the way He sees you! Ask Him for a vision for your life that makes your heart come alive and for faith to lay hold of it.

LEARN   Read 1 Samuel 15:10–23.

FLOURISH   When you're tempted to squander your time or doubt your worth, picture the prophet Samuel grabbing you by the shoulders, looking deep into your eyes, and imploring you, "Are you not absolutely beloved and called by God? Have you forgotten who you are? The Lord has anointed and appointed you!"

PRAY

Father,
   Like Saul, I can tend to cut corners, make excuses, and then attempt to strive my way back into Your good graces. But that's not how You operate. I'm already in Your mercy and grace. I humble myself before You. I choose to believe and obey You. Help my unbelief. Amen.

Don't Miss Your Assignment

But Samuel asked, "How can I do that? If Saul hears about it, he will kill me."

1 Samuel 16:2

God anointed and appointed Saul as king. Yet Saul's constant and continual bent toward himself sabotaged his own destiny. If we don't praise God, the rocks will cry out. If we don't step into our God-given assignment with a heart of faith and trust, perhaps deliverance for those we're assigned to help will come another way. I don't want to miss a thing God has for me, do you? While Saul was busy misusing his power, young David was in the wilderness learning how to fight lions and bears. He was both chosen and growing into God's man to replace Saul. Yet when God told the prophet Samuel that it was time to anoint another king, Samuel froze in fear. Samuel's fear made sense given Saul's crazy, impulsive ways. And yet, the odds, the circumstances, the opposition are all meaningless when the Lord has issued a charge to us. Though it's true that your God-given assignment may involve uncertainty, opposition, and a few giants, don't let your fears keep you from moving forward. If God has called you to it, He will see you through it.

LEARN Read 1 Samuel 16:1–7.

FLOURISH In what ways have you recently pulled back in fear? *That's* where God is calling you to engage your faith. What steps of obedience will you take today?

PRAY

King Jesus,
You are all that I need. So often I forget that if You call me out beyond my natural abilities, You will hold me up. I'm ready to follow You today. I'm all in. Lead me on. Amen.

The Lord Looks at the Heart

"The LORD doesn't see things the way you see them. People judge by outward appearance, but the LORD looks at the heart."

1 Samuel 16:7

*W*hen God sent Samuel to anoint the next king, He cautioned the prophet to listen with His spiritual ears so he wouldn't be misled by what he saw. We so often get it wrong. Our filter is profoundly skewed by our hurts and fears, our culture's trends, and our own judgments. But if our eyes opened up to see what God sees, we'd marvel at the things God values, and at what He finds distasteful. We'd see Him ministering to a convicted felon humbly praying on a prison floor, while distancing himself from the polished minister who lives for man's praise and pridefully guards his territory. We'd see Him draw near to the humble-yet-messy mom who just cannot keep up with the house or the laundry, and watch Him distance himself from the girl who has everything and wonders why everyone else is such a mess. May you discern what God sees when you look at others. And may you be who God is looking for when He's ready to appoint the next influencer.

LEARN Read 1 Samuel 16:4–13.

FLOURISH What you look for, you will find. Start looking for honor, humility, grace, and joy in others. You'll find it.

PRAY

Father,
I don't want to live by my assumptions and skewed perspectives. Open up the eyes of my heart so I can see what You see. Help me to discern honor, humility, grace, and joy when I see it. Help me to value those things too. I want to be more like You in every way. Lead me on, dear Jesus. Amen.

Promoted Gradually

Saul sent messengers to Jesse to say, "Send me your son David, the shepherd."

1 Samuel 16:19

Samuel went to the house of Jesse and anointed young David to be the next king. Yet it would be years before David actually took the throne. Even so, God was actively working behind the scenes. While the Spirit of the Lord came powerfully upon David, that same Spirit had lifted from Saul. It seemed the king was losing his mind. His men suggested he bring in a young warrior/musician to soothe his fears and anxiety. You wonder if David thought, *Is this the day my call comes to fruition?* This wasn't to be the day, but it was the start of his preparation process. David would go back and forth between his father's house and the palace as he was needed. He learned the ways of the kingdom and he learned to wait on God's sometimes hard-to-understand timing. Most often, after we've received a vision or sense of calling from the Lord, we too will see movement in that direction, only to see it short-lived. Did we hear wrong? Is this all there is? No! More often than not, you'll go back and forth between the palace and your home until the time is ready for you to take your place. Don't lose heart. Stay humble. Stay ready.

LEARN Read 1 Samuel 16:14–23.

FLOURISH What is your current waiting season bringing up in you? Take it to the Lord and keep your heart ready and in the right place. You'll be glad you did.

PRAY

Father,
  I know You make me wait because You're making me ready. Help me to discern Your voice and see Your movement all around me. Promotion comes from You. I'll wait on You. Amen.

What Emerges from Us

When Saul and the Israelites heard [Goliath's rant], they were terrified and deeply shaken.

1 Samuel 17:11

Someone once said that when we get bumped, what's inside spills right out of us. It's true: What's in us emerges from us when we're tested. Saul may have been tall, dark, and handsome, and he may have held the title of king, but when faced with a giant, his inexperience and insecurity surfaced. Saul's perpetual tendency toward self-doubt and self-preservation revealed a consistent thought life bent toward himself. David, on the other hand, was a different story. When Saul questioned David's capacity to take on a giant, David rehearsed his victories and reminded everyone listening that God was greater than any giant he'd ever face. David wrote, sang, and spoke of God's continual faithfulness. What emerged from David in the face of battle? Courage, honor, and faith. Every step you take matters, because it's taking you somewhere. Every thought you entertain is shaping you and framing your perspective, which impacts your future choices. But you may not realize the importance of your past choices until you face a giant or find yourself in a storm. Your choices matter profoundly because *you* matter. Your life matters. Your influence matters.

LEARN   Read 1 Samuel 17:1–11.

FLOURISH   What have you been holding, rehearsing, and believing all these years? Is it time for a change? *Every* step toward wholeness matters.

PRAY

Lord Jesus,
Show me my heart. Show me all of the inputs that have weighed me down and held me back. Give me a fresh dose of faith and a fresh vision for flourishing! I believe and therefore speak . . . You are mighty in me! Amen.

A Right Perspective in Battle

David asked the soldiers standing nearby, ". . . Who is this pagan Philistine anyway, that he is allowed to defy the armies of the living God?"

1 Samuel 17:26

When Goliath arrived on the scene, he hurled insults at the warriors of Israel. He spoke out of both sides of his mouth. He challenged them to battle, and he asked them why they'd even consider fighting him given he was a champion and they were only servants of Saul. Do you see how the enemy works? First he baits you into battle, then he diminishes your status by calling you names, hitting you where you're weak, and making it personal. But look at young David. It didn't even occur to him to take things personally (even though his own brothers, who were supposed to be on his side, hurled very personal accusations his way). Because David saw the bigger picture, he asked a faith-filled question: *Who is this Philistine that dares to defy the armies of the living God?* He understood that his battle wasn't personal. It was spiritual. It's the same with you. Don't let your enemy single you out. Stay in step with the Holy Spirit. See the bigger picture. And call on your giant-killer of a God to fight powerfully through you.

LEARN   Read 1 Samuel 17:12–27.

FLOURISH   Refuse to read between the lines or allow the enemy's intentions to hit their mark. Just say no. Look up and discern what God is asking of you.

PRAY

Lord Jesus,
Teach me how to stand in battle. Help me to raise my shield and stand in faith when the arrows zing my way. I don't have to let things in. I can be unaffected by scenarios that once made me insecure. I am strong in You! Amen.

When Jealousy Arises

When Eliab, David's oldest brother, heard him speaking with the men, he burned with anger at him and asked, "Why have you come down here? And with whom did you leave those few sheep in the wilderness? I know how conceited you are and how wicked your heart is; you came down only to watch the battle."

1 Samuel 17:28 NIV

*D*id Eliab know his brother at all? It was David, the younger brother, who, because he saw the bigger story, was more concerned about the reputation of his nation (and his God) than he was about his own safety. Yet his scared big brother accused him of neglecting his duties at home, of being conceited, and of having a wicked heart. When you mature in faith, your heart of conviction will grow; you'll start to care about things like honor, justice, and God's glory. One day you'll step out in faith, and you will excite the jealousies of others. They may accuse you of things *they're* actually guilty of, and they'll assign motives that don't belong to you. What to do? Pull out your shield of faith and use your capital NO. Don't let their words in—even for a moment. Keep your head up. Stay humble. And know that God disciplines His own. You stay obedient. He'll deal with your critics.

LEARN Read 1 Samuel 17:28–37.

FLOURISH Read this story and note the difference between scared pettiness and focused faith. You're called to be a difference maker. Keep the faith.

PRAY

Lord Jesus,
Break my heart for what breaks Yours. Give me Your passion and purpose to do what You would do if You were in my shoes. I entrust my critics to You and I lay hold of Your promises for me. Amen.

A Mantle that Fits You

"I can't go in these," he protested to Saul. "I'm not used to them." So David took them off again.

1 Samuel 17:38–39

avid's past battles had prepared him for his present battle. He feared God, knew His voice, and trusted His ways above all else. God knew what He was doing with David, and He's just as intentional with you. What can we learn from David's example? Follow Jesus wholeheartedly and trust His timing. Stay in pace with His grace and embrace a humble, teachable heart. Do this, and Jesus will lead you forward into your next place of promise. Embrace this mindset as a way of life—always seeking first His kingdom and His righteousness—and your life will be marked by power and will bear much fruit. People will start to notice. They'll have opinions about how you ought to walk this thing out. And while there's wisdom in many counselors, there's also wisdom in discerning whether or not something fits who you are and what God has asked of you in this particular season. You'll know when something doesn't fit because it'll feel forced and foreign, and even clunky. Wisdom's path is peace. Don't be afraid to be you. Your past battles have prepared you for this moment.

LEARN Read 1 Samuel 17:38–51.

FLOURISH You're not called to blend in. God made you unique for a reason! Stay humble, gracious, and teachable, and at the same time embrace the YOU God created. You're a masterpiece.

PRAY

Lord,

Help me to discern when You're calling me to learn new things and when You want me to stay true to what I already know. I am Yours. I want to be like You. Teach and train me, Lord. Amen.

The Test Before the Triumph

"Now's your opportunity!" David's men whispered to him. "Today the LORD is telling you, 'I will certainly put your enemy into your power, to do with as you wish.'" So David crept forward and cut off a piece of the hem of Saul's robe.

1 Samuel 24:4

David knew he'd be king one day. David also feared God. Saul feared only for himself and relentlessly pursued David with the intent to kill him. David's men assumed God had delivered Saul right into his hands. Self-defense, right? Thankfully, David had enough conviction and restraint *not* to kill Saul, but he did cut off a piece of his robe to make a point. But even that gesture ultimately bothered David. He was so given to the Lord's will and timing for his life, he knew that any effort to grab for himself would be a faithless one. Oftentimes on the way to your breakthrough, you'll be faced with opportunities to grab for yourself and force an outcome, but it will not be God's best timing for you. How do you protect against wrong assumptions? You fear God and walk intimately with Him. You fully trust His timing. You wait for Him to establish you. His Spirit within you will convict you and clarify your steps.

LEARN Read 1 Samuel 24.

FLOURISH The most important thing you can do today and tomorrow is to honor and fear the Lord. Spend time pondering His greatness and trust His timing.

PRAY

Lord,
*   Help me never to get ahead of You! Spirit of the Living God, fall afresh on me! Awaken my heart to sense Your direction and cherish Your protection. Lead me in power and purity. My soul waits for You. Amen.*

Keep Your Heart in It

In the spring of the year, when kings normally go out to war, David sent Joab and the Israelite army to fight the Ammonites. They destroyed the Ammonite army and laid siege to the city of Rabbah. However, David stayed behind in Jerusalem.

2 Samuel 11:1

*T*here's a time for engagement and a time for rest. But there's never a time for disengagement. When we walk through a storm, all we can think about is getting to the other side, experiencing some kind of relief from the battle. Yet it's the storms that teach us how to stand strong. It's the battle that teaches us how to fight. Our best lessons are taught through our hardships, and we learn to depend on the Lord through the things we suffer. But because God is good, He'll bring us through and give us rest from our trials. However, we're especially vulnerable after an intense battle or a great victory. And that's exactly when we tend to loosen our grip on what we know to be true. We forget that we're just as dependent in the good times as we are in the tough times. Our very breath comes from the Lord Almighty. No doubt, David was weary from battle. But his disengagement made him vulnerable. May you wisely discern the difference between restorative rest and undisciplined disengagement. It may save your reputation.

LEARN Read 2 Samuel.

FLOURISH Have you let your guard down? Left your post? Reengage and activate your faith. Don't leave yourself exposed to the enemy's schemes.

PRAY

Lord,
Lead me not into temptation and deliver me from evil. For Yours is the kingdom, power, and glory, both now and forever. Amen.

He Will Come for You

He led me to a place of safety;
he rescued me because he delights in me.
2 Samuel 22:20

*D*avid was a man after God's own heart. And because of it, he had a target on his back. The devil hated him, Saul hated him, and David even got himself into some serious trouble on occasion. Yet he knew enough to humbly cry out to the Lord. Humility in our heart activates the mercy in God's heart. He doesn't rescue us because we're good or because we've earned it. He rescues us because we need it. His compassion runs deeper than the deepest sea. His love reaches higher than the highest heaven. He is God. He has no rival. He's all powerful. What in the world would we do if the one true God were anything but good? I can't imagine! But thankfully, He is good. When we cry out to Him, He comes for us. He shrouds himself in darkness and veils His approach before He breaks through. You may not see Him coming, but neither will your enemy. But make no mistake about it. He will come for you.

LEARN Read 2 Samuel 22:1–40.

FLOURISH If you're in a desperate situation, cry out to God today, and don't hold back. Shift your weight onto His goodness and trust Him to carry you through. Let your thoughts linger on His compassion all day today. It'll nourish your heart.

PRAY

Father,
I need You to rescue me! I tend to put more weight on my performance than on Yours. Yet it's You who saved me. You're the One who rescues me. You're not looking for perfection, You're looking for faith; raw, humble, surrendered faith. So here I am, Lord. Come for me! Amen.

Ask for Wisdom

The Lord was pleased that Solomon had asked for wisdom.

1 Kings 3:10

olomon could have asked God for anything, yet he asked for wisdom. Why do you suppose that is? Why didn't he ask for relief from his enemies or wealth beyond compare? Solomon had enough wisdom to know that too much ease and too much material comfort would weaken him over time if he didn't also have wisdom to steward those blessings. God's promise of wisdom is one of the best-kept secrets of the Bible. He offers lavish amounts to anyone who asks for it. Why not throw your arms open wide and ask Him for abounding wisdom every single day of your life? What would you do with more wisdom? You'd be less apt to react and more likely to respond. You'd be slower to commit and firmer in your commitments. You'd refuse the rat race and instead run the sacred race. There are certain prayers God loves to answer. Pray for what's on His heart and you'll marvel at how He works in your life.

LEARN Read 1 Kings 3:6–14.

FLOURISH Get into the daily habit of boldly asking God for great amounts of wisdom. Then fine-tune your ears and listen for His answer.

PRAY

> *Lord,*
> *Pour out daily wisdom on me! Fill me with compassion. Break my heart for what breaks Yours. Awaken me to see the value in others. Anoint me to preach the Good News to the lost, the hurting, and the broken. Help me to live a wise, discerning life. Amen.*

Stunned by His Presence

The priests could not continue their service because of the cloud, for the glorious presence of the LORD filled the Temple of the LORD.

1 Kings 8:11

*S*omeone once said that the reason we don't experience the kinds of miracles many Christians do in other parts of the world is that we're so comfortable, not desperate enough, and so *vanilla* in our faith. Do you suppose that's true? Experts say that if you don't feel physical hunger at least twice a day, you're eating too much and too often. How much more so with our spiritual life? If we're not hungry because we feed on that which does not nourish, how will we long for the kingdom of heaven? If we don't hunger for the presence of God, how will revival come? What if we stopped propping ourselves up with all of our faux comforts and paid attention to what surfaces within us? We might feel anxious, irritable, and even uncomfortable. Is God's presence enough to meet us here? Absolutely. Maybe the question to ask ourselves today is this: *What am I trying so hard not to feel?* You have to feel it to heal it. Jesus is the Great Healer. What parts of our redemptive story are we missing because we're not missing His presence at all? It's in *His presence* where the fullness of joy is found.

LEARN   Read 1 Kings 8:10–11, 22–23.

FLOURISH   Give up something for twenty-four hours each week. Incorporate fasting as part of your regular practice. But don't just fast—pursue, press in, and wait on the Lord.

PRAY

Lord Jesus,
I hunger and thirst for You! Forgive me for the countless ways I numb out and miss You. Stir up a passion in my soul. I want to know Your presence, Lord. Amen.

Finish Strong

In Solomon's old age, [his wives] turned his heart to worship other gods instead of being completely faithful to the LORD his God, as his father, David, had been.

1 Kings 11:4

One of the daily prayers of my heart is this: *Dear Jesus, may I abound in love more and more. May I increase daily in all wisdom, knowledge, and depth of insight. May I understand the times and know what to do. May I wisely discern Your wisdom, Your will, and Your truth. May my life bear the fruit of righteousness, and may I live and die honoring Your name.* None of us do it all right all of the time. But more than anything else, I want to finish well. David sinned in profound ways. So why was God so taken with him? Because David's heart was *for* God. David was humble, repentant, and deeply in love with the Lord his God. He finished well. William MacDonald writes, "Solomon's beginning was better than his ending. A good start does not always guarantee a good finish. He had been raised to the pinnacle of greatness, but he plunged off into idolatry. If only the king would have practiced what he preached."*

LEARN Read 1 Kings 11:1–13.

FLOURISH What would it look like for you to finish well? What choices do you need to make today to ensure a strong finish?

PRAY

I'm prone to wander, Lord, I feel it! Help me lose my taste for that which weakens me and acquire a taste for that which strengthens me. Lead me not into temptation and deliver me from evil. Help me to finish well. Amen.

---

*William MacDonald, *Believer's Bible Commentary* (Nashville: Thomas Nelson, 1990), 369.

Discerning God's Voice

But the old prophet answered, "I am a prophet, too, just as you are. And an angel gave me this command from the LORD: 'Bring him home with you so he can have something to eat and drink.'" But the old man was lying to him.

1 Kings 13:18

God instructed His prophet to denounce the evil practices taking place at the altar of Bethel and pronounce the coming of King Josiah. The prophet was not to eat or drink anything while he was there. On his way home, a so-called prophet offered him a meal. He declined. Yet this man replied, "Actually, I too have heard from God, and you're supposed to eat with me." We live in a day when most anyone will claim they speak for God. What was happening during this prophet's mission is happening today. People manipulate their faith to match their lives and then claim it was God. They justify their sin and call it good. After all, God wants them to be happy, right? But there's only one true God, and He never contradicts himself or speaks contrary to what He's written in His Word. God's Word is *life* to you. May you grow increasingly discerning of the times and sensitive to His voice so you'll not be deceived by the many who claim to speak for Him. Your calling and influence depend on it.

LEARN Read 1 Kings 13.

FLOURISH Make it a daily practice to read God's Word. Pray before you read. Lean in and listen with a receptive heart.

PRAY

Lord,
I want to hear Your voice above all others. Open my eyes to see You and my ears to hear You. Heighten my discernment and give me a fresh love for Your living Word. Amen.

Something Out
of Practically Nothing

But she said, "I swear by the Lord your God that I don't have a single piece of bread in the house. And I have only a handful of flour left in the jar and a little cooking oil in the bottom of the jug. I was just gathering a few sticks to cook this last meal, and then my son and I will die."

1 Kings 17:12

God had gone ahead of Elijah and instructed a widow to care for his needs. Let's consider her story for a moment. She had run out of options and resources, and thus was preparing to die. But she forgot a critical point: We should never put a period at the end of a sentence that God is still writing! Her story wasn't over yet. When Elijah asked for help, she knew she had little help to offer. Still, she followed the prophet's instructions and experienced a divine miracle right in the midst of her impossible situation! God can make something out of nothing. He can take your measly resources and multiply them miraculously. There is a time to endure and a time to start afresh. But may we never base our perspective solely on our circumstances. If we do, we'll likely despair. What is the Lord saying to you in this particular season of life? He's asking for faith, trust, obedience. With Jesus on your side, the odds against you are meaningless.

LEARN Read 1 Kings 17:8–16.

FLOURISH In what area of your life have you lost expectancy? Revisit that place and ask God to breathe fresh faith and vision into your heart.

PRAY

Jesus,
You're always up to something new. Intervene in my life in the most miraculous, impossible ways! Show me Your glory! Amen.

Answer Me, So That They Will Know

"O LORD, answer me! Answer me so these people will know that you, O LORD, are God and that you have brought them back to yourself."

1 Kings 18:37

Elijah asked God to show himself strong on Elijah's behalf, both to show that He was the one true God, and to draw people back to himself. Oftentimes when we're in a predicament, we minimize it. We assume that since we're not facing down giants or evil kings, God's intervention on our behalf won't be as significant. But did you know that others are watching your life from a distance? They know you profess Christ, and they want to know how you'll handle things when life pushes up against you. What if you stood back, considered your observers, and dared to pray Elijah's prayer: *Father, this isn't just for me, it's for those who are watching me! I am Your servant. Intervene in my life so that others may see that You are the one true God. Show Yourself strong on my behalf because I belong to You! Draw others to You because of Your very real power in my life.* If you're in step with the Lord and obeying His Word, you're on solid biblical ground to pray such a prayer.

LEARN Read 1 Kings 18:1–40.

FLOURISH Pray audaciously today. And tomorrow. And the next day. The God of heaven knows your name and loves you, profoundly so.

PRAY

God of heaven,
Show me how to pray big-story prayers! I want my whole life to bear witness to Your redeeming power. Stir up a fresh passion in my soul! Amen.

A Fist-Sized Cloud

Finally, the seventh time, his servant told him, "I saw a little cloud about the size of a man's hand rising from the sea."

1 Kings 18:44

One morning during prayer the Lord whispered to my heart something that actually surprised me. *What have you done with the promises I've made to you? It seems you've set them aside for a season. What happened to your persistence? You've written them down. Go review them and let's start talking about them again.* So I picked up my journal from the previous year and worked my way through the list of promises I was sure the Lord had made to me. To my surprise, He'd already answered some of them; but since those answers came subtly and not suddenly, I practically missed them. God remembers His promises and He collects our prayers. Yet most answers do arrive faintly at first. God not only showed me that He'd been faithful even when I'd forgotten about my prayers, but He also compelled me to reengage and pray these things all the way through to completion. Don't miss the subtle answers to your prayers. They're often a sign of things to come.

LEARN Read 1 Kings 18:41–46.

FLOURISH Have you stopped praying about something God has promised you? Have you already experienced a few subtle answers? Celebrate. Thank Him. And reengage your faith.

PRAY

God,
Thank You for Your constant and continual faithfulness. Even when I forget, You never do. I'm eternally grateful for Your goodness. Make me into a mighty prayer warrior! Amen.

Remedy for Discouragement

Then the angel of the LORD came again and touched him and said, "Get up and eat some more, or the journey ahead will be too much for you."

1 Kings 19:7

*W*hen we find ourselves in a funk, we tend to let go of healthy, life-giving habits. We make poor food choices (or stop eating altogether), we waste time but don't sleep well, we pull away from community, and we stop asking God for fresh revelation of himself. Elijah was there. He'd just experienced a major victory, but with the triumph came a threat on his life. So Elijah ran and hid, and curled up in a ball and asked to die. Yet God's kind and compassionate direction was both practical and spiritual. He provided bread and water and told Elijah to eat and drink. Then, with a full stomach, he put his head down and took another nap. Once again, the angel of the Lord told him to get up and eat some more, otherwise the journey would be too much for him. Elijah still had a purpose. You still have a purpose. When you're worn out and discouraged, get some restorative rest, eat a good meal, and ask God to speak to you. Your story is not over until God says it is.

LEARN Read 1 Kings 19:1–8.

FLOURISH What does your soul need today? Do what nourishes it. Loosen up your calendar. Reinstate a good bedtime. Ask for a fresh God-given revelation.

PRAY

Jesus,
I am both physical and spiritual. Help me to tend to both aspects of who I am. Show me what habits are healthy and life-giving. Strengthen me once again. Speak, Lord. I'm listening. Amen.

When the Subtle Is Most Sacred

And after the earthquake there was a fire, but the LORD was not in the fire.
And after the fire there was the sound of a gentle whisper.

1 Kings 19:12

Elijah had big, giant faith. He'd seen God move in sensational ways. Yet here, in this place, Elijah felt beat up by the world and worn down by its problems. He needed a fresh revelation from above. God told Elijah to go out and stand on the mountain before the Lord. When the Lord passed by, a mighty windstorm kicked up with such a fierce blast of power that the rocks tore loose from the mountain. Imagine! Then there was a fire. But the Lord was not in the quake or the fire. After the sensational came the subtle. The Lord met and ministered to Elijah through a gentle whisper. Some of the most sacred, intimate encounters God has with His people are largely missed by the rest of the world. He meets us in the nooks and crannies of our lives and reveals His hidden secrets to us. How blessed are we? Though God is quite capable of the sensational, we'll often miss Him if we only look for Him there. *He's right here.* With you. Right now.

LEARN   Read 1 Kings 19:10–13.

FLOURISH   Elizabeth Barrett Browning once wrote, "Earth is crammed with heaven; every common bush afire with God. But only he who sees takes off his shoes. The rest just sit around and pluck blackberries." Have the wisdom to take off your shoes today.

PRAY

Jesus,
Forgive me for being so captivated by the big experiences that I miss You in the small, sacred ones. I don't want to miss You. Open my eyes. Touch my heart. I wait for You. Amen.

The Danger of Self-Pity

And a voice said, "What are you doing here, Elijah?"
1 Kings 19:13

We sometimes find ourselves in a predicament through no fault of our own. Oftentimes, while in that place, we make reactionary choices based on a faulty perspective. Yes, times were tough for God's prophet. But self-pity had set in because he believed he was the only one left who followed God. It's scary how closely connected self-pity and self-importance are. While God is patient with our frailties and compassionate about our weaknesses, He doesn't tolerate our self-sins because they'll kill us and diminish our God-given influence. We don't need pity when we have the promises of God! We don't need pity when we have access to the very presence of God! When we find ourselves coddling our hardships more than we cling to the promises of God, we're on a slippery slope. Lament and grief are healthy and an important part of the healing process. Pity, on the other hand, is a parasite and will suck the passion and life right out of us. Be ruthless with your self-sins. They're not your friend and you don't want them at your party.

LEARN Read 1 Kings 19:13–18.

FLOURISH If you've wandered over to self-pity or self-importance, reset your course today. Holy confidence and humble dependence are great safeguards for your heart.

PRAY

Search me, O God, and know my heart. Point out anything in me that offends You; lead me in Your everlasting way. I want nothing in my heart that offends You or hurts me. Revive and renew me, Lord! Amen.

This Is Easy for the Lord!

This is what the LORD says: This dry valley will be filled with pools of water!

2 Kings 3:16

*E*lijah told the kings who were heading into battle, "Without great fanfare, God will fill this drought-ridden valley with pools of water. You'll have plenty for yourselves and for your livestock. *This is an easy task in the eyes of the Lord.* And He will make you victorious over your enemy!" At every turn, our enemy seeks to steal what's ours, kill what God is birthing in our lives, and destroy what God is doing in our lives. And sometimes he gets away with it. If you're staring at a drought-ridden valley, don't despair. Just whisper a prayer. Jesus came not just to save you, but to destroy the work of the enemy in your life. Picture it. Imagine your valley suddenly filling with water. Imagine splashing your feet in pools of blessing. And don't forget that the Lord intends to put your enemy under your feet. None of this is hard for Him. Remember His strength today. Count on His goodness. Rely on His love. And pray big prayers today.

LEARN Read 2 Kings 3:1–24.

FLOURISH Dare to dream again. Droughts and barrenness don't last forever in God's economy. Get a fresh vision for what redemption may look like in your story.

PRAY

Mighty God,
I call on Your name! Deliver me from the hand of my enemy! Fill my deep valleys with water; offer fresh pools of blessing until I'm overwhelmed once again with Your goodness. Remind me of Your faithfulness. Show me Your strength today. Amen.

Prepare for Provision

And Elisha said, "Borrow as many empty jars as you can from your friends and neighbors."

2 Kings 4:3

Sometimes the situation in our lives is so desperate, we need to engage the faith and help of our friends. The poor widow in this passage not only grieved the loss of her husband, but she also faced the threat of losing her sons to slavery. She cried out to Elisha the prophet. Elisha instructed her to borrow as many jars from friends and neighbors as she could find, which she did. Her husband had served Elisha, which made her part of the family of God. When your circumstances feel like they'll swallow you whole, don't isolate, and don't shrink back. You're part of the family of the living God! Rise up and call your fiercest warriors. Borrow their faith. Ask them to gather on your behalf with open hands and full expectancy that God will move as you seek Him together. Desperate times call for passionate prayer and fierce faith. What if you borrowed faith jars from your friends and you all asked God to fill them on your behalf? Your jars would fill, your hearts would quicken, and you'd experience the clarity and provision you need. Maybe that's your battle strategy today.

LEARN Read 2 Kings 4:1–7.

FLOURISH Even if you're not in crisis, plan a prayer meeting with some of your godliest friends. Seek God together and watch what He will do.

PRAY

Precious Father,
Forgive me for defaulting to worry when I have You! I'm asking for a miracle. And I want to participate in a necessary miracle for someone else. Show me who my jar girls are and teach us how to pray. Amen!

Let Hope Arise!

She fell at his feet and bowed before him, overwhelmed with gratitude. Then she took her son in her arms and carried him downstairs.

2 Kings 4:37

This wealthy woman of God recognized that Elisha was a man of God. She and her husband built a small room for him to use whenever he was in town. She'd been so kind and generous to him that Elisha asked what he could do for her. She let him know that her needs were met. It wasn't until Elisha spoke to her about having a child that she fell apart. That desire had long been buried and it was almost too painful to talk about it now. She replied, "O man of God, don't deceive me and get my hopes up like that." Do you have such a desire buried deep within you? Sometimes it feels *easier* to live with loss than it does with hope. But is it better? I don't think so. What if God wants to breathe fresh life into your hopes? What if He intends to resurrect your long-buried dream? Will you let Him? Are you willing to have that conversation? What is that thing for you?

LEARN ▶ Read 2 Kings 4:8–37.

FLOURISH ▶ God's promises don't apply to our unrealistic expectations, but they do apply to our impossible situations. May you separate the two in your heart and then invite God to breathe fresh hope in you once again.

PRAY ▶

> *Father,*
> *You know the kind of courage it takes for me to even have this conversation. I don't want to go there—to be disappointed again. But I don't want to miss Your provision either. So here I am. Show me what hope looks like here. What are You up to? I'm listening. Amen.*

Detoxifying the Poison

Elisha said, "Bring me some flour." Then he threw it into the pot and said, "Now it's all right; go ahead and eat." And then it did not harm them.

2 Kings 4:41

*E*lisha detoxified the poisonous stew with some flour. I know a bit about the detox process. We initially thought that my second health battle was Lyme disease, but it wasn't. It was mold toxicity. I have the genetic inability to process mold, which makes exposure dangerous for me. Doctors treated my illness with binders that not only bound to the mold spores but pulled them out of my system. When one of my toddler sons tried to drink a bottle of Benadryl, the ER doctors gave him activated charcoal to bind and deactivate the dangerous levels of medicine he'd ingested. Sometimes we're exposed to toxic people and circumstances, and their influence *gets in us*—it deeply impacts us, and we feel poisoned. What will deactivate the toxins in our system? The spoken Word of God! Scripture says that what we bind on earth is bound in heaven and what we loose on earth is loosed in heaven.* If you've recently been poisoned by a toxic experience, pray God's Word, say God's Word, and bind the enemy's influence in your life. He *has* to obey.

LEARN Read 2 Kings 4:38–43.

FLOURISH Detoxify every day by speaking and praying God's Word over your life. *I am loved, called, anointed, and appointed. GREATER is He that is in me than any toxins that come against me!*

PRAY

Jesus,

Help me to guard my steps so I don't walk into toxic situations. But when I do, give me the firepower to pray boldly and confidently. My heart is bound to You. Poisonous circumstances cannot harm me. Thank You, Lord. Amen.

*See Matthew 18:18 NIV.

Healing the Powerful

> One day the girl said to her mistress, "I wish my master would go to see the prophet in Samaria. He would heal him of his leprosy."
>
> 2 Kings 5:3

A captive Jewish girl served in the home of a commander of the Syrian army (enemies of the Jews). He was a mighty warrior, but he battled leprosy. This dear girl, though she was taken from her homeland, cared about her master's plight. She pointed him toward healing through the one true God. God used this seemingly insignificant girl to shake things up in the kingdom. Maybe you feel like a captive yourself. You're not valued at home, nor are you in a position of great influence. And yet you can still impact those around you. You have the capacity to speak life, to point the way, and to initiate a healing process. But maybe those in authority over you are prideful and undeserving. Aren't we all sometimes? Naaman went to Elisha for healing and God dealt with his pride as well. You don't have to worry about a thing. God misses nothing. Who knows? Maybe the reason you're where you are today is to speak life into a broken situation. Outcomes are in God's hands. And one day you will see the impact and fruit of your obedience.

LEARN Read 2 Kings 5:1–14.

FLOURISH Sometimes the idea of helping the prideful stirs up our own pride. If that's the case, humble yourself today and thank God for grace. Then speak life into a difficult situation.

PRAY

Jesus,
Forgive me for my selective grace. I want to be more like the unnamed girl in this story. I want to help whoever You entrust to me! Show me what to do. My eyes are on You. Amen.

Spiritual Eyes to See

"Don't be afraid!" Elisha told him. "For there are more on our side than on theirs!"

2 Kings 6:16

*E*lisha, the prophet of God, walked so closely with God that he knew about the Syrian army's strategy before they took their first steps. As a result, Israel's king was always one step ahead of his enemy. The Syrian forces decided to go after Elisha. They surrounded his city; he seemed to be outnumbered. Elisha's servant was distressed, but not Elisha. In so many words, Elisha prayed, *O Lord, let my servant see what I already know!* So the Lord opened the young servant's eyes and he saw that the hillside around Elisha was filled with horses and chariots of fire. Our spiritual reality is far more substantial than our physical reality. Things are rarely as they appear in the natural, and God is always nearer than we perceive. Here's what's true: God has assigned angels to care for you *and* to fight for you. The precious, powerful Holy Spirit resides inside of you. God's promises are true for you. If your spiritual eyes opened up, you'd see that the enemy and your circumstances are no match for the forces that are standing guard on your behalf this very moment. Don't be afraid. Only believe.

LEARN Read 2 Kings 6:8–23.

FLOURISH Which circumstances are weighing too heavy today? Ask God for a fresh revelation of His presence and provision in your life.

PRAY

Lord,
Teach me just how secure I am in You! Help me to remember that when I face opposition, I can stand my ground and watch You fight for me. Give me spiritual eyes to see my spiritual reality. Amen.

Always Bracing for Impact

> The king got out of bed in the middle of the night and told his officers, "I know what has happened. . . . They are expecting us to leave the city, and then they will take us alive and capture the city."
>
> 2 Kings 7:12

*T*he Lord caused the enemy army to hear the clatter of speeding chariots and galloping horses and the sounds of a great army approaching. So the men panicked, abandoned all of their supplies, and fled for their lives into the night. The Lord delivered an abundance of resources into the hands of the starving Israelites. But Israel's king was more impacted by the famine than by God's voice and direction in his life. He assumed that this victory was no victory at all, but rather a setup by the enemy. After a long battle, it's almost instinctive to believe the worst and to continually brace for impact. But that's no way to live. "We must avoid becoming skeptical of God's provision. When our resources are low and our doubts are the strongest, remember God can open the floodgates of heaven."* If it's been a while since you've received some miraculous, breakthrough news, start by celebrating the small victories and believing expectantly for your big victory.

LEARN Read 2 Kings 6:24–7:17.

FLOURISH A weary heart is different from a hardened, skeptical heart. If you're weary, run to Jesus. He will restore you. If you're skeptical, run to Him too. Repent and receive His grace.

PRAY

Lord,
My long battle has taken its toll. Forgive me for the ways I've gotten cynical. I don't want to believe that the bad news is truer than Your good news. Revive my heart and perspective today. Amen.

Life Application Study Bible (Carol Stream, IL: Tyndale, 2004), 768.

Break Free and Believe

There was a man named Jabez who was more honorable than any of his brothers. His mother named him Jabez because his birth had been so painful.

1 Chronicles 4:9

*Y*ou are not your insecurities. You're not your past mistakes. You're not your family tree. You're not who other people say you are. Do you believe this to be true? You're not even the sum of all of your accomplishments. *You're something altogether more wonderful than these.* Truth is, most of us need a complete identity overhaul. Jabez's mother had a difficult, painful delivery. I had one too. But I still cannot imagine naming my son after that excruciating experience. Imagine being reminded of your painful birth every time your mom called your name. Talk about feeling branded. Yet somehow, Jabez broke free from his given label and lived more honorably than his brothers. Moreover, the God of heaven knew Jabez's name and his heart. And we're still talking about Jabez today. No matter what you've come from, look up, dear one. No matter what words have been spoken over you or what labels have been a reproach to you, break free and believe God anyway. He *loves* your faith, and He's a miracle-working God.

LEARN Read 1 Chronicles 4:9–10.

FLOURISH Ask God to show you any labels still attached to you and any self-limiting beliefs hovering over you. Then refute them one by one with God's Word.

PRAY

Father,
Show me my heart. Show me what hinders my progress and what blocks my view of You. Help me break free so I can be and do everything You've dreamed of for me.
In Jesus' name, I pray. Amen.

Do More in and through Me!

(Jabez prayed), "Oh, that you would bless me and expand my territory!
Please be with me in all that I do, and keep me from all trouble and pain!"
And God granted him his request.

1 Chronicles 4:10

I love Bruce Wilkinson's book *The Prayer of Jabez*. Though some find this a selfish prayer, nothing could be further from the truth. If you've not read Bruce's book, pick it up and soak it in. Whatever we've experienced of God, we hold a Dixie cup and the ocean remains. The more deeply we get to know the heart of God, the more profoundly our prayers start to echo His heart for us. He is the God of inexhaustible supply, the God of compassions that never fail, the One whose love will never dim, even a little bit. And He's the God who *loves* our faith. The more we pray God's heart, the more His answers change us and change the world through us. Ask God to expand His territory *in you and through you*, to expand your influence, and to deliver you from evil. Pray prayers that overwhelm you—impossible prayers that only He can answer. Stretch your arms open wide and pray, *Lord Jesus, do the impossible in and through me!* Jealous people will call that selfish. Kingdom people will call it gutsy.

LEARN Read 1 Chronicles 4:9–10 (one more time).

FLOURISH It's one thing to occasionally pray a scary prayer. It's a whole 'nother thing to pray this way continually. You want to change the world? Pray crazy prayers and wholeheartedly follow Jesus.

PRAY

Jesus,
Bless me, indeed! Do the impossible through me! Expand my terri-
tory, increase my influence, and deliver me from evil. Change the world
through me! Amen.

The Importance
of the Impossible

The Jebusites threatened David, "You shall not pass through these gates." Nevertheless David captured the stronghold (Zion), now known as the city of David, and made it his capital.

1 Chronicles 11:5 VOICE

*J*oshua and his armies never captured the city of Jebus during their conquest of the land of Canaan, and Jebus remained in the hands of the Canaanites until David became king.* The enemy told David, "You'll *never* break through these gates." *Nevertheless*, David broke through and made it his capital. He not only claimed his God-given territory, but he also renamed the city Jerusalem, which became hugely significant for future Christians. Jerusalem was the birthplace of the church. It's where Christ was crucified and rose from the dead. It's where Jesus poured out His Holy Spirit upon His followers. From *that* city, the gospel has gone out to the ends of the earth.† The locked gates before you are nothing more than an opportunity for faith. If the land before you is God-assigned, then no demon in hell will keep you from it. Your possession of your promised land has historical implications. Your story and your breakthroughs are never just about you. May God open your eyes to see the significance and the importance of the impossible tasks before you. May mountains move, gates open, and waters part before you.

LEARN Read 1 Chronicles 11:1–9.

FLOURISH Identify your impossible situation. Embrace expectant faith. Wait on God. Discern God's timing and strategy. Take the next step.

PRAY

Jesus,
Your Spirit in me ensures that nothing will be impossible for me! You go before me. I'll follow You. Awaken my faith today. Amen.

*Paraphrase of study note from *Life in the Spirit Study Bible* (Grand Rapids, MI: Zondervan, 2003), 584.
†*Life in the Spirit Study Bible*, 585.

Miracles and Rulings

Search for the LORD and for his strength;
continually seek him.
Remember the wonders he has performed,
his miracles, and the rulings he has given.
1 Chronicles 16:11–12

The ark was finally back home in Jerusalem. David had learned some valuable lessons along the way.* God is not only a *miracle-working* God and the Creator of the heavens and the earth, He is also the ultimate King and not to be trifled with. When we become too casual about His presence, we operate in our own strength, lean on our own understanding, take credit for the things He's done, and miss what He intends to do. He's the same yesterday, today, and forever. Shout to your soul today, *The God who parted the sea lives inside of me!* Remember His miracles, seek His face, pursue His strength, and rely on His faithfulness. Far too many Christians live underwhelming lives because they've wandered from the beauty of holy expectancy (they've forgotten that He's still moving mountains) and holy fear (they've forgotten that He is God and we are not). Want to reignite your faith? Recapture the essence of God's greatness, not only for what He does, but for who He is. Embrace a holy expectancy and believe that His presence in your midst changes everything.

LEARN Read 1 Chronicles 15; 16:1–36.

FLOURISH Ask God to increase your capacity to understand what He's capable of. Ask Him for a fresh revelation of His majesty and greatness. May He grow within you a heart of expectancy and reverence.

PRAY

Lord,
Reignite my heart to believe You for great things! Help me better grasp Your majesty and power. I want to live a holy, powerful, reverent life. I bow low and wait for You. Amen.

*Read 1 Chronicles 13 for context.

Counting Your Followers

Satan rose up against Israel and caused David to take a census of the people of Israel.

1 Chronicles 21:1

Our enemy is a legalist. If he finds an opening, he'll take it. David was tempt-able because deep inside, he wanted to shift his weight off of dependence on God and onto his great accomplishments. And so it goes today. We live in a day when folks obsess over numbers, followers, likes, and shares. Yet Jesus never called us to *get* people to follow us. He called us to follow Him and to feed His sheep. He calls us to count our blessings, not our followers. Things in this world are not as they appear. Scripture is clear that some with large ministries will see their work burn to ashes because they did it all to make a name for themselves, while others, whom the world knows nothing about, will be celebrated and honored for all to see. It matters what we do, but even more so why we do it. King David was a man after God's own heart, but in that moment, he tried to validate his own heart. "There is a thin line between feeling confident because you are relying on God's power and becoming proud because you have been used by God for great purposes."* How much can He bless you before you make it about you?

LEARN Read 1 Chronicles 21:1–17.

FLOURISH Forget about the number of your followers and feed His sheep.

PRAY

Father,
Forgive me for allowing the wrong things to validate (and invalidate) me. You are all that I need! Help me to be faithful here. I know You'll establish me. Amen.

*Life Application Study Bible, 861.

Everything Comes from You

Everything we have has come from you, and we give you only what you first gave us!

1 Chronicles 29:14

King David was nearing the end of his earthly life. He instructed Solomon to follow the Lord wholeheartedly. David gave God credit for his victories and thanked Him for his blessings. When I think back to my young adult years, I cringe over how I strived to prove myself when, in fact, I had nothing to prove and all of eternity to live for. Though David certainly had his own regrets, his heart was one with almighty God. David knew the Great Redeemer and could therefore rest in His care. The sooner you come to believe that every good gift comes from God and that you have *all* you need *in Him*, the sooner you can live with a heart of freedom, peace, and rest. And the sooner your life will become a pure and beautiful offering to the One who made you and who has entrusted *great* gifts to you. Don't muddy the waters by grabbing for validation, striving to prove something, or straining to manage others' opinions of you. Open your hands, receive everything God has promised, and then offer it back up to Him. It's the only offering that echoes into eternity, and it's the only way to live.

LEARN   Read 1 Chronicles 29.

FLOURISH   Look around and consider every good gift God has given you. What are some new ways you can offer your life back to Him in thanksgiving for all He's done?

PRAY

Father,
*   I don't want to waste a moment living out of a lie. Put my heart at ease in Your presence and use every part of my life as an offering to You. Amen.*

If We, Then He

Then if my people who are called by my name will humble themselves and pray and seek my face and turn from their wicked ways, I will hear from heaven and will forgive their sins and restore their land.

2 Chronicles 7:14

When our kids were young, we stood in a circle as a family and held hands. Then I looked at our sons and said, "Your place in this family matters so very much. In fact, whatever you allow in your life, you allow in ours." My husband and I explained that no one lives on an island and nobody's choices stand alone; they affect a whole community. We long for a revival in our nation, but it needs to start with us. What we allow in our lives, we allow in our community, even if those around us never know. We have a responsibility, especially as believers, to guard not only our hearts, but to also guard the city gate. How do we do that? We walk humbly with our God. We keep short accounts with our sin. We pray big-story prayers for our city and our nation. And we ask God to break our hearts for what breaks His. Scripture is full of promises that are contingent upon our attitudes and actions. What needs to change in your heart today so God can move in your midst? Your life deeply impacts your community.

LEARN Read 2 Chronicles 7:11–22.

FLOURISH Determine to press in more earnestly today. Carry a portion of the Lord's burden for your nation. Seek His face and appeal to His kindness and mercy.

PRAY

Lord Jesus,
  I come humbly before You and ask for mercy and blessing upon my nation. Forgive us our sins, cleanse us from unrighteousness, and heal our land. Amen.

Rest from Your Enemies

They earnestly sought after God, and they found him. And the LORD gave them rest from their enemies on every side.

2 Chronicles 15:15

*M*uch like the Israelites, many of us have a history of following God, wandering from Him, building our idols, and then smashing them again. We suffer because of our own wandering ways. And yet every time we seek the face of God, He makes himself available. God's mercies and kindness are breathtaking. King Asa took seriously the Lord's invitation to seek Him earnestly and follow Him wholeheartedly. And as a result, the Lord gave King Asa rest from his enemies. Jesus promised we'd endure hardship, trials, and opposition when we follow Him. But He also provides seasons of rest from battle, restoration after the storm, and relief from our enemies. However, we'll never know such rest if we continually dabble in two kingdoms. Have you given the enemy access to your life in any way? Shut him down, shut him out, and earnestly seek after God once again. God wants to reveal himself to you in fresh new ways. He wants to restore and strengthen you. May the Lord bring you into a season of rest from battle and relief from your enemy.

LEARN Read 2 Chronicles 15.

FLOURISH Sometimes we give our enemy access in the subtlest of ways (an unforgiving heart, a prideful assessment, an obsession with something other than God). Humbly search your heart today and then pray.

PRAY

Lord,
Show me my heart. Show me where I've let my guard down. Help me to shore up my life once again. And give me rest from my enemy. Amen.

The Lord Will Fight for You

This is what the LORD says: Do not be afraid! Don't be discouraged by this mighty army, for the battle is not yours, but God's. . . . You will not even need to fight. Take your positions; then stand still and watch the LORD's victory.

2 Chronicles 20:15–17

*T*he nation of Judah faced total annihilation. Enemy armies marched toward them fully intending to destroy them. King Jehoshaphat earnestly appealed to the Lord for guidance. He ordered everyone in Judah to fast. People from all over sought the Lord's intervention. King Jehoshaphat declared to God His greatness and faithfulness and, on that basis, cried out for His intervention once again. Then the Spirit of the Lord came upon one of their men and he prophesied God's promise to fight for them. The people began to worship *before* the breakthrough came. God inhabits the praises of His people and the devil flees. The enemy soldiers turned on each other and defeated themselves. It took God's people three days to collect the spoils from their war. God turned their battleground into a valley of blessing. Dare to practice restraint when you want to strike your own defense. Seek God's direction, protection, and intervention. You'll be amazed at what He does for those who wait on Him.

LEARN   Read 2 Chronicles 20:1–30.

FLOURISH   If you're in an impossible battle, assemble the troops, declare a fast, seek God, and wait for Him to speak. Worship Him before the breakthrough comes. You're about to experience God's power like never before.

PRAY

Lord,
*   You are faithful and true! I don't know what to do, but my eyes are on You. Intervene on my behalf; fight for me and deliver me. My soul waits for You. Amen.*

When the Wicked Prosper

When she arrived, she saw the newly crowned king standing in his place of authority by the pillar at the Temple entrance.

2 Chronicles 23:13

*J*ehoram, one of Israel's kings, married Jezebel's daughter, Athaliah. His union with her became his downfall. He became as corrupt as his wife and eventually died a brutal death. In an effort to seize the throne after both her husband and son had died, Athaliah sought to *kill* the rest of the royal family. Imagine! Yet God promised that a descendant of David would sit on that throne. Jehosheba, the wife of a priest, hid one of the royal children. The boy stayed hidden until his seventh year, when the priests finally staged a coup and dethroned the woman who'd wreaked havoc in God's kingdom. Because of Israel's disobedience and continual idolatry, God, on occasion, allowed enemies to usurp the throne. But He always comes back to His promise. The wicked queen was removed, and godly leadership was established once again. If you're disheartened by ungodly leadership or by the prosperity of the wicked, don't lose heart. God already has someone in the wings—someone He's hiding and preparing for just the right time. The wicked won't rule forever.

LEARN Read 2 Chronicles 22; 23:1–15.

FLOURISH Just as God is always preparing His leaders, He wants people praying for that process. Maybe He's preparing you! Pray big and trust His timing.

PRAY

Father,
You are still on Your throne! I declare it till my soul believes it. You will dismantle the schemes of the enemy and establish godly influence once again. Use me, Lord! Show me how to pray. Show me how to stand. I wait for You. Amen.

Don't Go Through with It

Amaziah asked the man of God, "But what about all that silver I paid to hire the army of Israel?"

The man of God replied, "The LORD is able to give you much more than this!"

2 Chronicles 25:9

*Y*ou've made a plan, you've invested resources, and you've enlisted the help of your friends. But partway through the process, you realize it's the wrong decision. Do you know how many people have gone ahead anyway because they've already spent the money? And for some, it's not about the money—it's about saving face. I've heard many stories of regret from people who didn't have the courage to turn back the minute they realized they'd misread the situation. King Amaziah was in the process of hiring and assembling troops from Israel to form a great army. But a man of God came to him and cautioned him against that decision because the Lord was no longer with Israel. They'd abandoned Him. If Amaziah went into battle with a people under God's discipline, he'd be soundly defeated. He asked the man of God, "What about the money I've already spent?" The prophet assured him that God could restore him and then some! Don't be stubborn about your plans if it's becoming clear that God is not in them. Never mind what you've spent. Honoring God matters most of all. If you honor Him, He'll restore you. And then some!

LEARN   Read 2 Chronicles 25:1–9.

FLOURISH   Never rush ahead into *anything*. Stay at the pace of grace. Seek God and follow His lead.

PRAY

Lord Jesus,

Forgive me for my tendency to control outcomes and assume You're in it. I will slow down my pace today. I'll seek Your face today. Show me the way that I should go. Amen.

He'll Work It Out

This is what King Cyrus of Persia says:

"The LORD, the God of heaven, has given me all the kingdoms of the earth. He has appointed me to build him a Temple at Jerusalem, which is in Judah."

Ezra 1:2

God's purposes will prevail in the end—*no matter what*. He works through His people. And when necessary, He works through His enemies. The Israelites had so rejected God and His ways that God gave them over to their desires and they were carried off into captivity. Yet He had a plan to redeem their story long before they understood just how lost they were. After seventy years, He planned to bring His exiled people back to their homeland to rebuild the temple. He prophesied that King Cyrus of Persia would issue the decree and guarantee their safe passage home. Imagine that! The king of Persia *happened* to be reading some of the prophetic scripts that had been removed from the temple, and he saw his own name! God stirred in Cyrus's heart and he instituted the decree for a remnant of God's people to return home. One way or another, God will work out His plan. God is in control; He's always been in control. And while He allows men the freedom to follow Him or disregard Him, He will ultimately bring every detail together and work it out to serve His ultimate purposes.

LEARN Read Ezra 1:1–4.

FLOURISH Determine to be someone through whom God can work with power, authority, and conviction. Though God's purposes will prevail, may you determine never to be a side note in the bigger story.

PRAY

Lord,
Your patience with Your people is breathtaking. Here I am. Use me in powerful ways. Work out Your greater plan through my life. Amen.

Remember Your Inheritance

Then God stirred the hearts of the priests and Levites and the leaders of the tribes of Judah and Benjamin to go to Jerusalem to rebuild the Temple of the LORD.

Ezra 1:5

*K*ing Cyrus's proclamation of freedom went to all the original 12 tribes, but only Judah and Benjamin responded and returned to rebuild God's Temple. The 10 tribes of the northern kingdom had been so fractured and dispersed by Assyria, and so much time had elapsed since their captivity, that many may have been unsure of their real heritage. Thus, they were unwilling to share in the vision of rebuilding the Temple."* God had stirred in Cyrus's heart to give all twelve tribes the freedom to leave their captivity and reclaim their inheritance. Yet only two tribes caught the significance of the invitation. And so it goes today. Though much time has passed since God's Word was first written, Jesus hasn't returned yet. As a result, many Christians have lost sight of their homeland. They identify more with the trappings of this world—even if it holds them captive—than they do with the promise of a new heaven and a new earth. But we are on a pilgrimage *now*. You are not made for this world. You're simply passing through. Recapture your kingdom identity. Remember your kingdom inheritance.

LEARN Read Ezra 1:5–11.

FLOURISH Consider the life that waits for you once God calls His people home. How you live here deeply impacts how you'll live there. Live like His promises are true today.

PRAY

Jesus,
Somehow You lived in this world without being captive to it. Help me to do the same. Awaken me once again to the reality of heaven. Amen.

*Life Application Study Bible, 958.

Both Sorrow and Joy

The joyful shouting and weeping mingled together in a loud noise that could be heard far in the distance.

Ezra 3:13

*W*hy was there both joyful shouting and sorrowful weeping at the same celebration? The younger saints worshiped and rejoiced with glee because they took part in rebuilding the temple. What a testimony to God's faithfulness! The older saints were likely heartbroken over the sin that caused the destruction in the first place. Perhaps they remembered the temple's former glory and wondered if they'd really ever be able to capture it again. Or maybe some wept over God's goodness in spite of their own badness. Oftentimes, those who've suffered the most feel things most deeply. If all we ever feel is joy or hype when we come into God's presence, we're missing a significant part of our relationship with almighty God. There's a time for joyful celebration, but there's most definitely a time for sober reflection—though never in condemnation. But it is always and ever for the sake of remembering, and to move us to a place of deeper intimacy and appreciation for what God has done for us. There's a time for rejoicing and a time for weeping—and sometimes both are called for on the same day. God welcomes your expression and He loves your heart. Enter in, fully engaged, today.

LEARN Read Ezra 3.

FLOURISH Consider approaching God more thoughtfully than you typically do. Ponder His goodness and remember what He saved you from and what He saved you for. Surrender your whole heart to Him.

PRAY

Father,
  I raise my hands in worship and I praise You with everything in me! You're so good! I honor You for all You've done and all You're about to do. Thank You, thank You, Lord. Amen.

Predictable Enemy Tactics

Then the local residents tried to discourage and frighten the people of
Judah to keep them from their work.

Ezra 4:4

*T*he enemy of our souls is all about counterfeits, deception, and distraction—primarily because he has no new ideas. When the tribes of Judah and Benjamin set out to rebuild the temple, their enemies first sought to distract them by trying to align with them. When that didn't work, they used two age-old tactics that the devil still uses today: fear and discouragement. "Discouragement and fear are two of the greatest obstacles to completing God's work. Most often they come when you least expect them. Discouragement eats away at our motivation, and fear paralyzes us so we don't act at all."* Discouragement condemns our present moment. Fear threatens our promised future. Discouragement comes when we compare and then despair, or when we lose heart over where we find ourselves at the moment. Fear goes after the vulnerable or unhealed places in us, or after the truths about God that we're still unsure of. To combat these, we need a higher vision of who God is and what He is up to, and we need a revelation about the enemy's strategy against us. Soon and very soon we'll be wise to the enemy's schemes.

LEARN   Read Ezra 4:1–4.

FLOURISH   Take inventory of your soul. If you find even a hint of discouragement or fear, identify its source and put it in its place.

PRAY

Jesus,
Thank You for making me wise to the enemy's schemes. His threat to me is always tied to my threat to him. Grant me fierce faith and divine discernment so I can be and do all You've called me to. Amen.

*Life Application Study Bible, 966.

The Prophet in All of Us

And the prophets of God were with them and helped them.

Ezra 5:2

Prophet: *A person regarded as an inspired teacher or proclaimer of the will of God.*

Imagine the journey for the tribes of Benjamin and Judah. They trusted God, left captivity, returned to their homeland, and began to rebuild the temple *for His glory*. And yet their efforts were met with obstacle, opposition, and accusation—to the point that the work actually came to a halt. It stopped completely. Where was God? Why did He allow the wicked and the liars to prosper? Because obstacles are a normal part of life in a fallen world. The arc of the covenant story of God with His people has always been one of risk, faith, setbacks, and breakthroughs. And it's no different today. The Lord raised up prophets not only to encourage the tribes of Benjamin and Judah, but also to engage with the work at hand. The kingdom needs more people who are so in step with the living God that they can speak an accurate word in due season. May you look for ways to encourage others and call out the best of God's influence in them. May you wisely discern the times and know what to do. And may you step in and help where God invites you to be part of the solution. The world needs your influence.

LEARN Read Ezra 5:1–4.

FLOURISH Privately immerse yourself in God's Word, rest in His presence, and listen for His voice. God will use you mightily in your public life.

PRAY

Father,
Pour Your Spirit out on me! I want to be in the right place at the right time with a right word at the right time. Speak prophetically and powerfully through me.
Amen.

Holy Vindication

Do not disturb the construction of the Temple of God. Let it be rebuilt on its original site, and do not hinder the governor of Judah and the elders of the Jews in their work.

Ezra 6:7

*T*he enemies of God's people appealed to King Darius and tried to get him to stop the construction of the temple. They used fear, discouragement, and threats. They assigned evil motives, tried to enlist help from the authorities, and even suggested the king search the records to see if Cyrus *really* signed the decree for them to move forward with the temple. They overplayed their hand. Once King Darius found the records, he enforced the will of God. He decreed not only the rebuilding of the temple, but also that all of the expenses be paid, and that all of the items taken from the temple to Babylon be returned to Jerusalem and put back where they belong. Furthermore, if anyone tried to stand against this decree, their home and lives would be reduced to a pile of rubble. Look at what God did! Vindication. Compensation. Restoration. Divine protection. He's the same yesterday, today, and forever. If you've stepped out to obey God and have encountered one impossible obstacle after another, you're in great company. Hold your ground. Stand in faith. Watch God turn things around.

LEARN Read Ezra 5:17–Ezra 6:12.

FLOURISH If events have shaken your faith, find your footing once again on the solid rock of Christ. You are secure in Him. May He move mightily on your behalf.

PRAY

Lord,
You are God Almighty, and I trust You! Shut the mouth of my enemy. Redeem my circumstances. Restore my resources. And provide safe passage so I can continue onward. I trust You, Lord. Amen.

More Than a Moment of Grace

> But now we have been given a brief moment of grace, for the LORD our God has allowed a few of us to survive as a remnant. He has given us security in this holy place. Our God has brightened our eyes and granted us some relief from our slavery.
>
> Ezra 9:8

*E*zra fell facedown before the Lord and repented for the sins of his people. When he realized how they'd continued to sin in light of God's amazing grace, he was overwhelmed with both grief and gratitude. He called this a *brief moment of grace*. The Israelites had been carried off into captivity because of their own blatant sin. While their sin was in full motion, God had worked out a plan to redeem them. While our sin was in full motion—before we ever knew we needed saving—Christ died for us. While condemnation and consequences were falling into place, Christ took our place. He redeemed us from the law of sin and death, and He redeems us every day with new mercies and grace. In Christ, we're surrounded by more grace than we'll ever need; God made sure of it. Even though we, like the Israelites, wander from God's best ways for us, He still brightens our eyes, grants us relief from suffering, and makes us secure in His presence. This is why we call Him our Redeemer.

LEARN Read Ezra 9–10:1.

FLOURISH Picture God's grace as an endless ocean. Go swimming today. Revel in the reality that Christ has *redeemed* you!

PRAY

Father,
You've been so good, so patient, kind, and true. You knew I'd wander before I did. And You made a way back for me. You've ransomed and redeemed me. You've always loved me. Thank You, Lord. Amen.

Rebuilding Your Wall

"The God of heaven will help us succeed. We, his servants, will start rebuilding this wall . . ."

Nehemiah 2:20

*W*hen God is about to bring renewal in some area of our lives or in the kingdom, He first speaks to us about it privately. He'll drop a burden in our hearts or grant us insight into a particular situation. Enough to make us look up and take notice. Someone may casually offer an update that to the untrained eye seems inconsequential, but to the heart prepared, it's further confirmation that God is doing something significant and we ought to pay attention. God stirred Nehemiah's heart to rebuild Jerusalem's wall. He'd spoken privately to Nehemiah before Nehemiah went public with his plan. Perhaps God has gotten your attention about a broken-down area in your family, neighborhood, workplace, or community. Lean in and listen. Pay attention to this newly stirred interest. Don't look for signs; look for God. But rest assured He can bring you a sign if you need one. If God is calling you to be a part of the solution, it may be through fasting and intercession, sowing and praying, speaking up and stepping up. Just know He'll make sure you have all you need to tend to what's on His heart. God cares about many things, and He intends to heal some of the world's hurts through you.

LEARN Read Nehemiah 2.

FLOURISH Ask God to show you which wall in your life He wants you to rebuild. Somebody or something needs your influence.

PRAY

Lord,
Use me according to Your will. Open my eyes to how You're moving in my midst. Make a way, stir hearts, and give me faith to tend to what's on Your heart today. Amen.

Guard the Low Places

> So I placed armed guards behind the lowest parts of the wall in the exposed areas. I stationed the people to stand guard by families, armed with swords, spears, and bows.
>
> Nehemiah 4:13

God's people worked on the wall, and with every step in the right direction, their enemy raged against them. Sanballat and Tobiah stopped at nothing to hinder their progress. But Nehemiah had heard from God and would not be moved. He cried out to God for intervention, and he did the practical thing and stationed armed guards behind the lowest parts of the wall in the exposed areas. We as God's people need to do that for each other. When we dare to move out into the purposes of God, we will enlist the rage of our enemy. He will unleash his fury on us to the point that we may feel beat up and worn out. These are the low, exposed places in life for us. Here's where we tend to look inward and wonder if we heard from God. And we look outward and feel overwhelmed by the impossible task before us. But we need to look upward and cry out to God like Nehemiah did. Then we need to call our warrior friends and ask them to stand guard with us until we feel built back up again. If you're in a low place, don't isolate. That's what your enemy is hoping for. Call in the guard and stand in faith. You'll get through this.

LEARN ▸ Read Nehemiah 4:1–13.

FLOURISH ▸ Connect with your warriors today. See if they need anything from you. Let them know what you're up against.

PRAY ▸

Mighty God,
Protect me when I'm vulnerable; fight when I am weak. Intervene the way You do. I'm calling on You! Amen.

Don't Fear the Enemy; Remember God

"Don't be afraid of the enemy! Remember the Lord, who is great and glorious, and fight for your brothers, your sons, your daughters, your wives, and your homes!"

Nehemiah 4:14

*T*he enemy is the author of chaos and confusion. But fighting the enemy isn't a game of Whac-A-Mole. We're not meant to be in a state of flurried confusion turning this way and that, chasing symptoms and reacting to circumstances. God has not given us a spirit of fear, but of power and love and sound mind.* Nehemiah's enemies intended to surprise the people working on the wall, but God gave them a heads-up; He'll do the same for us. Nehemiah rejected fear and stood in power. He charged the people to battle their fears by *remembering God*. Nehemiah knew the people were tired, but it was time to stand in faith and fight for their inheritance. It's grueling to work hard on the task in front of you and endure opposition and warfare at the same time. But that's when the enemy gains the most ground against God's people, so that's where we need to learn how to stand in battle. Don't fear your enemy. Remember the God who fights for you.

LEARN   Read Nehemiah 4:14–20.

FLOURISH   Stay engaged until God says it's time to rest. God has given you authority over all the power of the enemy.† With God, you have the upper hand; fight for your inheritance.

PRAY

Lord,
   Help me to keep my wits about me. I will not fear the enemy; I will remember You. You are great and glorious, mighty and true. I stand with You and You stand with me. Thank You, Lord. Amen.

*2 Timothy 1:7.
†Luke 10:19.

Give Generously;
God Remembers

Remember, O my God, all that I have done for these people, and bless me for it.

Nehemiah 5:19

The Jewish people returned to their homeland to rebuild their temple and restore their city, only to have some of their wealthy countrymen take advantage of them. They needed loans and assistance to reestablish themselves in a new city, and their wealthy neighbors, fellow Jews, charged them exorbitant interest and seized their land when they could not make a payment. These people traded one form of slavery for another. They complained to Nehemiah, who not only confronted the injustice, he shared generously from his own resources. Nehemiah worked hard like everyone else, and he earnestly tended to the needs before him. He was a giver, not a taker. Why? Because he feared God and determined to honor Him with every resource entrusted to him. Self-preservation and kingdom life are not compatible. It's tempting to grab what you want and turn a deaf ear to those in need, but right now, we're stewards, not owners. One day we'll be owners based on how we stewarded what doesn't belong to us. You can't do everything, but you're definitely called to do something. God keeps great records and He cares deeply about those in need. Live and give generously. God remembers.

LEARN   Read Nehemiah 5.

FLOURISH   You don't have to do everything, just the very things God asks of you. Rise up today and give with a heart of faith and love. You'll be changed in the process.

PRAY

Lord,
   Forgive me for my tendency to think solely of myself. Show me where to sow, who to help, and what to do. I'm Yours, Lord. Amen.

Discern Distraction

"I am engaged in a great work, so I can't come. Why should I stop working to come and meet with you?"

Nehemiah 6:3

*N*ehemiah loved and feared God and felt prompted by Him to leave the corporate world to take on a project that seemed impossible from any point of view. Yet he knew God was in it, so he took the great risk and returned to Jerusalem to begin the process of rebuilding. We love shiny new things. It takes grit and grace and vision to take on an old thing and make it new again. Yet that's what Jesus has done for us. He met us in our mess and brokenness, and He made us new again. We are His masterpiece, created anew in Christ Jesus *so that* we can do the wonderful things He's planned for us.* But if we never grasp the value of our lives, we'll never comprehend the importance of our work. And if we never comprehend the importance of our work, we'll not discern the enemy's attempts to distract us from that work. May you walk so intimately with God that you're acutely aware of your value and divinely aware of your calling. May you be able to say along with Nehemiah, *"I'm doing a great work and I will not be distracted by the enemy of my soul."* Not today. Not any day!

LEARN   Read Nehemiah 6:1–14.

FLOURISH   Take inventory of your soul today. Ask God to show you the value of your life and of your assignment. Be awakened to their importance and stand strong.

PRAY

> *Lord,*
> *I've lost sight of the value of my soul and calling. Ignite my heart once again! Give me fierce faith and deep conviction to stay the course! Amen.*

*Ephesians 2:10.

Celebrate along the Way

And Nehemiah continued, "Go and celebrate with a feast of rich foods and sweet drinks, and share gifts of food with people who have nothing prepared. This is a sacred day before our Lord. Don't be dejected and sad, for the joy of the LORD is your strength!"

Nehemiah 8:10

The people were as broken as the city walls. Nehemiah knew they needed the word of the Lord. When the people heard the word of God, they realized afresh just how far they'd fallen away from God. And yet, they'd returned to Him! They were fighting their battles, standing in the strength of the Lord, and persevering in faith. They'd already repented for their downfall. Now was not a time to be dejected; it was a time to celebrate. When we're worn down, we can feel especially sensitive about our shortcomings. Repentance restores intimacy with God whereas dejection assumes we're still a long way from Him. He's always only one prayer away. If you're following Jesus, obeying His ways, and doing your best with the tasks set before you, *rejoice*. In fact, plan a time of celebration for all God has done and for how you've persevered thus far. God is not disillusioned with you. He loves you. He'll never have unrealistic expectations of you. And your faith-filled-heart-of-gratitude celebrations mean as much to Him as do your moments of humble repentance.

LEARN Read Nehemiah 8.

FLOURISH Take time this week to celebrate your progress and God's faithfulness. Don't just think about it. Do it. ☺

PRAY

Jesus,
How far we've come! I rejoice today for the victories won and the lessons learned. I'm not who I was. Thank You, Lord. Onward and upward I go. Amen.

Provision and Decision

"You gave them bread from heaven when they were hungry and water from the rock when they were thirsty. You commanded them to go and take possession of the land you had sworn to give them."

Nehemiah 9:15

The Jewish people gathered for a sacred assembly to confess their sins and to remember their history with God. Leaders charged the people, "Stand up and praise the Lord your God, for He lives from everlasting to everlasting." The people recounted the ways God guided and provided for them. He gave them bread from heaven when they were hungry and water from a rock when they were thirsty. And He charged them to take possession of their promised land. Jesus is *our* Bread from heaven—our eternal provision. He satisfies our deepest hunger. He traded His life for ours. We are now eternally secure. He's also the Rock on which we stand. Our place of refuge and strength. And when we *truly* believe that Jesus is who He says He is and follow Him, streams of living water flow through us to a parched and desperate world. Stand up and praise the Lord your God, for He lives from everlasting to everlasting. Since you're a partaker of such divine, eternal provision, you also must make a decision. Will you lay hold of the land God has designated for you?

LEARN   Read Nehemiah 9:1–15.

FLOURISH   Push away the clutter today and ponder the wonder of Christ *in* you, your hope of glory, your secure foundation. What will you do with such a treasure?

PRAY

Father,
   How easily I forget about the power of Your love and the reality of my inheritance. You made a decision to save me. With awe and humble gratitude, I make the decision to trust You. Amen.

A Gracious Woman Retains Honor

> When it was Esther's turn to go to the king, she accepted the advice of Hegai, the eunuch in charge of the harem. She asked for nothing except what he suggested, and she was admired by everyone who saw her.
>
> Esther 2:15

God invites us to approach the throne of grace humbly, but boldly, and audaciously too. He invites us to see ourselves as He does: without fault and with great joy. He invites us to ask, seek, knock, and believe. We're invited to be ourselves before Him and to trust that He'll transform us into the royal heirs of the kingdom that we truly are! However, when we find ourselves in very real situations on this fallen planet that involve ego, competition, and people who do not fear God, it's wise to be less audacious and a bit more cautious. Proverbs 11:16 says that a gracious woman retains honor. There's something powerful about a woman who entrusts her honor and her outcomes not to man, but to God. She doesn't grab for herself or expect too much from others. She's not petty or common. She's uncommon. When she humbles herself, she knows God will lift her up at the proper time. When she dies to her imagined rights, God will defend her and deliver her. There's a time to stand and fight, but there's also a time to bow and let God fight for you. May you wisely discern the difference.

LEARN Read Esther 2:1–20.

FLOURISH Wisdom's path is peace. May you find your place of strength in Him today.

PRAY

Lord,
I hide myself in You. Give me strength when I need to stand and flexibility when it's time to bow. You will always be my Great Defender. I look to You. Amen.

124

When a Leader Abdicates Responsibility

The king said, "The money and the people are both yours to do with as you see fit."

Esther 3:11

King Xerxes, who was out of touch with reality, gave Haman, his second in command, way too much power. Leaders are appointed by God and are greatly accountable to God. It's a mystery why God allows certain people to remain in position when they do more harm than good. But He is God and is sovereign in His ways. Many leaders tend to be a blend of both glaring weaknesses and surprising strengths. (Aren't we all?) And they can either surround themselves with humble, capable, God-fearing associates, or pick passive-aggressive yes-men who will use their position to get their way. It's heartbreaking how many pastors and ministry leaders have hired a number-two guy who controls the narrative between the people and their leader. Morale and trust fall by the wayside as the go-between misuses his power. The leader doesn't really want to know what's going on and likes it that way, all while good people suffer. The results are heartbreaking. Does God see? Does He care? Absolutely. Will He *do* something about it? Yes. God always has His saints in the wings. He's preparing them and, when the time is right, will use them to thwart the enemy's plan. When it seems evil has won, it's only because the story isn't over yet.

LEARN Read Esther 3.

FLOURISH If you're aware of an unjust situation, fast and pray. Ask God to raise up someone to stand in the gap.

PRAY

Great King,
Intervene like only You can! Humble the proud, promote the humble, and foil the enemy's plan against the innocent. Move, O God! Amen.

When a Facade Won't Do

> When Queen Esther's maids and eunuchs came and told her about Mordecai, she was deeply distressed. She sent clothing to him to replace the burlap, but he refused it.
>
> Esther 4:4

*T*he wicked Haman had convinced King Xerxes to issue a decree against every single Jew. They were to be slaughtered, all on the same day. Imagine! Obviously, there was great mourning among the Jews. Mordecai wailed loudly and wept bitterly. Word got back to Queen Esther; she worried that Mordecai would get into trouble for mourning so close to the gate. The burlap and ashes weren't fitting for the palace gate, so she sent clothing to clean up his appearance. But a new set of clothes was not the answer. And *this* is where the kingdom story turns on its heels. Esther communicated to Mordecai from the privilege of the palace. This was no time for self-preservation or for putting on a good face. Mordecai didn't need to step up to the expectations of the privileged. Esther needed to come down to the needs of the oppressed. Ignorance is bliss. But once we know about oppression and injustice, we must not look the other way. Hiding in our wealth is to turn our backs on God. He is *for* the oppressed. May you lovingly dare to enter into a suffering that's not your own for the greater good of the kingdom.

LEARN ▸ Read Esther 4:1–4.

FLOURISH ▸ Ask God to open your eyes to something that breaks His heart.

PRAY

Father,
Break my heart for what breaks Yours! I refuse "blessing guilt," but I embrace a kingdom mindset. Thank You for Your gifts to me. Help me to live within the tension of my blessed life and my responsibility as Your child. Amen.

For Such a Time As This

"If you keep quiet at a time like this, deliverance and relief for the Jews will arise from some other place, but you and your relatives will die. Who knows if perhaps you were made queen for just such a time as this?"

Esther 4:14

Queen Esther's life was on the line. Her fears were real. Her people faced extermination, yet if she dared to appeal to the king on their behalf, she could die and the plan against the Jews could still succeed. She had much to lose. Most of us will never face that kind of pressure. But we do have a calling that requires faith, risk, and trust in an unseen God. People need Jesus. The lost need to be found. The rejected, accepted. The sick, healed. The broken, restored. Those facing death need to know about resurrection life. There's much to do and not enough of us to do it all. Jesus himself said, "The harvest is plentiful, but the workers are few."* There are storehouses in heaven virtually untapped because God's people are more interested in their earthly lives than their eternal ones. Lord, have mercy! He's still a miracle-working God. His promises are as potent as they've ever been. He's searching the world over, looking for faith, looking for conviction in the hearts of His people so He can bring healing, deliverance, and salvation to a lost and broken world. Make no mistake about it. God will bring deliverance. But the uninvolved will miss the miracle.

LEARN ▶ Read Esther 4:5–17.

FLOURISH ▶ Ask God to show you what impossible things He wants to do through you.

PRAY

> *Father,*
> *Give me boldness, courage, and strength to step into all You've planned for me! I'm available, Lord. Amen.*

*Matthew 9:37 NIV.

He Uses the Night Hours

> That night the king had trouble sleeping, so he ordered an attendant to bring the book of the history of his reign so it could be read to him.
>
> Esther 6:1

*T*he king extended his scepter to Esther and invited her into his presence. She asked for a dinner party with the king and Haman. There are varying opinions as to why she didn't tell the king on that first night about Haman's evil plot. My guess is that she felt the inner nudge to push pause. She asked for a second dinner the following night. That evening the king had trouble sleeping, so he read the record books of his reign and remembered afresh how Mordecai had saved his life. God used this delay to add weight to Esther's appeal. Time and again we read how God uses either insomnia or dreams to bring revelation to those who need it. Scripture says that He grants sleep to those He loves,* but He'll also interrupt sleep on occasion to get a message to us. Determine to reclaim your night hours. Keep a notepad ready in case He speaks. Before you turn in for the evening, bow low, thank God for your day, and claim His protection over your sleep. In Jesus' name, forbid the enemy to speak or interfere with your sleeping hours. You belong to Jesus, and He promises that even at night our hearts will instruct us.†

LEARN Read Esther 6.

FLOURISH Establish a healthy, consistent bedtime practice. Guard and protect that time.

PRAY

Jesus,
I claim my night hours for You! I command the enemy to stand down and be silent. I forbid him to speak or interfere with my sleep. My nights belong to You. Amen.

*Psalm 127:2.
†Psalm 16:7.

When God Turns the Tables

And as soon as the king spoke, his attendants covered Haman's face, signaling his doom.

Esther 7:8

God is full of mystery. He spoke the galaxies into place and entrusted His Son to a world that He knew would kill Him. He's altogether holy yet made himself intimately accessible to us. He is a God of justice who will one day set the records straight, but until then, He gives the vilest of sinners a chance to repent *because He loves them.* Somehow, He knows exactly where and how to bring discipline or deliverance. Nothing gets by Him. He knows what He's doing at all times. Back to the story of Esther. Haman was wicked to his core. He ordered the annihilation of an entire people group because one Jewish man dared to honor God above him. For a while, it seemed he'd get away with such a gross mismanagement of power, but then God used a humble Jewish girl turned queen, who dared to trust God and risk her life for her people. Take some risks and stand in faith against the evil in your day. When the King decides it's time, He'll cover the face of your enemy and signal his doom. He'll turn the tables, dismantle every scheme, and in a matter of moments, we'll see the redemption of all things. That great day is coming.

LEARN Read Esther 7.

FLOURISH What part of your story are you most excited to see God redeem? Envision it. And thank Him ahead of time. Praise Him now. It's coming!

PRAY

Lord,
You are a God of justice and love. Cut off the strength of the wicked; increase the power of the godly.* I know one day You will redeem all things. Amen.

*See Psalm 75:10.

Power for a Purpose

Then Mordecai left the king's presence, wearing the royal robe of blue and white, the great crown of gold, and an outer cloak of fine linen and purple. And the people of Susa celebrated the new decree.

Esther 8:15

Haman's wicked plot was exposed, and Mordecai's integrity revealed. In a sudden turn of events, King Xerxes gave Haman's property to Esther and his signet ring—a symbol of authority—to Mordecai. Since the decree against the Jews could not be reversed, the king issued another decree, allowing the Jewish people to defend themselves. Mordecai traded his sackcloth for royal robes. But this wasn't just about vindication, it was about salvation. The enemy army assumed it would overpower God's people, but quite the opposite happened. The Jews overpowered their enemies! Similarly, the enemy has issued a decree against God's people, to steal, kill, and destroy everything God intends to do in our lives. But God has issued a superior decree, giving us full authority over him. Because we're wrapped in God's robe of righteousness, we have the power to defend ourselves. We wear His signet ring. He's entrusted power and authority to us, but it's not just for us. We're called to contend for those who cannot or don't know how to fight for themselves. While I was interviewing Andy Crouch, executive editor of *Christianity Today*, he asked the question, "Who flourishes because I have power?" You've been given power for a purpose. All of heaven is on your side. Use your God-given authority and stop the enemy.

LEARN Read Esther 8–10.

FLOURISH See yourself in the bigger story. Stand in your authority and pray with power.

PRAY

Father,
Show me what You've entrusted to me. Help me to appropriate Your power and authority for the greater good. Amen.

Fear God, Shun Evil

There once was a man named Job who lived in the land of Uz. He was blameless—a man of complete integrity. He feared God and stayed away from evil.

Job 1:1

*P*roverbs 3:7–8 says, "Don't be impressed with your own wisdom. Instead, fear the LORD and turn away from evil. Then you will have healing for your body and strength for your bones." To be wise in your own eyes is to become either a pagan or a Pharisee. You'll either dabble in things you shouldn't while saying, "I've got this," and find yourself in a ditch, or you'll be impressed with yourself and say, "I already know this," and find yourself in the other ditch. True wisdom starts with knowing and fearing God and mistrusting yourself enough to know that you must turn away from evil. Job understood his own limits and trusted a God who knew no limits. He was a man of complete integrity and though a wealthy, successful businessman, was not arrogant. I asked this question earlier, but I'll ask it again: *How much can He bless you before you make it about you?* God wants to bless His children, but we are painfully prone to wander. If it's been a while since you've embraced a reverent, awe-filled attitude before God, humble yourself today. If you've been impressed with your own wisdom, humble yourself today. Doing so will honor God and bring strength to your soul.

LEARN Read Job 1:1–5.

FLOURISH Play the most reverent song you know, and bow low, with open hands. Remember God today.

PRAY

Mighty God,
I bow before You. You are matchless, mighty, and true. I have no wisdom that You've not given me. I give all that I am back to You. Amen.

A Wall of Protection

You have always put a wall of protection around him and his home and his property. You have made him prosper in everything he does. Look how rich he is!

Job 1:10

*T*he enemy had been patrolling the earth, looking for opportunities to attack. He found no opening in Job's life. The Lord himself called Job the finest man in all the earth.* Satan hated Job and resented the fact that God shielded him so. It almost seems like Satan baited God into lifting His protection from Job, but God falls into no one's trap. He's always in control, always knows what He's doing. If anything, Satan fell prey to God's wisdom. We'll explore Job's story over the next few days, but today let's remember that God *does* put a shield around His people. Psalm 125:2 says, "Just as the mountains surround Jerusalem, so the LORD surrounds His people, both now and forever." Psalm 3:3 says, "But you, O LORD, are a shield around me; you are my glory, the one who holds my head high." Here's one more. Psalm 5:12 says, "For you bless the godly, O LORD; you surround them with your shield of love." Any pain God allows, He redeems. Any trap He allows the enemy to set is meant for the enemy himself. God is on His throne, He has His heart set on you, and He *has* put a hedge of protection around you. Believe it.

LEARN Read Job 1:6–12.

FLOURISH Memorize one of the verses above and pray it every day.

PRAY

Lord,
You surround me with Your favor as with a shield. Thank You for all You've prevented and all You've provided. Thank You for the countless ways You protect me. Amen.

*See Job 1:8.

Grounded in the Things of God

"The LORD gave me what I had, and the Lord has taken it away.
Praise the name of the LORD!" In all of this, Job did not sin by blaming God.

Job 1:21–22

*I*t's hard to imagine the trauma Job and his wife endured in just a matter of moments. Yet Job's righteousness went so deep that at his worst moment, Job's instinctive response was to bow low and recognize God's sovereignty in his life. He actually fell to the ground to *worship*. Worship! Job had walked so intimately with his heavenly Father that he was more grounded by his spiritual life than he was shaken by his earthly life. That kind of intimacy doesn't happen overnight. Our instinctive responses are born out of a million similar choices—life-and-death choices we make every day that either acknowledge God or push Him aside. The reason Job didn't sin by blaming God was because he knew that everything good about his life came from God. Once we stop acknowledging God, we tend to grab for ourselves; when we don't get what we want, we blame God. It's a cycle of sin and shallowness that starts when we drift. If we want to stand strong in the changing seasons of life, we must stay connected to the Power Source—God himself—the Giver of life and the Protector of our souls. Stay intimately engaged with God. The world may shake but you don't have to.

LEARN Read Job 1:13–22.

FLOURISH Acknowledge God's involvement in your life every time you think of it. Practice the presence of God until it grounds you like never before.

PRAY

Father,
I want more of You. Draw me nearer, Lord. Take me deeper still. My heart longs for You. Amen.

When Silence Is Best

Then they sat on the ground with him for seven days and nights. No one said a word to Job, for they saw that his suffering was too great for words.

Job 2:13

*J*ob lost his family, his wealth, and his health. Imagine his grief, torment, and unfathomable discomfort and physical pain. Yet in all of it, he did *nothing* wrong. Job's friends heard of the tragedy and traveled from their homes to comfort and console him. Now, we know that later in the story, they opened their mouths, which became a problem. But for seven days and nights, they simply sat on the ground with him and said *nothing* because his suffering was too great for words. We tend to have empathy only until it's upstaged by expectation. We can't believe God would allow a long battle (even though we read about one such instance right here in Scripture). It doesn't fit our tidy Christian formula, so we back up, lose patience, and try to figure out where they went wrong. Is it a lack of faith? Lack of want-to? Lack of skill for managing life's problems? Does it matter? Lord, forgive us for the ways we assess another's suffering, especially when we've known only strength where they're weak. What if we gave up a week of days and nights and simply sat with the sufferer? No words. No fixes. No judgment. Only presence. The world needs more presence and less assumption.

LEARN Read Job 2.

FLOURISH Find someone who needs presence more than they need fixes. Do for them what God asks of you.

PRAY

Lord,
Forgive me for my tendency to step back and judge when You call me to step close and serve. Grow Your heart of love within me. Amen.

When the Numbness Wears Off

"What I always feared has happened to me.
  What I dreaded has come true.
I have no peace, no quietness.
  I have no rest; only trouble comes."

Job 3:25–26

*W*hen someone goes through a major trauma, God often shields them from the brunt of the impact because it would be too much to absorb all at once. People who've walked through unfathomable loss and hardship speak of a supernatural grace and peace that surrounds them immediately after the incident. It's like God carries them along in unseen arms; they don't seem to feel what everyone expects them to feel. Some call it denial, but more often than not, it's a gift of supernatural grace. In due time, however, the weight of their loss or hardship catches up with them. They're suddenly thrust into a season where they feel *everything*, like their nerves are exposed and highly sensitive. This becomes a trauma all its own. Where onlookers initially wondered about denial, now they assume overreaction. So what's the proper response to someone who's walked through a crisis? Let them be and feel as messy as they are. Then draw near and let them know you're not going anywhere. Withhold judgment. Suspend assumptions. And resist assessments. Grief after loss is not pretty, yet it's a necessary, sacred journey. The Church needs more brave souls to weather the storm with the brokenhearted. Mercy triumphs over judgment.*

LEARN   Read Job 3.

FLOURISH   Practice mercy by connecting with someone who's walking through a storm. Listen to their story.

PRAY

Jesus, Your compassions never fail. Your empathy runs deep. You meet people in their need and weep with them. Make me more like You, Lord. Amen.

*See James 2:13.

Bible Snobs
and Christian Bullies

"We have studied life and found all this to be true.
Listen to my counsel, and apply it to yourself."
Job 5:27

*I*s it possible to be an eloquent orator and a pompous windbag at the same time? Job's friend Eliphaz fits that description. He mingled beautiful truths about God with marred opinions about suffering. Yes, there are consequences when we sin and blessings when we obey. But we must never use those truths to assess the suffering of another. People thought Jesus suffered because of His own sin, but it was *our* sins He carried.* How do you know if you've encountered a Bible snob or a Christian bully? They use lofty, high-browed phrases when they talk about God, yet they're quick to fling their assessments of others from a thirty-thousand-foot view. They lack brokenness, empathy, accessibility, and humility. They present a punitive God who punishes us as our sins deserve when Scripture actually says that He *doesn't* punish us as our sins deserve.† They're impatient with those who have questions and suspicious of those who see things differently. Just because someone claims to speak for God doesn't mean they reflect God's heart. Seasoned followers of Christ in *any* denomination will have a twinkle in their eye and humility in their heart, and they will inspire you to walk intimately with Jesus, not run away from Him.

LEARN   Read Job 4–5.

FLOURISH   Who is the godliest, humblest person you know? Give them a call. Have lunch. Spend time with them.

PRAY

> *Humble me, Lord. Help me to rightly assess the circumstances around me. Help me to reflect Your precious, tender heart to a lost and broken world. Amen.*

*See Isaiah 53.
†Psalm 103:10.

Dangerous Assumptions

"Does God twist justice?
Does the Almighty twist what is right?
Your children must have sinned against him,
    so their punishment was well deserved."

Job 8:3–4

Bildad, Job's second friend to speak up, was also exasperated by Job's lament. Job knew in his heart that he hadn't sinned against God. For the life of him, he couldn't figure out why God had made him a target for suffering. He wondered aloud, "God, if I've sinned in some way that I don't know about, why not just forgive me and remove my guilt? Am I that much of a burden to you?" Job felt he had a handle on his own heart, but he started to wonder about God's heart. What's so painful about intense suffering is that it's sometimes unexplainable and often complicated. It's one of the great, universal questions around God's goodness and sovereignty. If He's good, why does He allow so much pain? We often want a God we can predict and explain so we don't have to live with the uncomfortable mystery surrounding Him. Job's friends insisted on a theology that made God utterly predictable and explainable. Therefore, they felt they were on solid ground to make an assumption about Job's children. In the end they'd be wrong, but in the moment, they inflicted much pain. When it comes to the goodness of God and the suffering of man, we don't know what we don't know. And it's wise to say so.

LEARN Read Job 6–8.

FLOURISH If necessary, put less weight on your own opinion and lean harder into the mysteries of God.

PRAY

Father,
*   I am like a vapor, a puff of wind. Yet I think I know so much. Forgive me, Lord. I bow low in humility. Show me more of You. Amen.*

My Redeemer Lives!

"But as for me, I know that my Redeemer lives,
and he will stand upon the earth at last.
And after my body has decayed,
yet in my body I will see God!"

Job 19:25–26

*W*e often forget that Job declared God's resurrection power while he was *still* suffering. He had no new answers, no idea why God had seemingly lifted His hedge of protection. Yet Job held on to his faith. "Although Job struggled with the idea that God was presently against him, he firmly believed that in the end God would be on his side. This belief was so strong that Job became one of the first to talk about the resurrection of the body."* At this point of the story, Job had no idea that the enemy had asked for permission to test Job *because* he was so righteous, or that God would restore him to an even greater place than before. Some parts of your inheritance are reserved for that great day, but God *still* has good things planned for you in the land of the living. God has already planted graces and gifts in every one of your tomorrows. Declare His goodness now, before He gives you what you hope for. One day you'll stand with Him and you'll be glad your heart trusted Him when your eyes couldn't see Him.

LEARN   Read Job 19:25–27; 23:10.

FLOURISH   Declare God's goodness and faithfulness over the very situations that break your heart.

PRAY

Lord,
I will one day see what escapes me now. That's why my faith is precious to You. I declare that You are good, and soon my eyes will see it. Amen.

*Life Application Study Bible, 1072.

He's Just and He Knows Me

"But he knows where I am going.
And when he tests me, I will come out as pure as gold."

Job 23:10

*E*liphaz condemned Job. He assumed Job's suffering was a result of some hidden sin in Job's life. I picture Job mustering up all of his courage and strength to reply to this toxic accusation. Job's response is also a good one for us: "I admit I'm walking through a difficult time right now. I acknowledge that God seems painfully silent and hard to find. Though I cannot find Him, I know that He knows where to find me. He knows where I am, and He knows where I'm going. And when He tests me, He'll bring me forth as gold. I'll know Him better and love Him more than I did before." Job knew in his heart that he was not blatantly sinning and trying to cover it up. Yet he also knew God's holiness in a way that made him tremble with holy terror, for who can stand self-assured before the Most Holy God? If you're walking through unimaginable suffering right now or are feeling unfairly assessed, two things are called for: holy confidence and humble dependence. Trust God's opinion far above man's. And remember, humility is always appropriate when approaching the throne of God. He's a God of justice and He knows you intimately. This should assure you and undo you, all at once.

LEARN   Read Job 23.

FLOURISH   Embrace holy confidence. Jesus will defend your honor. He will deliver you. Embrace humble dependence. He is God and He is holy.

PRAY

Father,
   You know me. You love me. And You will defend and deliver me. When You test me, You promise to bring me through pure as gold. Thank You, Lord. Amen.

Playing the
Performance Card

"Everything I did was honest.
  Righteousness covered me like a robe,
  and I wore justice like a turban."

Job 29:14

When tragedy first hit his life, Job went facedown to the ground and worshiped. He declared God's goodness in both times of favor and hardship. But as the battle raged on, and "friends" accused and assessed, Job lost his footing. He'd had enough. Instead of remembering the majesty and goodness of God, he began recounting the goodness of Job. He's not alone here. When pushed far enough, we all reach for that performance card in our back pocket. We pull it out and ask, "You allow this after all I've done for You?" Every time we rely on past laurels in order to defend our case before God, we build a case against God. As if we know our hearts better than He does. It's not God's harshness that allows us to endure a storm that brings out the worst in us; it's His goodness. He knows how deep our self-reliance goes, and if He doesn't uproot it, the enemy will use it against us in a way that will cost us more than the storm we're in. If you catch yourself defending yourself to God by measuring your good deeds, turn them into seeds and make them an offering once again. It's the only way you'll see a harvest. God is not only your Defender; He's your Deliverer. And He will come for you.

LEARN Read Job 29.

FLOURISH Ponder Christ's performance during His short time on earth— His surrendered life, His obedience, His suffering, and His victory.

PRAY

Jesus,
  I stand on Your grace, and Your grace alone. I can't save or deliver myself. Only You can. My soul waits on You. Amen.

Encountering
the Living God

"I had only heard about you before,
but now I have seen you with my own eyes."

Job 42:5

When it was God's turn to speak, He spoke of heavenly storehouses, earthly phenomena, and the ability to put intuition into the heart of man—all far beyond Job's ability to even understand, let alone perform. Job repented, not because his friends were right about him, but because he'd been wrong about God. Still, Job knew God. He even declared God's sovereignty amidst his own suffering. But he actually *encountered* God during this exchange. We long for an encounter with God—as we should—but are we prepared for what His presence will reveal to and in us? Never condemnation, but definitely revelation. We don't know what we don't know, and we can't see what we can't see. When the God of heaven moves in close, our hearts melt, our knees buckle, and we realize we're not nearly as wise as we thought ourselves to be. For God to change us, we need to know *Him*—the Person and His heart. Job found God to be more than enough for him. Beyond anything he'd lost, he'd gained something more of God. The Lord met Job in the ashes of his pain, opened his eyes, *and then* restored him to greater honor, wealth, and health than before.

LEARN Read Job 42.

FLOURISH Tell God He's more than enough for you! Ask Him for fresh revelations of who He is. Trust Him to redeem your story.

PRAY

Lord,
I want to encounter You in a way that changes me! Open my eyes that I may see You with greater clarity. Show me Your glory. Amen.

Walk, Stand, Sit

Blessed is the one
    who does not walk in step with the wicked
or stand in the way that sinners take
    or sit in the company of mockers. . . .

Psalm 1:1 NIV

God *wants* us to flourish. He wants to bless us. He wants to restore our souls, redeem our lives, and see our God-given purposes fulfilled. Though we're saved and empowered by grace, the choices we make impact the quality of our lives and relationships and influence whether or not we flourish in our circumstances and to what extent we fulfill our God-given purpose. Notice the progression in Psalm 1: *Walk. Stand. Sit.* If we *look* to anything besides Jesus to find our worth and satisfaction, our feet will take us there. Eventually, we'll stand at a crossroads and have a decision to make. If we still don't see the error of our ways, we'll end up sitting and commiserating with those who have no fear of God. But as Christ-followers, Jesus calls us to *walk* in His way, with the wise, and in a manner worthy of our calling. He reminds us to *stand* in faith with our feet securely on the Rock of our salvation. And He paid a high price for us to *sit* at the table of grace and to be *seated with Him* with all of His authority and right standing before the Father. Why would an heir walk any other way? *Profoundly blessed* is the one who walks His way.

LEARN ▶ Read Psalm 1.

FLOURISH ▶ Pay attention to your gaze, for soon your feet will follow. Look up and live.

PRAY

King of Kings,
    You are mighty to save and so very good! I look to You for all I need. Keep me close to You. Amen.

But You, O Lord

But you, O Lord, are a shield around me;
you are my glory, the one who holds my head high.

Psalm 3:3

*B*rokenhearted and weeping, David fled his kingdom. His own son betrayed him, usurped his authority, and undermined his throne. Armies chased him, people doubted him, and circumstances looked grim for him. Though some of David's troubles were the consequence of his own sin,* he was still a man after God's own heart, and God still listened to his prayers. David knew that God was always on His throne, and if He intended to restore David to his throne, nothing and no one could stop Him. Even so, to be betrayed, undermined, and tossed aside (especially by someone you loved and trusted) is excruciating. If you stare too long at your circumstances, they'll overwhelm you. That's why David only glanced at his situation and then set his fierce gaze on the One who would deliver and defend him. Never look at your hardships and injustices in isolation. Acknowledge them, yes, but always with this caveat: "But you, O Lord, are a shield about me; you are my glory, the one who holds my head high." Your circumstances may be true, but truer still is God's presence and power in your life. Stay humble and hopeful that you will see God—the One who fights for you—intervene on your behalf. You will and He will.

LEARN Read Psalm 3.

FLOURISH Write down the greatest angst of your soul and follow it with Psalm 3 (pray it until you believe it).

PRAY

Lord,
You are greater than my circumstances and more powerful than my enemies. You're my shield, my glory, and the One who fights for me. My eyes are on You. Amen.

*See 2 Samuel 12:11.

He Trains You for Battle

He trains my hands for battle;
he strengthens my arm to draw a bronze bow.

Psalm 18:34

*D*avid was able to look back over his life and recount the faithfulness of God. He described God as a Rock—a firm place to stand, a Refuge—a safe place to hide, a Shield—the power that saves, and *the Lord*—who is worthy of praise. This is *our* God. When you're going under, when the enemy looms large, call on the Lord, *knowing* that your cry will reach His ears. He will arise in your defense and will startle His enemies with a surprise counterattack. He will rescue you and put you in a safe and spacious place. And once you're healed and recovered, He will begin to train you for your next battle. He'll teach you how to carry your assignment in a way that doesn't injure you and actually strengthens you. He'll make you spiritually agile by showing you how to respond to sudden change and how to walk on uneven terrain with surefooted confidence. He'll show you what you're capable of when you're carrying His shield of faith. And before you know it, you'll be such a fierce warrior that your enemy will stumble and come trembling from his stronghold. God will use every twist and turn in your story for your good and for His glory.

LEARN ▶ Read Psalm 18.

FLOURISH ▶ What's your current battle stirring up in you? Identify your training ground and engage your faith.

PRAY

Mighty God,
  You're making me into a mighty warrior! I trust You! Show me how to best engage my faith amidst my current battle. I will not be defeated or discouraged, because You are with me. Thank You, Lord! Amen.

He Speaks

The heavens proclaim the glory of God.
The skies display his craftsmanship.
Day after day they continue to speak;
night after night they make him known.

Psalm 19:1–2

*K*ing David wisely understood the dichotomy between his own smallness and God's greatness. The more David reflected on God's majesty, the more he realized his own tendency to miss Him. God has made sure that anyone who wants to know Him, will know Him. The One who spoke the galaxies into existence has made himself available to *us*. Imagine. His magnificent creation reveals His lavish love and meticulous attention to detail. His handiwork is all around us—in the glory of sunrises and sunsets. The beauty of a butterfly, the joy of laughter, the sound of a bubbling brook. When we acknowledge His creation, we get a very real sense of His presence. *Every* good gift comes from Him. Those who seek Him, find Him. He speaks through His Word, through others, through the inward nudge of the Holy Spirit within us, through a song, a sense, and even a subtle shift in circumstances. But we'll miss Him if we we're not watching and listening for Him. We must slow the pace of our lives if we wish to see Him, and we must address the inner tempo of our thoughts if we wish to hear Him. Slow your pace today and look for evidences of God all around you.

LEARN Read Psalm 19.

FLOURISH Write out a journal prayer thanking God in detail for the parts of creation you're most grateful for today. It honors God and is good for your soul.

PRAY

Glorious God of heaven,
Thank You for Your lavish love, the beauty of nature, and the gift of Your presence. I will enjoy all of these today. Amen.

Honor, Anointing, and a Cup That Overflows

> You honor me by anointing my head with oil.
> My cup overflows with blessings.
>
> Psalm 23:5

David's younger wilderness seasons prepared him for promotion. He learned to embrace courage and to rely on the Lord's provision. He also learned how to guard what the Lord had entrusted to him when an enemy preyed upon his territory. We must learn these things as well. That's why we have a Shepherd, one who cares for us *always*. He steers us away from evil, to places of rest and restoration. He leads us off the overused pathways to roads where truth and righteousness remind us who we are to Him. The closer we follow Him, the more we rely on Him until our heart beats in rhythm with His. Over time, we're transformed into the royal heirs we were always meant to be. In the face of our enemy, He claims us as His own. He stands by us, continually pours out fresh anointing on us, and equips us for battle. From preparation to promotion, from the valley of the shadow to the mountain where His sun shines, in the face of enemy attack and around the victory table of celebration, we will *always* have all that we need. We, like David, will one day look back over our lives and declare that we never—not for a moment—lacked any good thing because God's goodness and mercy followed us every step of the way.

LEARN Read Psalm 23.

FLOURISH What do you need at this moment? Look to your Shepherd today. He's leading you even now.

PRAY

Precious Shepherd,
You've always been faithful. I've never lacked a thing. Even now, I will trust You. I have all that I need. Thank You, Lord. Amen.

Strength and Resilience

The LORD is my fortress, protecting me from danger,
so why should I tremble?

Psalm 27:1

My husband is a giant of a man. He's solid as an oak, and as righteous as one too. When our sons were adolescents, they'd overconfidently barrel into their dad and try to knock him over. But he never budged. All of the force they'd muster against him would only reverberate within them as they bounced off him and landed in a heap on the floor. What a picture of sturdiness and strength! King David was as resilient. His many enemies taught him to be strong in the strength of the Lord. Even when you have to leave a space that you love because of an enemy attack, know that it's only temporary. God will make sure He moves you toward your promised land. You don't have to be mighty in stature to be mighty in battle. You just need to stand in the strength of your God. The more time you spend in the sanctuary of God (constantly and continually acknowledging His presence in your life), the less the offenses and attacks of men will affect you. Imagine them, in their foolishness, mustering up their strength to knock you over, only to land themselves in a heap on the ground. Refuse to be derailed by mere humans. *Be strong in the strength of the Lord.* Don't fear. Don't fret. Expect to see His goodness in the land of the living.

LEARN Read Psalm 27.

FLOURISH If you're thinking too long about the negative opinions of another, run into the sanctuary of God. Strengthen yourself in Him. Envision your victory.

PRAY

Mighty God,
You are my defender, my deliverer, my strong tower. I will remain confident in You. Teach me how to trust You for greater things. Amen.

The Eyes of the Lord

But the LORD watches over those who fear him,
those who rely on his unfailing love.

Psalm 33:18

When we rightly honor, fear, and revere the Lord Most High, His eyes are instinctively *drawn* to us. Think about that for a moment. When you wake in the morning, open your Bible and bow your head; God's eyes are drawn to you. When you go about your day and you whisper a prayer and acknowledge His presence, His eyes are drawn to you. When you're faced with a choice to walk in His way or your own, and you choose His—because you love Him—His eyes are drawn to you with great affection and tenderness. Just imagine! God is aware of everything that goes on in the earth today. He made us so He understands everything we do and why we do it. But He's especially drawn to the sons and daughters who walk this earth with reverence in our hearts. He leans in, breathes fresh life, establishes us in His purposes, and delivers us from death. When we fear the Lord, we know enough not to put our trust in lesser things. *He* is our help and our shield. We trust in His holy name. We rely on His love. The beautiful thing about walking intimately with God and reverently honoring Him is that we are continually drawn to Him, and He to us.

LEARN Read Psalm 33.

FLOURISH Remind your soul to rightly honor and fear God, and smile at the thought of Him fixing His eyes on you.

PRAY

Father,
I am Yours. I'm more spiritual than I am physical. Help me to walk in Your ways, to rightly honor You, and to remember Your heart for me. Amen.

Delivered from All My Fears

I prayed to the LORD, and he answered me.
He freed me from all my fears.

Psalm 34:4

I'd never thought it possible to be delivered from *all* of my fears. I didn't even think it was possible to be delivered from most of my fears. But as I've continually looked away from the roar of my enemy and set my gaze on the Lord, He has—over time—set me free. God wants to occupy more space in your life. He wants to bring freedom to those places the enemy has boldly claimed. Envision your freedom. It *is* possible for God's voice in your ear to ring truer than the enemy's roaring threat against you. It is possible for the peace of God to flood your whole being, right in the midst of your storm, and to calm the angst within your soul. How do you cultivate a life that easily accesses the truth about God? You taste and see that He is good. Every day, in multiple ways, note the goodness of God all around you. Acknowledge His influence. Picture fear, shame, and anxiety shriveling to nothing and falling right off of you because your face is radiant with God's all-consuming power and presence. Your fears are real. Your battles will be significant. But there's a *super*natural power on your side—God himself. Don't wait for heaven to be free. He's here for you right now.

LEARN Read Psalm 34.

FLOURISH Make it a regular practice to look to God. Picture your fears coming to nothing. Believe it's possible. He will deliver you.

PRAY

Lord,
I never want to settle for less than Your best for me! I want freedom!
Deliver me from all my fears. May my countenance reflect Yours. Amen.

Your Heart's Desire

Take delight in the Lord,
and he will give you your heart's desires.

Psalm 37:4

Whe hen I first read this passage as a new believer, I pictured a grandma with more lipstick than lips, holding up a package of chewing gum, pointing to her cheek and saying, "You give me a kiss and I'll give you this." I didn't at all understand the magnitude of this promise. God's not pining away, trying to bait us into an occasional visit or a swift kiss on the cheek. He's the unequaled, untamable, unfathomable, powerful life Source from which everything in creation originated. He needs nothing, holds everything in His hand, and loves us with a passion that cannot be contained. Any gift from His hand pales compared to the treasure of knowing His heart. We pine for gifts, for answers, for change. *God wants us to more deeply long for His presence.* We're so temporary in our wishes. He's eternal when it comes to His desires for us. The more we delight in His presence, *in Him*, the less we pine for lesser things. And the more our souls get filled up with His goodness, the more our hearts beat in rhythm with His. Suddenly His desires become our desires, and we find ourselves praying His kingdom right to earth. Nothing compares to the greatness of our God. Nothing we desire on earth compares to Him. Enjoy His presence. Delight in Him. It'll change everything.

LEARN Read Psalm 37.

FLOURISH Ponder the galaxies and your desires and the fact that God is interested in both. Find your greatest delight in Him today.

PRAY

Unstoppable God,
I marvel at Your goodness. You're my greatest gift and I already have You! Thank You, Lord. I bless Your name. Amen.

Wait Joyfully, Expectantly

He has given me a new song to sing,
a hymn of praise to our God.
Many will see what he has done and be amazed.
They will put their trust in the LORD.

Psalm 40:3

*T*ruly *new* songs rarely come out of times of ease. They rise up out of the ashes, or settle in during times of Sabbath, or thunder through us in a time of battle. God invites us to sing a new song when circumstances cloud our view of Him. Worship breaks through the overcast sky and connects us once again with the warmth of His presence. Just this morning I battled some discouragement because I've waited long for full healing. I want to be symptom free, but I'm not. Not yet, anyway. The Lord whispered to my heart, *Active waiting produces perseverance, but perseverance won't do the miraculous in you unless it's coupled with joyful expectancy.* I've persevered through many battles. I'm persevering even now. But I'd settled into a mode of biding my time until my breakthrough, and this morning I found myself in the muck and mire of disappointment. Such passive waiting happens every time we count the days of our war when God would rather we count the promises He's made to us. If you identify more with the length of your trial than you do with the height of God's love, it's time for a new song.

LEARN Read Psalm 40.

FLOURISH Find your song today. Embrace joyful expectancy today. God IS up to something altogether *new* in your life. Soon your eyes will see it.

PRAY

Lord,
I thank You by faith that You're coming for me! You're breaking through for me! Help me to persevere with joy. Do the miraculous in me. Amen.

Be Still and *Know*

"Be still, and know that I am God!"
Psalm 46:10

*H*ow do you know when it's time to double down, hang on, and fight for victory, or when it's time to let go, rest your heart, and let the Lord fight the battle for you? Pay attention to the state of your soul. If restlessness drives you to strive, then you know it's time to *be still and know* that He is God. This translates to a simple yet different formula: let go, sink down, relax, and in some cases, be quiet. When our souls are stressed, our words tend to follow suit. And before we know it, our own declarations defy the goodness and faithfulness of God. Sometimes the most faith-filled thing you can do is to quiet your heart, close your mouth, and let go of the thing that stresses you so. Jesus doesn't drop things, so you can trust Him to hold whatever you entrust to Him. We'll talk another day about discerning when it's time to rise up and run to the battle line, but today there are some things God wants you to let go of. He wants to make a trade—your stress for His peace, your burden for His grace, your earthbound perspective for His eternal one. His yoke is easy and His burden is light. May your precious, restful heart of faith honor Him greatly today.

LEARN Read Psalm 46.

FLOURISH Today's going to be a great day. Let go, relax, and be still. You'll be glad you did.

PRAY

Lord,
You want my soul to be a flourishing, healthy place. Forgive me for the angst I've allowed there. I'm ready to make a trade—my stress for Your grace. You are so good to me. I love You, Lord. Amen.

Your Great Unearthing
Is the Devil's Undoing

You crown the year with a bountiful harvest;
even the hard pathways overflow with abundance.

Psalm 65:11

*W*e don't determine the seasons of our lives; God does. We need a faith perspective in every season. Maybe you're walking through a time when you feel undone, exposed, and scattered. Your once well-defined boundaries have been replaced with holes in the ground, dirt mounds, and boulders that have surfaced. You wonder what in the world happened to your tidy life. It's during these seasons that God sets the plow a little deeper into the soil of our hearts because He's about to do a *new* thing. Beneath the surface, you've got buried hurts, embedded lies, and weeds that choke the life right out of you. It's a messy process, and the enemy wastes no time in leveraging his lies to make you feel worse than you already do. But if you could look up and listen for the Lord, you would hear Him say, "My dear child. This isn't about who you are; it's about who you're becoming. Your great unearthing will soon be the devil's undoing. Hold on. Listen for My voice. And know that this season will not last forever. A time of great flourishing is ahead for you." Believe it, friend. You will get through this.

LEARN Read Psalm 65.

FLOURISH Lean in and do the inner work of the soul. Sort through your losses, your buried traumas, and the lies you picked up when life let you down. Hang on to hope. A new day is coming.

PRAY

Precious Lord,
Meet me here. Give me faith to believe You for greater things! Heal me from the inside out. My soul trusts in You. Amen.

When God Seems Silent

But then I recall all you have done, O LORD;
I remember your wonderful deeds of long ago.

Psalm 77:11

*I*t's one thing to stay attentive to God's presence when the heavens seem to be open over us, when His words are plentiful and His voice is crystal clear. But how about when He's gone silent—like He's lost our address? This so often happens when we're suffering, and we wonder, *Why now? Now's when I* need *a word from You!* During such times, we instinctively turn inward. Our self-focused nature emerges when God stops talking. Like Asaph, we sometimes blame God for our suffering, our insomnia, and for His lack of involvement in our lives. We accuse Him of forgetting to be himself—kind, compassionate, and loving. Negative accusations and assumptions about God will always be destructive to our soul. So why does God allow the painful, silent season? Because we need to learn to turn on a dime like Asaph did. We won't mature in our faith until we learn to stop in our tracks and redirect our focus, our thoughts, and our words. If you're there today, remember God. Remember His goodness, recall His miracles, and revive your trust in Him. Don't confuse His silence with His absence. He's right here and He's developing gritty faith in you. Rise up, dear one.

LEARN Read Psalm 77.

FLOURISH If your thought life is on a track that's taking you downward, stop now and redirect your gaze. Declare God's goodness. *Rejoice* in His faithfulness.

PRAY

Lord,
I notice how others seem to be flourishing while I'm floundering. I wonder what You're up to. But my heart trusts You! You are mighty to save. Do a new thing in me! Amen.

Your Pilgrimage

What joy for those whose strength comes from the LORD,
who have set their minds on a pilgrimage to Jerusalem.

Psalm 84:5

Our souls were *not* made for aimless wandering. If we wander too long, we'll wear out, lose heart, and eventually lose our way. The Israelites wandered into trouble time and time again because they relied on their own strength and trusted in their own ability to reason. They forgot about their heritage, which made them forget about their inheritance. Two things will keep us from making the same mistakes in our own lives: dependence and vision. "What joy for those whose strength comes from the LORD, who have set their minds on a pilgrimage to Jerusalem." Conversely, if you're in a season when the wind is at your back and all is flourishing, walk wisely, carefully, and stay humbly dependent on the Lord. Remember who all this is for. And if you're feeling dry, barren, and lifeless, don't worry. That's the perfect atmosphere for God's power to awaken and establish you. He's not done with you. He's got more for you to do. Find your strength *in Him*. Through every twist and turn in life, remember that your purpose is powerful. Your pilgrimage, sacred. You're just passing through. Keep the vision of eternity before you, and in every season rely humbly and wholeheartedly upon His strength. Jesus will get you safely home.

LEARN   Read Psalm 84.

FLOURISH   God gives grace *and* glory. *No* good thing will He withhold from those who walk uprightly before Him. Check your course and your heart today.

PRAY

Precious Father,
I'm prone to wander, Lord, I feel it! Bind my heart to Yours. I'm leaning in hard today, relying on Your strength, counting on Your goodness. Awaken eternity within me once again. Amen.

Divine Protection

This I declare about the LORD:
He alone is my refuge, my place of safety;
    he is my God, and I trust him.

Psalm 91:2

*T*here's a story about a godly young man, held captive in a Nazi prison camp. After he read Psalm 91 and asked the Lord, "Men are dying all around me. Will I die here too, Lord?" the Lord whispered back to his heart, "Rely on what you've just read and walk out of here." This brave soul approached the inner gates of the prison with his Bible clutched tightly against his chest. The guards aimed their guns at him and spewed, "*What* do you think you're doing?" He replied, "I'm under the protection of the Most High." The soldiers immediately dropped their guns and opened the gates. The same thing happened at the outer gates: The guards shouted with guns drawn, only to stand down and open the main gates to his freedom. The man found out after the war that he was the only one to get out of that camp alive. He also learned that Hitler insisted that his inner circle refer to him as "Most High." It was God Most High who orchestrated his freedom. And He's done the same for you. No enemy can take you out even a minute sooner than God's appointed plan for your life. Walk free. Walk courageously. You're under the protection of the Most High God.

LEARN Read Psalm 91.

FLOURISH Prayerfully read Psalm 91 every day for a month. Let the idea of His divine protection sink deep into your bones.

PRAY

> *Most High God,*
> *Help me to walk free, to be brave, and to live courageously. You are my shelter and protection. My days are anointed and appointed by You! Amen.*

Strong As an Ox;
Anointed Too

But you have made me as strong as a wild ox.
You have anointed me with the finest oil.

Psalm 92:10

*I*t's good and important to start out your day giving thanks to God. Before one thing happens—good or bad—you have reason to celebrate God. He's worth it, He deserves it, and believe it or not, it's good for you. Gratitude profoundly impacts your health. Grateful people have a more optimistic outlook on life than most; they have fewer aches and pains, and they sleep better than ungrateful people.* *Proclaim* God's goodness in the morning and His faithfulness at night. When you get into the habit of declaring God's goodness over every situation that you face between sunup and sundown, you will find that God's presence in your life carries more weight than your temporary, fleeting circumstances. Another amazing benefit of keeping your perspective tethered to God's consistent faithfulness is that you'll recognize the countless ways He honors you in the face of your enemy. He claims you as His own, equips you to win your battle, and *refuses* to let your enemy triumph over you.

LEARN　　Read Psalm 92.

FLOURISH　　Declare out loud, "You have made me as strong as a wild ox and have anointed me with Your finest oil. I'm strong, blessed, called, and equipped!" It'll shoot adrenaline into your soul.

PRAY

Lord,
*　I declare Your goodness over my life. You've been so faithful, kind, and true. I am strong in You, anointed in You, secure in You. Thank You, Lord. Amen.*

---

*Amy Morin, "7 Scientifically Proven Benefits of Gratitude," *Psychology Today*, April 3, 2015, https://www.psychologytoday.com/us/blog/what-mentally-strong-people-dont-do/201504/7-scientifically-proven-benefits-gratitude.

Never Forget His Benefits

Let all that I am praise the LORD;
    may I never forget the good things he does for me.

Psalm 103:2

*I*t's impossible to fully fathom the staggering, radical nature of our salvation. Our finite minds cannot grasp what Jesus saved us from and what He has promised us. We have been made new, beyond our wildest dreams. We are destined for heaven, where every aspect of our story will be redeemed. His Word is *alive* in us! His power, available to us! So why do some live lives marked by power, insight, and authority, while others profess Christ but seem to live as earthbound as the rest of the lost world? A.W. Tozer once asked a similar question, and after much consideration and study, determined that those who rise up and do great things for God and with God possess what he calls spiritual receptivity. They cultivate a lifestyle of listening to God, and when He speaks, they do something about it. What if we did the same? What if we began to speak with precision, pray with power, and obey with the full assurance that God will do what He promises? What if we thanked God by faith for healing, redemption, renewal, and rescue? What if we asked for the impossible? Outcomes are up to Him. But our faith changes us and pleases Him. May we *never* forget all He's promised us.

LEARN Read Psalm 103.

FLOURISH Up your game. Err on the side of faith. Grab ahold of His promises. Live expectantly. Leave the results to Him.

PRAY

Faithful Father,
    I come to You in faith today. I'm reaching for You and grabbing hold of Your promises. I'm believing You for greater things. Awaken faith in me, Lord! Amen.

Wonderfully Made

Thank you for making me so wonderfully complex!
Your workmanship is marvelous—how well I know it.
Psalm 139:14

*Y*ou were God's beautiful, amazing idea. You were not an accident, a side note, or an afterthought. God put intricate thought into every nuance of your personality so that His precious plan for your life would divinely fit you. He determined your birthday and celebrated when you took your first breath. He sings and rejoices over you. Really, *imagine it*! He wired you with passions, convictions, and gifts to reflect His heart to a world in need. You've got some good work to do, battles to fight, and giants to confront. You have some gifts to steward, moments to enjoy, and wisdom to acquire. You were crafted by God's own hand. You may also have genetic predispositions handed down from your family line that may or may not make life tougher for you than most. But do not allow family sins, weaknesses, or tendencies to take precedence over God's promises! You may have to work harder than most to overcome a familial predisposition, but you can overcome. Determine that you will! The very power that raised Christ from the grave is alive and active in you. There's more right with you than wrong with you. You couldn't be more loved, empowered, or secure if you tried. Scripture says it: You are fearfully, beautifully, and wonderfully made.

LEARN Read Psalm 139.

FLOURISH Celebrate with joy today because of the masterpiece God made in you. Picture His Fatherly smile when He looks at you.

PRAY

Father,
It's hard to comprehend the reality of Your Fatherly affection for me. Make it real to me. I want to live fully alive, knowing I'm profoundly loved, gifted, and called. Amen.

In All Your Ways, Know Him

Trust in the LORD with all your heart,
and do not lean on your own understanding.
In all your ways acknowledge him,
and he will make straight your paths.

Proverbs 3:5–6 ESV

My middle son, Luke, was a strong-willed little one who challenged us on every front. He's now a humble, gentle, submitted-to-God grown-up man, for which I'm grateful. During one of his childhood meltdowns, he lamented, "How will I know when God is speaking and when the devil is just trying to trick me? I seem to get into trouble a lot." I suppressed a smile and wrapped up my sobbing little boy in a hug. "Suppose we took a walk in the woods and at first you held my hand and we explored together, but eventually you let go and ran ahead. How easy would it be for someone else to whisper from the shadows and pretend they're me? In the same way, stick close enough to know God and His ways and you'll recognize His voice." The word *acknowledge* in this passage in Greek is *yada*—to know and experience intimately. To *trust* God is to be bold and secure—to be so confident in your relationship with Him that you trust Him more than you trust yourself. The promise is that when you live intimately with Him, fully reliant on Him, He'll make every crooked way within you and every crooked path in front of you straight. He will literally straighten out the path before you. What a miracle!

LEARN Read Proverbs 3.

FLOURISH Ask God to show you where you're trusting yourself more than Him.

PRAY

Jesus,
   Revive my relationship with You so I can enjoy You more fully, trust You implicitly, and follow You to new heights. Amen.

What God Loves

There are six things the LORD hates—
no, seven things he detests. . . .

Proverbs 6:16

One Sunday morning I noticed one of my mentors standing in line to receive prayer. Her eyes sparkled; her wrinkles revealed her hard-earned wisdom. She was a true matriarch. Someone in front of her took a sudden step back, causing her to do the same. The young woman behind her was so perturbed that she let out a huff and rolled her eyes. I was appalled. I prayed, *Lord, help me never to be so blind.* There are things God absolutely loves. And there are things He hates. He hates haughty eyes that look down on others, for any reason. He loves *humble eyes that reflect His.* He hates a lying tongue that destroys. He loves a *truthful tongue that sets others free.* He hates hands that kill the innocent. He loves *hands that help the vulnerable.* He hates hearts that plan evil schemes. He loves a *heart that plans good things.* He hates feet that race to do evil. He loves *feet that promote justice* and are quick to help those in need. He hates false accusations and a slandering tongue. He loves *those who courageously yet humbly stand up in truth and love.* He hates it when someone sows discord in any family. He loves the *one who humbly promotes unity in Him.*

LEARN Read Proverbs 6.

FLOURISH Ponder what God loves: humble eyes, a truthful tongue, hands that serve, a heart that plans good things, feet quick to obey, an advocate of justice, and one who promotes peace and unity among His brothers.

PRAY

Lord,
Help me love what You love, hate what You hate, do what You'd do, and say what You'd say. Make me more like You. Amen.

Search for Good;
Find Favor

If you search for good, you will find favor;
but if you search for evil, it will find you!
Proverbs 11:27

What you look for, you will find. In life, you'll experience good and bad, gladness and sadness, feast and famine. But in Christ, you can be sure that there's a redemptive aspect to every element of your life. God issues daily invitations and opportunities to be a blessing to a world in need. Look for the good and you'll find something more: *favor that comes from walking in God's power and reflecting His heart.* Those who relish division and drama, whose bent is gossip, whose heart beats for its idols, well, *evil will find them.* Sobering, yes? One day, we'll live forever with the Lord and enjoy opportunities to serve Him without enemy opposition and the hindrances we face in this life. But our search for good today is producing a beautiful grit in us that goes against the tide of culture and flies in the face of the enemy's intent for us. You are an ambassador of heaven. You have access to joy, peace, perspective, and power. You can change the atmosphere wherever you go when you go in the strength and perspective of the Lord. May you be a force to reckon with and may you enjoy favor wherever life finds you.

LEARN Read Proverbs 11.

FLOURISH Rise up today, lean in, and look for the good in your life. Ask God for opportunities to serve Him. Be glad about your status in Him. You're highly favored.

PRAY

Lord,
I often forget that You intend to change the world through me. Open my eyes to see redemptive possibilities all around me! Use me, Lord. I'm available. Amen.

Fill Your Space;
Run Your Race

Thieves are jealous of each other's loot,
but the godly are well rooted and bear their own fruit.

Proverbs 12:12

*T*hieves are jealous of each other's loot. . . . Yet we as God's people also tend to be jealous of another's fruit. We compare and despair. We wonder why God blesses them and not us. We spend too much time feeling disappointed about the success of others. But to allow ourselves to go there is to abandon our garden, go to the fence, and spend our time overanalyzing and wrongly assessing the blessings and impact of another. The truly godly are well rooted in the things of God, which yields fruit in our lives that nourishes others. One of the great hindrances to this process of depth, growth, and fruit is jealousy. It's the gateway sin to every other sin.* Oh, if we could see the heavenly deed with our name on it! We would not only be content to fill our space and run our race, we'd be inspired and encouraged and empowered to do so! Walk away from the fence and get excited about your own story. Ask God to use your current limitations, obstacles, and setbacks to conform you into His image. Ask Him to make you promotable. The depth of your roots will always correspond with the quality of your fruit. Enjoy Jesus. Enjoy the journey. Ask Him to empower you with what He's given you.

LEARN Read Proverbs 12.

FLOURISH Shut down every hint of jealousy. Love your story. Look to Jesus.

PRAY

> *Father,*
> *Find me faithful and grateful in this season! Forgive me for losing perspective when I look to others. Make me promotable. Draw me nearer, Lord. Amen.*

*See James 3:16.

A Reliable Messenger Brings Healing

An unreliable messenger stumbles into trouble,
but a reliable messenger brings healing.
Proverbs 13:17

I marvel that God entrusts the kingdom to such broken people. Yet He puts His Spirit in us and works wonders through us, all while we work out our salvation and gradually discover who we are to Him. I shudder to think back on how often His message of love got lost in translation through me because I was too broken, insecure, and self-focused to rightly relay His heart to others. Yet still, He loved me through it all. Because of His unrelenting love, I'm not who I was; I am someone altogether new. And I'm not who I will be. I'm counting on His goodness to continually transform me. The same goes for you. We *get* to be a work in progress without the condemnation. Let that sink in for a moment. And yet we *must* contend for freedom. Far too many Christians stay stuck because they prefer a known captivity to an unknown freedom. *A reliable messenger brings healing.* When we understand who we are to God and who He is to us, we more reliably communicate His message to a lost and broken world. The freer we become, the more clearly His kingdom is communicated through us.

LEARN Read Proverbs 13.

FLOURISH How is God revealing himself to you this season? Get a vision for who He is making you to be. Picture His kingdom message flowing through you and bringing healing to others.

PRAY

Thank You, Lord, for Your commitment to me. I marvel at Your patience and steadfast love. Transform me into someone I never dreamed I could be. Share Your message of love through me to a world in need. Amen.

The Miracle in the Mess

Without oxen a stable stays clean,
but you need a strong ox for a large harvest.
Proverbs 14:4

I once knew a business owner who was all about appearances. He had the nicest building. The nicest equipment. And he lived the life of the wealthy. Yet his employees were floundering and discouraged, underpaid and overworked. He's since gone out of business. When façade matters more than fruit, we sacrifice our influence and our impact. However, when we're committed to God's people, God's process, and God's purposes, we'll find miraculous life change, community impact, and kingdom movement. But it's often messy. People are broken. Relationships are complicated. Conflict is no fun. And growth takes time. But that's why godly, humble, and visionary leaders are so incredibly important in the kingdom of God. There's a big difference between a flashy appearance and a fruitful life. One is all show and no go, while the other is in the trenches, doing life with others, stewarding gifts, responding to needs, and moving forward in faith. Don't get discouraged by the messes in life. It just means you're alive and on the road to redemption like the rest of us. And it takes a strong person to stay the course, maintain perspective, and keep hope alive. Don't miss the everyday miracles in the messes of life. Jesus did life this way. He understands. And He's in it with you.

LEARN Read Proverbs 14.

FLOURISH Reframe your perspective on the messy parts of your life. Look for God in them. Watch for a miracle.

PRAY

Lord,
I sometimes want to trade the mess for a perfect-looking life, but there's no life in that! Help me to embrace the real and forsake the façade. Help me to see the beauty and the miracle in the mess. Amen.

Make Your Plans, Stay Flexible

We can make our plans,
but the LORD determines our steps.
Proverbs 16:9

I remember when I finally mustered up the courage to write the first words of my first book. Up to that moment, I'd had two agendas at war within me—obedience and procrastination. I sensed the inner invitation from God to trust Him and take the first steps toward publishing. At the same time, the self-preservation monster stirred up my fears, compelling me to stop so I'd never have the chance to fail. One day, my giant of a husband hovered over me and my bowl of popcorn and said, "It's time to get writing. You're out of excuses. God's made it clear. Get going." The next morning, I stared at a blank screen and nothing came to me. Except the still, small whisper that I knew was God. *Your neighbor needs you.* I knocked on her door and she answered with tears in her eyes. "How'd you know?" she asked. After some precious time with her, I headed back to my house, where the Lord reminded me that life with Him always requires flexibility and sensitivity to His Spirit. The words poured out onto the page after that simple act of obedience. Life with God is life, indeed. Ask for some God-given dreams. Make your plans. Stay flexible. Be interruptible. Jesus will lead you on a fruitful faith-adventure of a lifetime.

LEARN Read Proverbs 16.

FLOURISH Are you postponing obedience? Make some plans! Are you flexible? Pay attention to His divine interruptions.

PRAY

Lord,
   I don't want anything to stand in the way of Your highest and best for me. Awaken me to the next plans You have for me. Help me to respond to Your divine interruptions. Amen.

A Time for Everything

For everything there is a season,
a time for every activity under heaven.

Ecclesiastes 3:1

I'm not afraid of death. I'm afraid of dying." My dear brother-in-law held my hand as I sat next to his hospital bed. His skin was yellow, his eyes gaunt, and his smile weak. I didn't have the heart to tell him he *was* dying, and doing so, so very gracefully. Though we believed God still performs miracles today, we sensed this was Donny's time to pass from this life to the next. God decides and determines the seasons. It's ours to discern those seasons. There's a time to fight with everything in you, and a time to let go and let God—a time for pruning and a time for flourishing. There's a time to forge ahead with what little strength you have, and a time to wait on God when it makes no sense at all. There's a time to walk away quietly and allow God to vindicate you, and a time to stand strong in the face of persecution, knowing He'll deliver you. Here's what's true: Obedience to God will always strengthen your soul and sturdy your stance. You don't pick or decide your seasons. You can't force outcomes. And you can't rush through a season that God intends for you to glean from. But as you discern the season, you can embrace it too. Because He has set eternity in your heart. Every season is bursting with eternal possibility.

LEARN Read Ecclesiastes 3.

FLOURISH Prayerfully discern your current season. What do faith and obedience require of you here?

PRAY

Father,
You are good and Your ways are higher than mine. Show me what You're up to in this season. Help me to find You here. Amen.

Strong in Battle

A person standing alone can be attacked and defeated, but two can stand back-to-back and conquer. Three are even better, for a triple-braided cord is not easily broken.

Ecclesiastes 4:12

*W*hy won't you let me in? Who hurt you so deeply that you've built up such a wall?" I stared at the woman in front of me and marveled at her calm demeanor but her audacious question. Yet she was right. I'd been hurt enough that I'd subconsciously decided I didn't need any new friends. Yet I feared God and recognized His influence enough to know that He was behind her insistence that I open up and trust again. That was twenty years ago. And to this day, that woman is one of my closest, most trusted friends. I couldn't know the battles we'd both face in our lives, but God knew. We've journeyed through life's twists and turns; we've stood back-to-back and conquered our enemy. We've both suffered some pretty horrible storms, but the storms have passed, and our bond is stronger than ever. And our history with God is stronger still. Brady Boyd once said on my radio show, "It takes a long time to make an old friend." Especially a friend who loves and fears God. Those are the best kind. It's been said that the wolves attack the sheep that have wandered from the fold. We wander sometimes because of sin, other times because of pain. Either way, the devil hopes to find us alone. Don't let that happen.

LEARN Read Ecclesiastes 4:7–12.

FLOURISH Put some time into your most trusted relationships this week. Don't take them for granted.

PRAY

Lord,
You've wired me for togetherness. Help me to nurture deep, godly, in-the-trenches kinds of friendships. Be the center of them all. Amen.

Laboring from Envy

Then I observed that most people are motivated to success because they envy their neighbors. But this, too, is meaningless—like chasing the wind.

Ecclesiastes 4:4

Scripture says that a lazy person is as bad as someone who destroys things. Their apathy not only hinders flourishing, it destroys it. Imagine! Similarly, workaholism that springs out of a drive to outdo, surpass, or compete is also destructive. From the outside, a person may appear a great success. They may have a nicer home and a better reputation than the lazy man, but they'll destroy a few things along the way too. They'll ruin their relationships with those closest to them. They'll destroy their own faith perspective because they're not inspired by faith; they're driven by lust. They'll kill their own capacity to enjoy life because striving born out of envy is not a sustainable way to live. If God has gifted you, embrace those gifts. But enjoy them too. Consider everything you do as an offering back to God. Ask Him to multiply every offering. Believe Him for great things. Know that His will for you in one area of life won't contradict His will for you in another. God is all about harmony, health, wholeness, and flourishing. Deal with even the smallest hint of envy so it won't destroy you or your offering.

LEARN Read Ecclesiastes 4:4–6.

FLOURISH Check your motivation for doing what you do. If behind your motivation you find striving for the wrong reasons, reset your course.

PRAY

Jesus,
You paid it all! I have nothing to prove and all of eternity to live for. Help me to steward my gifts with a heart of faith and an assurance of who I already am in You. Help me to enjoy my life. Amen.

Better a Funeral
Than a Party

Better to spend your time at funerals than at parties.
After all, everyone dies—
so the living should take this to heart.

Ecclesiastes 7:2

*W*ho prefers a funeral over a party? Almost no one. Still, Scripture says it's *better* to go to a funeral than a party. Why do you suppose that is? Parties are fun. They make us forget our troubles, if only for a day, so we can enjoy our special occasion. God *calls* us to celebrate, feast, and remember His goodness to us. Celebration is a gift from God. It's good for the heart and healing for the soul. So what could possibly be *better* about a funeral? It's where all of life comes into clear view and we remember what's truly important. It's the place where life is reset for us. We're forced to reckon with all of our running, all of our striving, all of our performing. Who's it for? What's it accomplishing? Who's it helping? Funerals help us see life through an eternal lens. We tend to take our own life for granted until someone loses theirs. Loss is heartbreaking, especially when that person has squandered their life. But their funeral might be the very thing that wakes you up to the significance of your own life. You don't know how many days you have left on this earth. But you have today. Don't wait for someone else's funeral to make your life count.

LEARN Read Ecclesiastes 7:1–8.

FLOURISH Make life count today. Taste your food. Love well. Notice and be kind to a stranger. Give a gift. Thank Jesus for everything good in your life.

PRAY

Jesus,
You've given me this life and I want it to count! Awaken my heart to every eternal possibility before me. Amen.

It's Better to Fear God

Even though a person sins a hundred times and still lives a long time, I know that those who fear God will be better off.

Ecclesiastes 8:12

*W*hy do some people seem to get away with so much before God intervenes? There's a day of disaster coming for the wicked person who refuses to repent. Scripture is clear. But what about the *believer* who continuously tries to control and manipulate others? Or who harbors bitterness and refuses to forgive? Or who repeatedly uses others for his own gain? Do you ever wonder why God waits so long to intervene, to humble or to discipline His own? Especially when you feel like you can't get away with a thing. You feel the inner wince of conviction and you know you're out of line the moment you have a rogue thought or an impatient posture. So how does that work? *It's all about the fear of the Lord.* To fear God is to hold Him in high regard, with honor and reverence. You can love God from a distance without fearing Him. But you cannot truly walk intimately with God without reverently honoring Him at the same time. If you're quick to feel conviction over the slightest departures, it's because His light shines brightly in your heart. If you wonder why He's not disciplining another, know this: He will, at exactly the right time.

LEARN ▸ Read Ecclesiastes 8:9–13.

FLOURISH ▸ Entrust the impossible people in your life to God. He sees everything. He'll deal with everything. *You* fear God.

PRAY ▸

> *Lord,*
> *Forgive me for questioning Your timing and Your dealings with others. I know You don't miss a thing. I entrust _____ to You. Help me to honor You in all that I do. Amen.*

I Recommend Having Fun

So I recommend having fun, because there is nothing better for people in this world than to eat, drink, and enjoy life. That way they will experience some happiness along with all the hard work God gives them under the sun.

Ecclesiastes 8:15

*K*ing Solomon surveyed life and outcomes and came to a conclusion: Life isn't fair. It's downright hard sometimes. So what's a person to do? Have fun. Eat, drink, and enjoy life. Make room for happiness amidst the hardships of life. Don't forget to laugh—really belly-laugh. Slow down long enough to taste your food—really taste your food. Watch a good movie and enjoy a big bowl of popcorn. Stop at a lemonade stand and bless the child for her noble business venture. Build some margin into your schedule. Give yourself room to breathe. Put something on your calendar that you're excited about. Plan activities that nourish your soul and breathe life back into you. Every year, millions of earned vacation hours go to waste because employees never take their hard-earned time off. Where's the fun in that? Shouldn't joy and gladness be two of the most defining factors in our lives? Dallas Willard once gave this advice to John Ortberg: "You must arrange your day so that you are experiencing deep contentment, joy, and confidence in your everyday life with God."* Amen.

LEARN   Read Ecclesiastes 8:14–16.

FLOURISH   Plan something really fun this month. And next month too.

PRAY

Lord,
I need a fun mentor! Help me to engage with You in this way! You've provided countless ways for me to add enjoyment to my life. Help me arrange my days so they reflect Your joyful heart toward me. Amen.

---

*John Ortberg, *Soul Keeping* (Grand Rapids, MI: Zondervan, 2013), 85.

Dark, Yet Lovely

I am dark but beautiful.
Song of Songs 1:5

King Solomon's heart awakened when he saw the Shulamite woman. He pursued her and won her affection. She was both excited about new love and self-conscious about her imperfections. Her brothers forced her to work the vineyards under the hot sun, which darkened her skin. (Pale, delicate skin was the standard for beauty back then.) Do you see the parallel to our lives? The King loves us. Pursues us. Finds us in our hardship. Invites us out of the fields of striving and effort and into His kingdom of grace. As we move toward Him and align with His kingdom ways, we see all of the ways we fall short; how the hardships of life have marred us. The enemy spews from the shadows, "You are darkened with sin! I know where you've been!" How wonderful to become so secure in the Father's love that we can say, "I may be dark, but I am lovely." God wants to bring such inner healing to your soul that you can look at your painful history with a grounded sense of grace. You're enough for God. He's not surprised by or disappointed in you. He sees you through and through and loves you more than you love yourself. Imagine your healed self, whispering back to Him, "I *am* lovely." Let the healing begin.

LEARN Read Song of Songs 1.

FLOURISH Ask God to show you if there are any remnants of shame still lingering in your story. Ask Him to heal you.

PRAY

Lord,
I want to know that kind of assurance and holy confidence. In every way life has marred me, You want to minister to me. Bring life, healing, and wholeness to the deepest places within me. Amen.

The Season of Singing Birds

> The flowers are springing up,
> the season of singing birds has come,
> and the cooing of turtledoves fills the air.
>
> Song of Songs 2:12

*A*t the opening of this chapter, the Shulamite woman lapses back into an old mindset. She sees herself as a common, ordinary flower. But her lover tilts her chin upward that she might see herself once again through his eyes. She soon realizes that a new season truly is upon her. And that love, indeed, has found her. The winter is past, the rains are over, and flowers are now in bloom. The season of singing birds has finally come. This exchange so reflects our journey toward understanding what Jesus sees when He looks upon us. The thought of being known deeply enough to be truly loved is both terrifying and exhilarating. One moment we find ourselves running toward our Savior, but the next we're tempted to run away. One moment we're drawn to His loving voice as He sings over us, but the next we refute His words with our own earthbound assessments. But to move into the next place of maturity, we must also move with Jesus to a new place of intimacy, where we trust His perspective over our own. Wholeness comes when we see ourselves and the world through His eyes. *To know this love is to be filled with the fullness of God.**

LEARN ▶ Read Song of Songs 2:1–13.

FLOURISH ▶ Ask Jesus to give you a fresh revelation of how He sees you. And dare to listen for His response.

PRAY ▶

Jesus,
Open my eyes to see what You see in a way that heals and changes me.
Help me to trust You more than I trust myself. Amen.

*See Ephesians 3:19.

Let Me See Your Face

My dove is hiding behind the rocks,
>   behind an outcrop on the cliff.
Let me see your face; let me hear your voice.
For your voice is pleasant, and your face is lovely.

Song of Songs 2:14

*Y*ou don't have the voice for radio." After I dared to share a private dream with her, a woman from my church just stopped me in my tracks with these words. She had a scowl on her face and zero compassion in her eyes. Before I had the chance to inhale, her words landed like a punch to the gut. Later that day I heard God's whisper, *"Don't you dare hide. Let me see your face. Your voice is sweet, and you are lovely."* I faintly remembered reading that in Scripture, and my heart fluttered when I found it. I've worked in radio now for almost fifteen years, and one thing listeners most often say to me is, "I love your voice. It's so soothing. It puts my heart as ease." The church lady was wrong. If I'd listened to her and turned away from the dream that God put in my heart, I would have missed out on an opportunity to encourage hundreds of thousands of people over the years. Maybe someone has spoken words over you that are untrue. Don't you dare hide. Listen for Jesus instead. Hear your Shepherd as He calls to you, *"Let me see your face. Your voice is sweet. And you are lovely."*

LEARN ▶ Read Song of Songs 2:14.

FLOURISH ▶ Dismantle any destructive words others have spoken to you.

PRAY ▶

Lord,
I'm done hiding! I don't want man's voice to ring truer than Yours! I want Your dreams in my heart. Give me courage to follow You anywhere. Amen.

Catch the Foxes

Catch all the foxes,
   those little foxes,
before they ruin the vineyard of love,
   for the grapevines are blossoming!
Song of Songs 2:15

*W*hen God is doing a new thing, the devil hides in the shadows with a plan. He aims to demolish everything God creates. Thankfully, Jesus came to *destroy* the works of the devil.* One of the most important Scripture passages for the believer comes from Proverbs 4:23: "Guard your heart above all else, for it determines the course of your life." The word *guard* in this passage speaks of diligence, protection, and continual attention. How often are we *this* attentive to the condition of our hearts? Especially in a season of flourishing, we're tempted to let our guard down. If the enemy can't dismantle our destiny in big, traumatic ways, then he'll send in the little foxes—harassment, distraction, irritation, and temptation, just to name a few. We'll make little concessions here and there and think nothing of it. But then one day, a crisis hits, and we realize it could have been prevented had we paid closer attention to our hearts and to the work of God in our lives. Study where God is working in your life. Are there any foxes nipping at the vine? Is the enemy picking away at your resolve? Don't put up with it. Guard your heart. Guard your yard. Catch the foxes. And let love grow.

LEARN   Read Song of Songs 2:15–17.

FLOURISH   Refuse to underestimate the little foxes. Deal with them immediately.

PRAY

Father,
   Heighten my discernment and my awareness of the state of my life. Teach me how to walk wisely and powerfully before You. Amen.

*See 1 John 3:8.

Sober Reflection

"Come now, let's settle this,"
    says the LORD.
"Though your sins are like scarlet,
    I will make them as white as snow."
                                    Isaiah 1:18

From an earthly point of view, the nation of Judah appeared to be prosperous. But from heaven's point of view, the people of God were on the brink of destruction. Their sins? Perverting justice, oppressing the poor, turning from God to idols, and looking for military aid from pagan nations rather than help from God.* They'd so lost their way that God actually *detested* their religious practices! He doesn't want empty worship, meaningless sacrifices, or token gifts. He doesn't need anything from us. He longs for our hearts. Imagine God's heartbreak. His own people had turned their backs on Him. Dr. Warren Wiersbe writes, "Before passing judgment on worshippers in a bygone era, we should confess the sins of the worshipping church today. . . . The average church allocates about 5 percent of its budget for reaching others with the gospel, but 30 percent for buildings and maintenance. At a time when the poor and the aged are pleading for help, churches in America are spending approximately 3 billion dollars a year on new construction."† We'd be unwise to consider Isaiah's call an outdated one. God's invitation to return and repent stands just as true today. He'll wash away *every* sin.

LEARN Read Isaiah 1.

FLOURISH If you've wandered in any way, return to Him. And if not, pray for those who have. Pray for revival.

PRAY

Father in heaven,
    Purify my heart! Show me what You see! Awaken my nation for You!
Amen.

*Life Application Study Bible, 1418.
†Dr. Warren Wiersbe, The Wiersbe Commentary (Colorado Springs: David C. Cook, 2007), 1157.

Don't Fear What They Fear

Make the LORD of Heaven's Armies holy in your life.
    He is the one you should fear.
He is the one who should make you tremble.
    He will keep you safe.

Isaiah 8:13–14

*F*ear of invasion was a continual threat for the people of Judah.* They constantly braced for impact. Much like today. Terrorist attacks, anarchy, and godlessness seem to be the norm on the news today. And yet our souls aren't wired to live in a perpetual state of alert. When we look to ourselves and to the endless streams of news reports for perspective, we will lose heart and lose faith. Proverbs 3:7–8 says this: "Don't be impressed with your own wisdom. Instead, fear the LORD and turn away from evil. Then you will have healing for your body and strength for your bones." Fearing the wrong things puts incredible stress on our health and on our faith perspective. Though evil threats are real, God tells us to *tremble before Him*. He's the One we should fear; He's the One who'll keep us safe. Though it seems like an oxymoron to fear the One who will keep you safe, keep this in mind: When you tremble before Him, you'll tremble at nothing else. How do you live in this fear-driven world with a grounded sense of faith? Make Him holy in your life.

LEARN   Read Isaiah 8:11–22.

FLOURISH   Cut back on your social media and news consumption and increase your intake of worship, the Word, and times of reflection.

PRAY

Lord,
    How I think about things impacts me and those around me. Help me to steward my perspective in a way that rightly reflects Your power to intervene in this hour. Amen.

*Life Application Study Bible, 1436.

A Son, Given to Us

For a child is born to us,
a son is given to us.
Isaiah 9:6

A *Son* was *given* to *us*. We sing it, we say it, we pray it. But stop for a moment and consider God's gift. He surrendered His perfect, beautiful, joyful, grateful, obedient, sinless Son for an imperfect, disgruntled, ungrateful, disobedient, sinful people. Why? Because He loves us like He loves His own Son. He envisioned an eternity with us; countless hearts transformed, stories rewritten, lives reclaimed. Though the way would be costly, beyond our comprehension, the result would be breathtaking. Lost people found. Broken people restored. Sick people healed. Sinful people redeemed. Jesus—with a heart full of compassion, abounding in love, set out on a mission—came to earth that His light might shine in our hearts and light up the darkness around us. Jesus willingly offered to come to us, to die for us. All for the sake of love. The angels, no doubt, held their breath as He laid aside His robe and crown and entered our universe through the womb of a poor teenage girl. Much suffering awaited Him, and He knew it. Yet He came. God gave Him to us. *Unto us a Son was given.* And He carried the weight of the world on His shoulders. Unfathomable, astonishing grace. Thank You, Lord.

LEARN   Read Isaiah 9:2–7.

FLOURISH   Spend time today pondering God's gift of His Son. Recapture the awe and wonder of it all. Put on your favorite worship song and go all in!

PRAY

Wonderful Counselor, Mighty God, Everlasting Father, Prince of Peace, How is it that You love me so? I bow low and praise You with my whole heart. May my whole life be an offering back to You. Amen.

Perfect Peace

You will keep in perfect peace
all who trust in you,
all whose thoughts are fixed on you!

Isaiah 26:3

hat's *perfect* peace? The phrase in this passage translates this way: *Shalom.* When our thoughts are fixed on the Lord, He touches our hearts with His peace, tranquility, rest, safety, friendship, prosperity, and well-being. Wow. He is the essence of all these things, and He imparts himself to us as we draw closer still. We have everything we could ever possibly need, and then some, in Him. Picture ascending a mountain until you are up in the clouds. Imagine the startling white clouds are saturated with healing elements that settle your nerves, restore your soul, put your heart at ease, and open your eyes to the spiritual reality around you. You suddenly see yourself as the clean vessel of God that you are. You realize as you ponder the miracle of your remaking that absolutely nothing is too difficult for Him. You see the problems of this earth as fleeting while you grasp more firmly that the promises of heaven are sturdier than the mountain under your feet. God's provision is greater still. Scripture says that all of the riches of the heavenly realm belong to you.* We don't spend enough time pondering who God is and what He is willing to impart to us. His love changes everything.

LEARN Read Isaiah 26:1–19.

FLOURISH Decide today to upgrade your relationship with God. Spend more time with Him. Think about His greatness. Rely on His goodness.

PRAY

Mighty God of heaven,
I raise my hands and worship You. I lay hold of all You've promised me. I set my gaze on You. May Your power change my life. Amen.

*See Ephesians 1:3.

New Strength, New Heights

But those who trust in the LORD will find new strength.
They will soar high on wings like eagles.

Isaiah 40:31

My health relapse lasted about three years. During that time, I instinctively rehearsed my symptoms—how I was *feeling*. But when you think too long about how you're feeling, you'll feel more of the same, and on a deeper level. I longed for God's intervention. I prayed for it too. But in my weaker moments, I followed my feelings right into the ditch. One day as I stood at the base of our stairs, the Lord whispered to me, "Take those stairs! You're not as weak as you feel! In Me, you're stronger than you know." I sprinted up those stairs with so much strength, it surprised me! But I was still sick and tired. He whispered, "Let the weak say I am strong." The Lord challenged me that day to engage my faith at all times with everything in me. Waiting on God with hopeful expectancy is not meant to be a hit-and-miss proposition. It's a way of life. We're meant to go about our days with a deep conviction that God is who He says He is, and with a deep expectancy that any day now, He *will* break through. You want to rise up with new strength and soar to new heights? Actively wait on, hope in, and believe that the Lord is coming *for you*.

LEARN   Read Isaiah 40:21–31.

FLOURISH   Consider the distinction between passive waiting and active waiting. How might God want you to lean in and trust Him more?

PRAY

Father,
You give strength to the weak and power to the powerless. My soul actively waits on You. I know You'll come for me! Thank You, Lord. Amen.

A Pathway Through the Wilderness

For I am about to do something new.
 See, I have already begun! Do you not see it?
I will make a pathway through the wilderness.
 I will create rivers in the dry wasteland.

Isaiah 43:19

When the way is long and the battle rages on, we tend to identify more with our circumstances than we do with our heir status. But Scripture says we're pilgrims, traveling to a most holy city. We're just passing through. No one can snatch us out of His hand. No enemy scheme can keep us from His plan. We are firm and secure in His love and established by His grace. However, we *will* at times find ourselves in painful seasons, trying circumstances, and situations where there's no easy way out. We may stop dreaming, forget to look for the *new*. We may feel stuck and thus despair over the sameness of it all. Here's where we must make the distinction between surrendering to our circumstances and surrendering to God in our circumstances. One camps in the valley with no hope for change. The other declares, "This place does not define me. God will make a way where there is no way. I'm passing through the valley; I don't live here. I'm a child of God. And He's masterful at bringing beauty out of ashes, rivers in the wasteland, and solutions where I can't see one." He's *already begun* to do something new for you. Soon you will see it.

LEARN ▶ Read Isaiah 43:1–19.

FLOURISH ▶ Look for the new thing God is up to in your life. Watch for the subtle shifts in your circumstances. God is up to something *good*.

PRAY ▶

Lord,
 Open my eyes to see what You're up to in and all around me! Amen.

Jesus Paid It All

But he was pierced for our rebellion,
    crushed for our sins.
He was beaten so we could be whole.
    He was whipped so we could be healed.

Isaiah 53:5

I cannot read Isaiah 53 without tearing and choking up. I think about our suffering Savior, who took on the sin and rebellion of the world. And the world assumed His suffering was *His* fault. Too much for anyone to bear. But Jesus did. He bore the weight of the world along with our wrong assessments and flippant judgments. *He purchased our freedom* from our own rebellion, from our countless self-serving ways, from the wounds inflicted on us by others, and from everything that ails us in our bodies. As He hung on that cross, His blood trickled down to the ground and into the lowest nooks and crannies of the earth. Then the earth shook. The veil tore in two—from the top down. The sky darkened. And a guilt-ridden soldier realized this criminal was actually an innocent man. Our Savior *defeated* sin and death for us! No other religion honors a King who sacrificed for His people. If you are in Christ, *Christ is in you*. His blood flows through your veins. The power that raised Him from the grave is alive and accessible to you. So why do we live such earthbound lives? Maybe because we're still trying to earn our way. Jesus paid it all. May you live from that reality.

LEARN Read Isaiah 53.

FLOURISH Dare to believe that Christ's victory over sin, sickness, and the grave means more than you once thought. Ask God for revelation.

PRAY

Father,
    Open my eyes to what Jesus won for me! Heal me from the inside out.
May resurrection power mark my life in every way. Amen.

Beauty for Ashes

To all who mourn in Israel
>   he will give a crown of beauty for ashes,
a joyous blessing instead of mourning,
>   festive praise instead of despair.
In their righteousness, they will be like great oaks
>   that the LORD has planted for his own glory.

Isaiah 61:3

I watched my younger sister walk through the valley of the shadow of death when her husband was diagnosed with pancreatic cancer. He died ten months after his diagnosis. We sat at my kitchen counter and cried together. We laughed too as we remembered moments when Donny was alive. I asked her, "How are you getting through this?" She said, "I'm sure everyone grieves differently, but for me, here's what I've done: 1) I get out of bed every single day; 2) I've determined that God's goodness *will not* be up for grabs; 3) I tell myself, *You will get through this*; and 4) I tell myself, *You are stronger than you know*." I'm watching God restore her day by day. If you've walked through loss, hardship, or overwhelming adversity, I pray you've given yourself time to grieve and sort through your losses. For those who mourn, God promises to bring honor and beauty where you've known loss and heartbreak. He will strengthen you once again. Your life may look different than you imagined, but you'll be stronger than you ever dreamed. Jesus came to proclaim good news to those who've lived under the shadow of perpetual bad news. Your Redeemer has come.

LEARN Read Isaiah 61.

FLOURISH Where are the ashes in your life? Imagine beauty, honor, and praise emerging from that very place.

PRAY

Father,
>   *Thank You for promising redemption in my story. Awaken fresh hope within me once again. Amen.*

The Heavens Gasp

"The heavens are shocked at such a thing
and shrink back in horror and dismay,"
says the Lord.

Jeremiah 2:12

I followed the Bible study host to the kitchen for more refreshments. She leaned in and whispered, "I keep having affairs and I can't seem to stop." My jaw dropped. I looked around to see if anyone had heard her. I was at a loss for words. For a second, I thought I'd heard her wrong. Their little home was cozy. They had a young daughter. Christian plaques on the wall. We were there for Bible study. I learned later that her husband knew of the affairs and was fighting for his marriage. Who would turn away from a bubbling brook to drink water out of a mud hole? Yet daily, the heavens gasp because our lips are covered with dirt. Every time we turn to our idols to prop us up, we drink muddy water. Every time we shift our dependence onto our possessions, our status, or our associations, we're lapping up grimy water. God wants us to enjoy life, to flourish in the good gifts He entrusts to us. Yet time and time again, we turn His gifts into idols. I don't want the heavens to gasp; I want them to *rejoice* over my faith. May streams of living water flow through you because of Christ's transformative power within you.

LEARN Read Jeremiah 2:1–13.

FLOURISH Ask the Lord to show you your idols. Remember His commitment to you and reaffirm your commitment to Him.

PRAY

Father,
Forgive me for the countless ways I look to Your gifts to give me life. You are the Source of life, and all I'll ever need is in You. I thirst for more of You! Amen.

Take the Ancient Path

This is what the LORD says:
"Stop at the crossroads and look around.
　Ask for the old, godly way, and walk in it.
Travel its path, and you will find rest for your souls.
　But you reply, 'No, that's not the road we want!'"

Jeremiah 6:16

The prophet Jeremiah appealed to the people to come back to God, to do His will, His way. Meanwhile, the other so-called prophets promised a false peace without addressing any of the selfish, sinful tendencies of the people. Following Jesus isn't about rigid religion or pious self-denial; it's about understanding and believing God when He says that sin, rebellion, and self-sufficiency are devastating to the soul and in direct conflict to His kingdom ways. Imagine our holy God appealing to these rebellious souls, asking them to return to Him so He could bring rest to the souls and restoration to their lives. But they would have none of it. Every day we face a similar crossroad. Will we go our own way? Lean on our own understanding? Choose an earthbound perspective instead of an eternal one? God's ways will ultimately always bring life, rest, healing, and wholeness. The saints before us searched out and found the ancient path. Now it's our turn. Maybe you're at a crossroads today. Stop and look around. Discern God's way and walk in it. You'll be glad you did.

LEARN Read Jeremiah 6:1–21.

FLOURISH The ancient path of faith is not well traveled by the masses—only by those with a keen eye of faith. May you have the discernment and humility to walk in it.

PRAY

Father,
　Help me to discern Your highest and best will for me. Show me the ancient path that You've placed before me. Lead me onward. Amen.

Boast in *This*

"But those who wish to boast
should boast in this alone:
that they truly know me and understand that I am the LORD
who demonstrates unfailing love...."

Jeremiah 9:24

*A*s a young mom and new Christian, I understood that I was saved, but I didn't grasp that I was loved. It wasn't until all of my self-striving props were pulled out from under me and I found myself on a sickbed, in need of help, unable to return the countless favors I'd received, that I reckoned with the idea of God's unfathomable grace. I knew that ours was the one true God, that He sent His Son to save sinners. I couldn't fathom, though, how profoundly He *loved* me until He met me in my mess. I found that my greatest treasure was the intimate, personal, active love of God. Suddenly I saw all of my striving and feeble attempts at self-worth for what they were—dirty rags.* If you're in a season where the props have been pulled away, don't panic; see the gift of grace in it all. Here's your opportunity to know and experience God's love like you've never known before. His love is an endless ocean, and we've only dipped our toes in the water. As you experience your Father's love, you'll find that nothing else satisfies, nothing else is worth bragging about. If you're known for anything, be known for knowing Him.

LEARN Read Jeremiah 9.

FLOURISH If you currently are going without something you long for, see this as an opportunity to tap in to a deeper revelation of God's great love for you.

PRAY

God,
I've only touched the surface of a love that reaches higher than the heavens. Grant me a fresh revelation of Your love! Amen.

*See Isaiah 64:6.

You Will Speak for Me

"If you return to me, I will restore you
 so you can continue to serve me.
If you speak good words rather than worthless ones,
 you will be my spokesman.
You must influence them;
 do not let them influence you!"

Jeremiah 15:19

*H*ave you noticed that people who deeply fear God don't seem to fear man? They walk in power, talk in power, and pray with power. They're the true influencers in every generation. I remember reading about Catherine Booth. She co-founded the Salvation Army with her husband, William. She was a small, somewhat frail woman who battled health issues off and on. And yet she went boldly before the British Parliament and confronted those men for lowering the age of prostitution to thirteen. She challenged the men who had daughters to consider the implications of their decision. Another translation of the verse above reads, "*If you extract the precious from the worthless, you will be my spokesman.*" We are surrounded by decadent ways, irreverent attitudes, and reasons to react in fear. And yet, if we can stay connected to God's power and perspective, we will be able to extract the precious from the worthless, we will see what God sees, and we will be able to speak with precision and power. Oh, the world needs more lionhearted men and women of God! Extract the precious from the worthless and be God's spokesman.

LEARN Read Jeremiah 15:10–21.

FLOURISH Ask God if there's something precious you can extract from your battles; some treasure you've not mined yet.

PRAY

Lord,
 I want to be bold and brave for You. Refine me, heal me, prepare me, and use me! Help me be courageous for You. Use me, Lord. Amen.

When You've Been Scattered

"But I will gather together the remnant of my flock from the countries where I have driven them. I will bring them back to their own sheepfold, and they will be fruitful and increase in number."

Jeremiah 23:3

The priests and the prophets—who claimed to speak for God—were supposed to care for, lead, and protect the Israelites. But they did the opposite. They misused their position for their own gain, misled the people by their own poor example, and allowed good people to be driven off their land because of their sinful and poor leadership. God saw every bit of it, and finally He'd had enough. These things still happen today. Jeremiah prophesied that God would deal with ungodly leaders, and that those who'd been scattered would once again be gathered, drawn back to the land they lost. God promised to appoint faithful, godly shepherds to watch over them. He promised too that they'd be more fruitful and established than before. Maybe you've been scattered for the same reason. Know that God sees it all. And He will redeem it all. He may or may not bring you back to the land you lost, but one thing He *will* do: restore what the enemy has stolen from you. He will make you more fruitful than before, more established than you've ever been. God knows the whole story and He's in the process of redeeming it.

LEARN Read Jeremiah 23:1–8.

FLOURISH Believe God cares about your heart and that He is—right now—working to redeem your story.

PRAY

Good Shepherd,
Thank You for being my advocate. You are able to redeem and restore and to open new doors. Help me get excited about new fruit, new strength, and the new day ahead of me. Amen.

A Future and a Hope

"For I know the plans I have for you," says the LORD. "They are plans for good and not for disaster, to give you a future and a hope."

Jeremiah 29:11

*W*e often picture this beautiful passage on a greeting card or inspirational wall art. But Jeremiah prophesied this word to a people in *captivity*. He told them to plant gardens, have babies, and build homes. They were captives of Babylon, but God would in due time rescue them and restore them to their land. He said to them, "*Multiply! Do not dwindle away!*" Our tendency during troubled times is to shrink back, and when we're afraid, we react. When hardships press in, we tend to hunker down. Self-preservation instinctively kicks in. But faith plans for the future in the face of fear. Faith rises above the current circumstances and envisions a new place of promise, a new place to thrive, and a new strength in the Lord. One thing God asked of the Israelites amidst their captivity was to return to Him in all of their ways; to seek Him wholeheartedly. And He promised to listen to their prayers. If your circumstances have pressed you and you've hunkered down or shrunk back, rise up today. Dream today. God has purposes and plans for you. Don't react or pull back. Run to Jesus with everything in you and get a vision for where He's taking you.

LEARN Read Jeremiah 29:1–14.

FLOURISH Take inventory of your life. If you're dwindling instead of multiplying, rise up and run to Jesus. Plan now for a future harvest.

PRAY

Father,
How quickly I forget to trust You! I engage my faith once again. I'll obey today, seek You today, and plant seeds today. Your ways are always good. Amen.

God-Revealed Secrets

"Call to me and I will answer you and tell you great and unsearchable things you do not know."

Jeremiah 33:3 NIV

*T*hings are rarely as they appear. And we don't know what we don't know. We see from an earthbound perspective, and what we do perceive, we view as if looking through a dark glass.* Our perspective is skewed by our own experiences, painful memories, cultural tendencies, biases, and strong opinions. Thankfully, if we've walked with the Lord awhile and have spent time in His Word, we've experienced the wonder of gaining otherworldly wisdom that flies in the face of how things appear. What a privilege to be acquainted with the Most High God! He actually *confides* in those who fear Him.† He invites us to *call on Him* so He can tell us unsearchable things we do not know. The word *call* in this passage is *qara*, which means to shout out, to proclaim, to cry out to get someone's attention. It can also mean to *name* something. What if you cried out to God with passion and purpose? And what if you *named* Him for who He is and who you need Him to be? Cry out to God as your Healer, Defender, Deliverer, and Advocate. Then wait expectantly, for He will surely grant you unsearchable wisdom and the revelation you need.

LEARN ▶ Read Jeremiah 33:1–16.

FLOURISH ▶ If you've settled for an earthbound perspective in some area of your life, rise up, dear one, and call on God. He'll bring revelation to your soul.

PRAY

Holy God,
I cry out to You as my Healer, Defender, and Deliverer! Grant me unsearchable wisdom and revelation. Show me what You want me to know and see. I wait for You. Amen.

---

*See 1 Corinthians 13:12.
†See Psalm 25:14.

Oh, the Mercies of God!

The faithful love of the LORD never ends!
His mercies never cease.
Great is his faithfulness;
his mercies begin afresh each morning.
Lamentations 3:22–23

Our sin would consume us if not for the mercies of God. Our enemy would devour us if not for the mercies of God. Our troubles would swallow us whole if not for the mercies of God. Jeremiah looked at a nation and people in ruins—a consequence of their blatant sin and disregard for God. He was tempted to be overrun by the destruction before him. But then he *called to mind* the mercies of God. He *dared to remember* the inexhaustible love of God. He *thought about* God's unexplainable compassion. And do you know what rose up within him? *Hope.* Because God's heart beats so compassionately for us, our trials will not have the last say in our lives. Though the enemy levels his attacks against us, he will not finish us off. Though God disciplines us when we need it, and we sometimes endure consequences for our own destructive choices, God doesn't leave us there. His mercy draws us out, draws us near, and makes us new again. Oh, the mercies of God! If you're in a trial, under discipline, or feeling undone by the rubble around you, call to mind the mercies of God. His mercies are in motion even now.

LEARN ▶ Read Lamentations 3:17–33.

FLOURISH ▶ Call to mind the endless mercies and compassion of God toward you. Be as kind to yourself as He is to you.

PRAY

Precious Father,
Thank You for Your mercy and grace, compassion and kindness. Where would I be without them? I will not be consumed by my troubles because I'm already consumed by Your love. Amen.

He's Made You Equal to the Task

"But look, I have made you as obstinate and hard-hearted as they are. I have made your forehead as hard as the hardest rock! So don't be afraid of them or fear their angry looks, even though they are rebels."

Ezekiel 3:8–9

God called Ezekiel the prophet to confront a stubborn, rebellious people given to idolatry and apathy regarding the things of God. Imagine being called to an assignment that you knew would fail. God told Ezekiel to warn His people, but He also informed him that the people wouldn't listen. So why the assignment? Because every act of God changes the story on earth. Changes us. When we're tied up with the fear of man, we will look to others' responses for our cues. But when we look to the Lord and remember how He has conditioned us in our past battles, we'll stand firm in confidence that He is strong in us. If you're facing an impossible assignment with impossible people, dare to consider God's faithfulness in your present and how He's prepared you in the past. You're stronger than you know. And when you face opposition and seem to gain no ground, trust that something's changing in you and in the greater story. Some of these things we won't see until the other side. But ours is to trust and obey. Outcomes are in His hands. And you are equal to the God-given task before you.

LEARN Read Ezekiel 3:1–9.

FLOURISH What battles have changed and strengthened you? Let your mind linger on these triumphs awhile. Rise up with fresh confidence today.

PRAY

Jesus,
Thank You for Your mighty work in me. You've made me equal to the task before me. I will trust You. Amen.

Listen for Yourself First

Then he added, "Son of man, let all my words sink deep into your own heart first. Listen to them carefully for yourself."

Ezekiel 3:10

How often do we listen to sermons, read books, and take notes *for everybody else*? We hear a good point and we want to remember it for a friend. Or we hear a word of correction and wish so-and-so could hear it. But when we listen for others and not for ourselves, we skim the surface of what God is saying, and we miss the potency of God's living, breathing word *to us*. It's easy to view God as a content machine from whom we get tidbits of wisdom and meme-able phrases. He is the living God who spoke the world into existence. He gave us His living, active Word to teach us and train us so we could truly *know Him*. We need God's consistent voice in our lives like we need oxygen. And He does indeed want to speak through us, but He'll do so only to the extent that we allow Him to speak first *to us*. Some words will be just for us, not for public consumption. Others, God wants to season with time before we share them. And still others, well, they must be shouted from the rooftops. How do we discern the difference? The more secure we are in Him, the easier it'll be to know when to hold our words and when to share them.

LEARN   Read Ezekiel 3:10–11.

FLOURISH   Develop the habit of listening first for yourself. Trust the Holy Spirit to prompt you to share what He wants when He wants.

PRAY

Lord,
I want to know You more. Speak, Lord. I am listening. Amen.

A Time Is Coming

Tell the people, "This is what the Sovereign LORD says: I will put an end to this proverb, and you will soon stop quoting it." Now give them this new proverb to replace the old one: "The time has come for every prophecy to be fulfilled!"

Ezekiel 12:23

When our sons were teens, we packed up hot cocoa and snacks and took them to a place where two rivers collided and formed one raging river. That Thanksgiving morning, the boys tossed sticks into the water and watched them disappear in a matter of seconds. Then we wrapped ourselves up in blankets, hugged our mugs, and said to our kids, "Sons, we love you and we're doing our best to train you in the ways of the Lord. We can't watch you every minute, and only God knows your hearts. But we believe we're entering a day of acceleration when destructive choices will take us where we don't want to go faster than we ever imagined. Just as the strong current pulled those sticks downriver, we believe our sinful choices will do the same. It matters deeply that you guard your heart and walk in the fear of God." We prayed together and committed ourselves afresh to following Jesus. Things sped up exponentially in our culture after that day and have continued to do so. A day is coming when God will deal with sin, wickedness, apathy, and the decadence in our culture. He's been patient because He wants none to perish. May we live like Jesus could return any moment. Because He might.

LEARN Read Ezekiel 12:21–28.

FLOURISH Trust God more than you trust yourself. Don't dabble where you shouldn't.

PRAY

Father,
Help me to live ready for Your imminent return. Amen.

Sodom's Sins

"Sodom's sins were pride, gluttony, and laziness, while the poor and needy suffered outside her door."

Ezekiel 16:49

*T*he prophet Ezekiel had a seemingly impossible job. And the book itself is difficult to walk through. But we must, since it's the Word of God. Oftentimes when we think of the city of Sodom, we think of her sexual sin, which was blatant, and a huge problem in the sight of God. Yet it's interesting that Scripture notes that Sodom's core sins were as follows: pride, gluttony, and apathy—and particularly, all while the poor and needy suffered outside her door. That hits closer to home, wouldn't you say? These three sins open the door to greater decadence. Who hasn't elevated their own importance over another? That's pride. *Lord, forgive us.* And who hasn't consumed more than is necessary? That's gluttony. *Lord, forgive us.* And who hasn't shrugged their shoulders at a need or taken an easy road instead of the obedient one? That's laziness. *Lord, forgive us.* Sodom's sins are our sins, and until we're honest about our own tendencies, we will stay captive to them. Look how far Sodom fell because of her own prideful blindness. May we operate in an opposite spirit. May we live purely and humbly, may we consume only what we need and give generously to others, and may we engage in this faith journey with our whole hearts and tend to the needs around us. God empowers us to live differently from the rest of the world. May your life defy the gravity of the times.

LEARN Read Ezekiel 16:46–63.

FLOURISH Spend some time with the Lord. Ask Him to reveal anything buried in your heart that needs to go. Respond accordingly.

PRAY

Lord,
Forgive and cleanse me. Renew and restore me. I am Yours. Amen.

The Ones Who've Strayed

"I will search for my lost ones who strayed away, and I will bring them safely home again. I will bandage the injured and strengthen the weak."

Ezekiel 34:16

*T*his part of Ezekiel's prophecy came after he confronted the leaders who fed on the fruit of their high position while scattering those they were appointed to care for. The world is filled with Christian misfits who feel driven out, scattered, and untended by leaders who didn't understand them, didn't protect them, and didn't care for them. They've walked away from the faith disillusioned and disheartened. I have a son who wandered for a time for this very reason. He still loved Jesus, but he no longer trusted the church. Perhaps you love someone who fits this description. Know this: God sees them. He knows the whole story. Jesus himself has determined to go and find them, to bring them back into His fold, and to bind up their wounds. Though we often ponder God's unfathomable love (as we should), we must also consider His anger, which is born out of His fierce love for us. He is furious about the fact that His followers have been driven away by poor leadership. He sees and He cares. So don't despair. Just whisper a prayer to the One who loves your loved one more than you do. He won't forget about them.

LEARN   Read Ezekiel 34:1–16.

FLOURISH   Pray for every broken wanderer on the earth today. May the Lord bring them back, heal their wounds, and ignite their faith once again.

PRAY

Good Shepherd,
*   You don't miss a thing! Thank You, Lord. Hear my prayer and do what You said You would do. Bring back every wandering heart. Heal and restore them. Use them powerfully in the kingdom today. Amen.*

From Ruins to Redemption

"I will make a covenant of peace with my people and drive away the dangerous animals from the land. Then they will be able to camp safely in the wildest places and sleep in the woods without fear."

Ezekiel 34:25

*W*hy did the Israelites perpetually wander? How did they forget about God's love, time and time again? Since God is a loving, wise heavenly Father, He gave them over to their desires and allowed them to experience the consequence of their choices. They were ruined. They were captives. They were without hope if not for the love of God. It's the same with us. Our capacity to ruin our lives is staggering. Yet God knows the end from the beginning, and He is set on the full redemption of our story. He's made a covenant of peace with us, and one day we will *flourish*. We'll no longer live in fear. Our land will prosper, our fruit will be bountiful, our hearts will be whole. We will know in the depths of our soul that it was the Lord who broke our chains and set us free. We couldn't save ourselves, so He saved us. Jesus will take the rubble of our lives—the broken parts of our story that are still a part of our present reality—and remove it forever. We'll know only health, wholeness, and restoration. We'll live with the deep joy of serving in our giftedness without any hindrance, obstacle, or enemy. This is our God.

LEARN Read Ezekiel 34:25–31.

FLOURISH Picture yourself totally restored. Imagine the joy that awaits you. That day is coming.

PRAY

Mighty God,
Sometimes I forget just how wonderful You are. You've brought me into Your family and changed my life forever. Thank You, Lord. Amen.

A Tender, Responsive Heart

"And I will give you a new heart, and I will put a new spirit in you. I will take out your stony, stubborn heart and give you a tender, responsive heart."

Ezekiel 36:26

Over the years, I've interviewed some notable Christian leaders who were once prodigals. In their wild years, they didn't care who they hurt or how their choices impacted others, especially their own family. Then the Holy Spirit met them in their rebellion and asked questions like, *"Is this how you want your life to go?"* and *"Are you done yet?"* One by one, these world shakers responded to the voice of God, and He radically changed the trajectory of their lives. And what's even more amazing is how profoundly God tenderized their hearts. They can't talk about their past sin without a humble tremble in their voice. They know what God saved them from. And they can't talk about the grace of God without tearing up, because they know they could never earn their way. The New Testament talks about how a hard heart keeps us from seeing and understanding what we ought to know.* May every heart beat in rhythm with God's heart and every soul respond to His loving guidance. Nothing will change the world like a people with a tender, responsive heart toward God.

LEARN   Read Ezekiel 36:22–38.

FLOURISH   Thank God for the ways He's already tenderized your heart. Ponder the thought of who you're becoming because of Him.

PRAY

Heavenly Father,
I marvel at Your patience with the people You love! Tenderize my heart so it beats in rhythm with Yours. Soften the hearts of those around me that they too might respond to You. Amen.

*See Mark 6:52 and Ephesians 4:18.

Dry Bones, Hear the Word of the Lord!

Then he said to me, "Speak a prophetic message to these bones and say, 'Dry bones, listen to the word of the LORD!'"

Ezekiel 37:4

God called Ezekiel to prophesy to a valley of dried-out bones (they'd been dead a long time). Not just any dried, dead bones, but a nation buried in despair and hopelessness. God called it a grave of exile. Yet God can bring life to anything, anytime, anywhere. The wind of the Spirit blew, the valley of old bones reassembled, and they came to life and formed a great army! Note the progression of restoration. First there was the sound of rattling of old bones coming back to life. After the bones came together, muscles formed, and then skin. And then suddenly there was a great army. This is such a picture of God's order of things. First He builds an infrastructure, and then He adds the strength. Then He mobilizes us into our God-given purpose. As you speak life into your dead valleys, understand that God is a God of order, and He works from the inside out. He first puts lives back together, then He builds strength. After that, He mobilizes us to conquer enemy territory as the army of God. So dare to look at the barren parts of your life and the dead bones scattered in your valley, and speak life. Believe, wait, and watch for God to do the impossible.

LEARN Read Ezekiel 37:1–14.

FLOURISH Identify the valley in your life that needs the breath of God. Speak as though you are speaking the very words of God.*

PRAY

> *God of heaven,*
> *Breathe life in and through me! Show me how to speak life into every situation. Amen.*

*See 1 Peter 4:11.

Fasting in Times of Trial

"Please test us for ten days on a diet of vegetables and water," Daniel said.

Daniel 1:12

*D*aniel and his friends were deported to a foreign land. God allowed Daniel's homeland to be conquered as a consequence of that nation's rebellion against God. But even when a nation goes astray, God always has a remnant on the earth, some of His people who still honor and revere His name. Daniel was one such man. He and his friends were brought to the palace to be trained for royal service. During their time of preparation, they were ordered to drink wine and eat heavy foods (common to palace life). Who would have blamed them given all they'd lost? Yet Daniel had a conviction to follow God, and he wanted to be clearheaded so he could hear the voice of God. We tend toward comfort foods and other indulgences when we've been treated poorly, lost something unjustly, or have been overlooked completely. It's natural. But it's *super*natural to go against our flesh and to press in that we might hear from God in this place. If you're in a time of transition, or if you've recently been displaced somehow, don't pamper yourself in a way that's harmful, weakens your resolve, and dulls your hearing. Do the opposite. Engage in a fast. Lean in. Listen for the Lord. He will surely speak to you. His favor will surround you like a shield.

LEARN Read Daniel 1.

FLOURISH Practice fasting, not just for the sake of giving up something, but to lay hold of something more in Christ Jesus.

PRAY

> *Mighty King,*
> *Give me a Daniel-like heart! Help me to practice self-restraint, high conviction, and courageous faith. Amen.*

Unbound and Unharmed

"Look!" Nebuchadnezzar shouted. "I see four men, unbound, walking
around in the fire unharmed! And the fourth looks like a god!"

Daniel 3:25

*K*ing Nebuchadnezzar issued a decree that at the sound of music, all of
the people must bow and worship his statue. Daniel's three friends
loved and feared God and refused to obey the decree. These were just young
men, living as captives in a foreign land, but still more privileged than most,
because they lived and served in the palace. They had much to lose. This was
a test to the death. Though they had honored the king as a leader and served
him with nothing but excellence and integrity, they couldn't and wouldn't
give him ultimate allegiance above God himself. This enraged the king to
such a degree that he ordered the furnace turned up seven times hotter and
commanded his strongest soldiers to bind them as captives. They felt no need
to defend themselves because they trusted God to deliver them. And even
if He didn't, He was still the God of the universe. The soldiers who tossed
them into the furnace died from the heat. But God joined His sons in the
fire and danced amidst the flames with them. They prevailed unbound and
unharmed. With that image in mind, hold fast to your convictions. Trust God
to deliver you. You will come through the fire without smelling like smoke.

LEARN Read Daniel 3.

FLOURISH If you've compromised your convictions or kept your faith
hidden, may you stand a little stronger today and trust God.

PRAY

Jesus,
You were so brave on my behalf. Help me to be brave on Your behalf.
No matter what I face, I will emerge unbound and unharmed because
You are with me. Thank You. Amen.

Becoming Accusation-Proof

At this, the administrators and the satraps tried to find grounds for charges against Daniel in his conduct of government affairs, but they were unable to do so. They could find no corruption in him, because he was trustworthy and neither corrupt nor negligent.

Daniel 6:4 NIV

*W*hen you honor God and trust Him to defend and deliver you, He will lead you to high places and use you in profound ways, and this will surely excite the jealousies of others. Daniel was exceptional because above all, he honored God. He determined not to do the wrong thing. And he determined not to leave undone the right thing. When you walk with God in this way, you become bulletproof. Others can find no cause to accuse you. They'll try but their accusations won't stick. Your character and God's favor are a shield around you. Yet as we see in Scripture and in history, when persecutors can't find fault, they'll change the rules to justify their attack against God's people. In the end, their plans will come to nothing. Jesus said, "Don't be bluffed into silence by the threats of bullies. There's nothing they can do to your soul, your core being. Save your fear for God, who holds your entire life—body and soul—in his hands."*

LEARN Read Daniel 6:1–5.

FLOURISH Ask God if there are any open doors in your life that He wants closed. Living above reproach protects you and honors Him.

PRAY

Father,
You are my protection and shield. Help me to live in a manner worthy of Your name and of my high calling. My accusers and my destiny are in Your hands. Amen.

*The Message paraphrase of Matthew 10:28.

Anyone Who Prays Will Be . . .

"Give orders that for the next thirty days any person who prays to anyone, divine or human—except to you, Your Majesty—will be thrown into the den of lions."

Daniel 6:7

Daniel's accusers manipulated the king into issuing a decree: Anyone who prayed to anyone but the king must be thrown into the den of lions. Daniel went to his usual prayer spot, opened the windows toward heaven, and with nothing to hide, prayed as earnestly and consistently as he always did. There were both consequences and results to Daniel's prayer life. Daniel was thrown into a pit with ravenous lions known for tearing their prey from limb to limb. But what about the *result* of Daniel's prayers? The lions obeyed God, not their instincts, and thus, Daniel was spared, God was glorified, and Daniel was once again promoted. There will always be consequences to saying no to the ways of the world in order to say yes to God. But if you cultivate a consistent, earnest, sincere prayer life, you will hear from God. He will reward you publicly for the way you've pursued Him privately.* In the coming days, anyone who prays to God alone and who refuses to bow down to idols will be persecuted and may suffer consequences. Yet anyone who truly seeks His face will see mountains move, giants fall, and lions quieted.

LEARN Read Daniel 6:6–28.

FLOURISH Draw near to God and He will draw near to you. Seek Him in all you do. Get to know Him as your King and your friend.

PRAY

Mighty King,
I bow before You this day. I honor You as my King. I thank You for being my friend. Give me courage to be Your representative on the earth today. Amen.

*See Matthew 6:6.

O Lord, Hear, Forgive, and Act!

"O Lord, hear. O Lord, forgive. O Lord, listen and act! For your own sake, do not delay, O my God, for your people and your city bear your name."

Daniel 9:19

*D*aniel, much like Joseph of the Old Testament, could have been bitter and steeped in self-pity for having to bear the consequences of sinful people. Neither deserved to be dragged from their homeland to a foreign land. But both leveraged their hardship for the greater good of their people. They dug deep, rose up, and became great leaders in their time. We live in a day when no one wants to take responsibility for their actions, let alone the actions of their fellow man. Yet that's exactly what Daniel did here. He knew Israel's history enough to know of God's faithfulness and Israel's sinfulness. He didn't mince words, make excuses, or complain about his captivity. Facedown, he fully named and owned the sins of his people. He appealed to God based on His goodness and mercy and nothing else. Daniel stood in the gap for his people and his nation. That's what leaders do. Gabriel, the archangel, came to Daniel to bring further insight and understanding. When we move past our personal discomforts and into a place of intercession for the greater purposes of God, heaven moves, and God responds. Your city, your nation, and your people are desperate for redemption whether they know it or not.

LEARN Read Daniel 9:1–23.

FLOURISH Consider the sins of your nation. Humble yourself and pray. May God hear, forgive, and act.

PRAY

Father,
   We've abandoned You, neglected Your ways, and served idols of our own making. Forgive us, O Lord! Draw us back to You. Bring revival. Heal our land. Amen.

Shine Like the Stars

"Those who are wise will shine as bright as the sky, and those who lead many to righteousness will shine like the stars forever."

Daniel 12:3

*E*veryone wants their five minutes of fame. People don't seem to care if they're famous for all of the wrong reasons; it's attention they crave. Yet they're chasing after the wind. Even the true celebrities who've paid their dues, honed their craft, and earned their way will be in for a big surprise one day. The archangel Michael prophesied to Daniel about the anguish reserved for the last days. Nobody's stardom or platform will save them. But God will rescue His own. They *will shine bright for all the world to see,* and they'll shine like the stars *forever*. We as believers don't exhaust ourselves trying to be stars; we empty ourselves because we're servants. Our culture today values all the wrong things. Scripture says it this way: "Their destiny is destruction, their god is their stomach, and their glory is in their shame. Their mind is set on earthly things."* But we're of a different kingdom. May we, like Daniel, serve with wisdom, godliness, and integrity. He kept his heart pure. He lived in *Babylon*. You may feel like you live in Babylon, yet everything you do for the kingdom, every person you love and point to Jesus, adds to the future glory of your life. Keep living for Jesus. One day you'll shine for all to see.

LEARN Read Daniel 12.

FLOURISH Be inspired to shine for Jesus. A future glory awaits you.

PRAY

Mighty King,
Help me not to care about or be distracted by empty pursuits. I want to live for Your kingdom because it will last forever. Amen.

*Philippians 3:19 NIV

Settling for God

When she runs after her lovers
    she won't be able to catch them.
She will search for them
    but not find them. Then she will think,
"I might as well return to my husband,
    for I was better off with him than I am now."

Hosea 2:7

God instructed Hosea to marry a prostitute, one who would leave him time and time again and who would bear children from other men. Why? To reflect Israel's wandering ways. And wander, Gomer did. During one of her wandering, sinful pursuits, things fell apart. She returned to Hosea by default. How often this happens among God's people! Some never graduate beyond an adolescent relationship with Him. They're alternately running to Him when they find themselves in trouble and then running away from Him when they get bored or challenged, or both. God is patient with our growth process and loves us beyond measure. But He'll put up with immaturity only for a season. When it's time for us to progress in our faith and we stunt our own growth because we refuse to grow up, God will discipline us. If God peeled back the sky and we saw Him for who He is, every creature would fall to the ground. His majesty and power and glory are matchless, and He is not to be trifled with. He's not a distant relative we need to call on occasion. He's either Lord, or He isn't.

LEARN   Read Hosea 2:1–13.

FLOURISH   Ask God to show you how He's working in you to mature you.

PRAY

Mighty God,
   Grow me up in You! Show me any attitudes or mindsets that hinder my maturity and lead me to higher ground. I want to grow in grace and wisdom. Amen.

Led to the Desert

"But then I will win her back once again.
I will lead her into the desert
and speak tenderly to her there."

Hosea 2:14

God leads us into the desert—not to dismiss us, but to deliver us. After a time of discipline, God led Gomer to the desert to remind her who she was, to reset her course, and to reawaken her heart. Sometimes we arrive in the desert because we've lost our way. Sometimes it's through no fault of our own. One day we're thriving, and the next we feel cut off from community, from flourishing. And still other times, we feel dead on arrival. Our souls are parched, we're exhausted, and we wonder if we'll ever find our way back to a flourishing life once again. God does some of His best work in our desert seasons. He reminds us that we're not what we do, we're someone He loves. The desert is the place where we break unhealthy attachments to the things of this world—even attachments to ministry roles that have taken up residence in our sense of identity and value. We need the desert seasons because we need continual reminders that first and foremost, we're made for Him. We're prone to wander, prone to strive, and prone to find our worth in all of our accomplishments. But if we determine to embrace this season and listen for the Lord's tender voice, we will come out of this wilderness leaning on the arm of our Beloved.

LEARN Read Hosea 2:14–16.

FLOURISH If you're in the desert, look and listen for Jesus. This season will prove to be one of the most important in your life.

PRAY

Jesus,
Meet me here. Give me a fresh sense of Your love. Let me hear Your voice. Amen.

Prepare for His Blessings

I said, "Plant the good seeds of righteousness,
   and you will harvest a crop of love.
Plow up the hard ground of your hearts,
   for now is the time to seek the LORD,
that he may come
   and shower righteousness upon you."

Hosea 10:12

Throughout Scripture God appeals to His children to return to Him, follow Him, and trust Him so He can bless them. We're prone to wander. God sees it, knows it, and continually makes a way for us to return to Him. God longs to be gracious to us, to show us His kindness, mercy, and love. He is a good Father who withholds no good thing from those who walk uprightly before Him. In this world of small "g" gods, one might ask, "Why does He call for such allegiance? Why are His blessings so conditional?" Because He's the only true Source of life. He created us. He made us for His glory. His ways are higher than our ways and His paths are our road to healing and redemption. We cannot sustain His blessings when we're outside of His will. We'd either squander them or they'd crush us. So how do we prepare for the next season of God's blessings? We sow seeds of righteousness now. And we plow up the hardened places in our lives so that when His showers of blessings come, we're ready.

LEARN   Read Hosea 10:1–12.

FLOURISH   The word *plant* in this passage means to scatter seed so as to prepare for an increased harvest. Sow more seeds. Plow up the hard soil. Prepare for rain.

PRAY

Gracious Father,
   Show me where to sow abundantly. Show me where to plow. I want to be ready for Your showers of blessings. Amen.

After Repentance Comes Refreshment

Don't be afraid, O land.
Be glad now and rejoice,
    for the LORD has done great things.
Joel 2:21

The prophet Joel's message took a sudden turn. He went from calling for repentance, with a warning about the impending judgment, to charging the people *not* to fear. He even said, "Be glad *now*. For the Lord *has done* great things." Joel wanted the people to remember two things about God: He's holy and He's good. The Israelites would never know God's profound goodness until they came to grips with their capacity to defy Him. We'll never be free from sin that we refuse to acknowledge. And we'll never truly experience the depths of His goodness until we come to grips with the depths of our need for Him. But when we are sincerely, truly sorry for our wandering ways, and when we repent (have a change of heart and a change of mind), times of refreshing do come.* But we can't have it both ways. We'll either enjoy a season of sin that may ultimately destroy us, or we'll enjoy the refreshing, reviving, never-ending spring of God's goodness as we stay in the flow of His love. We don't keep with repentance to ensure our salvation or to secure His love; we're saved and we're loved because He can't help himself. He loves us because He made us. We bear fruit in keeping with repentance† because we love God and enjoy our oneness with Him.

LEARN   Read Joel 2:12–27.

FLOURISH   Ask God to search your heart. Respond to what He shows you.

PRAY

> *Precious Lord,*
>   *Search my heart. Show me what I need to see. Point out anything that offends You. Lead me onward, Lord. Amen.*

*See Acts 3:19.
†See Luke 3:8.

Your Sons and Daughters Will Prophesy

"I will pour out my Spirit upon all people.
Your sons and daughters will prophesy.
Your old men will dream dreams,
and your young men will see visions."

Joel 2:28

Many scholars believe that this prophesy was fulfilled in part at Pentecost.* Imagine the power of God's movement across ethnic, generational, and economic lines. He's no respecter of persons; He's a respecter of faith! Some scholars believe that another Great Awakening is coming, and that we will see an upsurge in the work of the Holy Spirit in our midst. But we don't have to wait until then to encourage someone with a prophetic word, to dream dreams, and to see visions. God is actively at work on the earth today in these very ways! Countless Muslims have come to Christ after seeing a vision that they knew was Jesus. Though I know there are differing views on this topic, I like to err on the side of faith and dare to believe God for more, not less. Several years ago my husband and I claimed this verse as our own: "Even at night, my heart instructs me."† We asked God to give us dreams in the night hours, strategies on how to pray, and what to believe Him for. He's answered our prayers in too many ways to count. Don't wait for a great outpouring. Pray and believe God for more now.

LEARN   Read Joel 2:28–32.

FLOURISH   Imagine seeing your children prophesy, you dreaming dreams, and God speaking with great clarity. Dare to ask Him for more.

PRAY

Precious Father,
Pour out Your Spirit on me and my family! May we prophesy, dream dreams, and discern Your ways with greater clarity! Amen.

*See Acts 2.
†Psalm 16:7.

Thousands Are Waiting in the Valley of Decision

Thousands upon thousands are waiting in the valley of decision.
There the day of the LORD will soon arrive.

Joel 3:14

Every single day, people die without knowing Jesus. They face a Christless eternity; once they've taken their last breath, there's no altering their eternal destiny. A friend once told me a story about a man who didn't know Jesus. A believer befriended him and spent regular time with him. He wanted to earn his trust before sharing the gospel (many have approached evangelism this way). A year passed and finally the friend shared Jesus with his unsaved friend. The friend's reply? "No way this is true. And if it is true, why would you wait a whole year to tell me? What if I would have died suddenly? It's like I've been in a burning building and you were waiting until we were close enough to death to warn me! What were you thinking?" Of course, the young man was jarred by his response, but it bears some consideration. The ship is sinking. Lives will be lost. It's time to save them, time to tell them about the lifeboat God has provided. It's up to them to decide if they'll trust Jesus for themselves or not. But right now, thousands privately wonder if there's a God in heaven who loves them. Be His ambassador today.

LEARN Read Joel 3:14–21.

FLOURISH Share your faith story with someone this week.

PRAY

Father,
I'm sorry I so often prefer comfort over risk when it comes to sharing my faith. Give me a heart for the lost and the boldness and courage to reach out to them. Amen.

God's Surprising Prophet

Indeed, the Sovereign LORD never does anything
until he reveals his plans to his servants the prophets.

Amos 3:7

*A*mos was not the son of a prophet; he was not the son of a priest. As a humble shepherd, he could have stayed in Tekoa, doing his job, providing for his family, worshiping God. But God gave Amos a vision of the future. . . . Amos, a fiery, fearless, and honest shepherd from the south, confronted (the Israelites) with their sin and warned them of impending judgment."* Imagine this God-fearing man, working on the hillside, shepherding his sheep, when suddenly he's ambushed with a great vision from God of impending judgment on God's people. He'd heard about the wandering ways of his brothers and sisters in the north—how they worshiped idols, cheated the poor, and exploited the vulnerable. Suddenly, he felt God's fire in his bones. He had to do something about it. He spoke with precision and power. Some listened. Others didn't. We are teetering on the edge of judgment as well. Yet, as Scripture says, God never does anything without first revealing His plans to His servants—at least to those who are awake, listening, and waiting for His word. And the ones God uses may surprise us. Maybe it won't be the person with the giant platform or spectacular ministry. Maybe it'll be a plumber, a farmer, or a stay-at-home momma.

LEARN Read Amos 3.

FLOURISH Ask God to speak to you about the times we're in. Write down your thoughts.

PRAY

Jesus,
Help us to be humble enough to hear You speak. Amen.

Life Application Study Bible, 1861.

Gloating Is Never Godly

"You should not have spoken arrogantly
in that terrible time of trouble."
Obadiah 12

I once heard a story about a yelling match that broke out at a Christian writers conference. The yellers were known Christian leaders who happened to stand on opposite sides of the political aisle. Their rant was so heated that it stirred up all kinds of angst and anxiety in the hearts of the other writers in attendance. Their conviction evolved into anger, which morphed into full-blown rage and prideful condescension. Things obviously got out of hand. We live in a polarized culture politically, racially, economically, and denominationally. Because this is where we live, it matters that we steward our perspective. It matters how we speak to and about those who vote, look, or think differently from us. There's no place in our hearts for arrogance, reactive rage, or selective love. Humble, bold conviction that compels us to stand up for the weak is one thing. But self-righteous, divisive angst is something altogether different. A good test of our hearts is to note how we react to political outcomes or the latest, hottest news report. Are we able to remember that God is on the throne and that He draws nearest to His humble servants? Or will we be ruled by fear and lash out? Will we gloat when the other guy loses? Our world desperately needs more saints who hold a godly perspective.

LEARN Read Obadiah.

FLOURISH Challenge your own perspective if you're anything but humble, hopeful, and expectant.

PRAY

Lord,
Help me to remember that if I have to let go of love to hold on to my cause, I've lost my way. Help me reflect Your Son's heart for this world. Amen.

An Impossible Mission

"Get up and go to the great city of Nineveh. Announce my judgment against it because I have seen how wicked its people are."

But Jonah got up and went in the opposite direction to get away from the LORD.

Jonah 1:2–3

*P*icture the most anti-Christian city in the world today. The people are heartless, cruel, and wicked to their core. In Jonah's day, that city was Nineveh, the capital of Assyria. What if God called you to bring the good news to North Korea, Russia, or the Middle East? What if He charged you to share the message of His cross with those who've tortured and killed countless Christians? Jonah didn't want this assignment. He didn't want such a wicked people to be saved. He wanted God's judgment—not His mercy to fall. So Jonah got up and went the opposite direction. Jonah hated the people of Nineveh and all they stood for. He'd built up angst in his heart and anger in his soul. The mission *felt* impossible. Yet here's what's true: *Hiding from God is impossible.* Doing what He asks is always possible with His strength. If you're postponing obedience, know this: You're heading into a storm. If you're willing to turn around and engage your faith once again, you'll find God more faithful than you ever dreamed possible.

LEARN Read Jonah 1:1–3.

FLOURISH Has your love grown cold toward a people group? Ask God for His loving perspective and compassion.

PRAY

Heavenly Father,
You care so deeply about this broken world. Give me faith, boldness, and courage to carry out my God-given assignments. I am running to You, not away from You. I know I can trust You. Amen.

What the Storms Reveal

The sailors were terrified when they heard this, for he had already told them he was running away from the Lord. "Oh, why did you do it?" they groaned.

Jonah 1:10

*I*n my book *Fully Alive*, I wrote about a word God gave to me in one of the greatest storms in my life: *The storms reveal the lies we believe and the truths we need.* Jonah tried to escape God's call on his life by launching out onto the great sea. But he soon learned that God is the God of the land and the sea. The lie Jonah believed was that he could run from God. The truth he needed was this: Though nothing could ever separate him from God's love, we will experience consequences when we run from Him. I serve as a ministry coach for a group of women online. Just the other night, one of them pondered, "Just as the men on the ship were paying a price for Jonah's disobedience, who's paying a price for mine? Who am I putting in harm's way? Who am I not blessing, serving, helping because I'm hiding?"* What a powerful observation! Once the sailors threw Jonah overboard, the storm instantly stopped. The men were awestruck by the Lord's great power, and God arranged for a fish to swallow Jonah. Getting swallowed by a fish can help a man swallow his pride. Jonah's story was not over yet.

LEARN Read Jonah 1:4–17.

FLOURISH Thank God for never giving up on you.

PRAY

Lord,
You are so patient, kind, and true. Make me more like You. I want Your heart to beat in my chest. Amen.

*Paraphrase from Jeni Fobart.

The Lord Spoke a Second Time

Then the LORD spoke to Jonah a second time: "Get up and go to the great city of Nineveh, and deliver the message I have given you."

Jonah 3:1

When the Lord spoke to Jonah, Jonah ran in the opposite direction. When a great storm came, Jonah was tossed overboard. When the Lord arranged for a great fish to swallow Jonah, he thanked God for not allowing him to drown. Once Jonah got his heart right before God, the Lord ordered the fish to spit Jonah out onto the beach. Then God spoke to Jonah a *second time*. We don't always get it right the first time. Most often we delay obedience because of self-protection. We prefer to save face or stay comfortable or avoid risk. And when we mess up, the enemy is right there to condemn us not only for a missed opportunity, but also for the consequences of our disobedience, as if he cares about a lost soul or lost opportunity. But the opposite is true. He relishes the idea of such things. He also loves to throw you into a self-defeating, self-condemning cycle. Determine to have none of it. God knows your frame and your steps before you take even one. Plus, He's the God of second chances. He cares far more about developing an intimate relationship with you, built on trust, than He does about you getting it right every single time. Accept God's grace and begin again. He's doing a great work in you.

LEARN Read Jonah 2–3.

FLOURISH Refuse condemnation for missed opportunities. Embrace and look for God's invitation to new ones.

PRAY

Father,
Your patience with me is breathtaking. I'm listening and watching. Show me my next assignment. Thank You for the chance to begin again. Amen.

Is It Right for You to Be Angry?

The LORD replied, "Is it right for you to be angry about this?"

Jonah 4:4

*J*onah warned the people of Nineveh. Judgment was coming. To Jonah's great surprise, the people responded. The king stepped down from his throne, took off his royal robes, dressed himself in burlap, and issued a corporate fast. No one was allowed to eat or drink anything, not even the animals. Everyone needed to earnestly seek God. And they did. Their response moved God's heart, and in His kind and compassionate way, He showed mercy to a city previously doomed for judgment. Jonah was furious. He was angry with God for making a fool out of him. His prediction mattered more than Nineveh's predicament. He cared more about saving face than saving grace. God asked, "Is it right for you to be angry about this?" I couldn't help but chuckle when I first read Jonah's response. "Yes. Angry enough to die!" Thankfully, Jonah's tantrum didn't hinder God's mercy. God's own kindness compels Him time and time again to send a warning through His prophets. His intent is always that people might respond and repent. And when we do, He rejoices. If we do not, we're the ones who need correction.

LEARN Read Jonah 4.

FLOURISH If there is a people group you don't want to receive God's salvation and mercy, ask God's forgiveness and pray for those people daily.

PRAY

Lord,
I can be so selective with my grace, and yet You never are. Burden my
heart with what burdens Yours. Teach me to walk in Your way. Amen.

A Beautiful Day Is Coming . . .

Everyone will live in peace and prosperity,
　　enjoying their own grapevines and fig trees,
　　for there will be nothing to fear.
The LORD of Heaven's Armies
　　has made this promise!

Micah 4:4

During an interview I did while promoting my book *Fully Alive*, I recounted the storm I walked through with my health, and I shared the fear and anxiety that accompanied that battle. I'm now about 90 percent healed, but when I have inflammatory surges, I've got to work to stay out of the ditch of discouragement. I yearn for full healing. The interviewer asked me this surprising question: "Do you ever just get sick of the battle? Don't you ever feel like saying to God, 'Enough, already!'?" Honestly, I do feel that way sometimes. But after losing a few loved ones to cancer, and after my own fierce battles, something has changed in me. I *know* now that life on earth is short and eternity is long. We're here for a blink of an eye compared to the eternity we'll spend in the presence of Jesus and in the absence of suffering. God has made sure that every single one of our moments has redemptive possibilities. A day is coming when every gesture of faith, every hoped-for outcome will be swallowed up in God's amazing grace and goodness. A day is coming . . .

LEARN　　Read Micah 4:1–8.

FLOURISH　　Refuse to waste precious strength on whining, complaining, or worrying about your life. Hidden within every trying circumstance is a potential for future reward.

PRAY

Lord Jesus,
　Help me to see the redemptive possibilities all around me. Help me trade defeat for victory, fear for faith, and discouragement for courage. Resurrection power, come alive in me! Amen.

Do Justly, Love Mercy, Walk Humbly

> Do what is right, to love mercy,
> and to walk humbly with your God.
>
> Micah 6:8

*Y*ou can hear God's heart in His appeal to His people: "Why have you turned away from Me? Don't you remember the miracles I performed to set you free? The people I provided to help you along the way? The protection I offered when others tried to curse you?" The *Study Bible* says, "Israel responded to God's request by trying to appease him with sacrifices, hoping he would then leave them alone. But sacrifices and other religious rituals aren't enough; God wants changed lives."* Appeasing our conscience will never change our hearts. The law was meant to show people their need for God so they'd turn to Him *so He could heal them*.† When we welcome God's presence in our lives, *He makes us new*. We begin to discern justice from injustice. We understand God's heart for the vulnerable. We also grow to love God's mercy for others, for without it, we ourselves would have no hope. And as we mature in Christ, we grow in humility, because He opens our eyes to what we deserve and what we've actually gained in Him. God doesn't want to be appeased. He wants to be loved, honored, followed, and even enjoyed.

LEARN Read Micah 6:1–8.

FLOURISH Love on God today. Tell Him how much He means to you. Honor His presence in your life.

PRAY

> *O Lord, how often I rely on outward performance when You're really after inward transformation. Heal me, change me, and grow Your likeness in me. Amen.*

*Life Application Study Bible, 1908.
†See Matthew 13:15.

After Discipline Comes Deliverance!

Do not gloat over me, my enemies!
For though I fall, I will rise again.
Though I sit in darkness,
the LORD will be my light.

Micah 7:8

God disciplines His children because He's a loving heavenly Father. And when He does, our enemies gloat. Sadly, if you're walking through a season when God is addressing something in your life, your fellow Christians may also puff out their chests, look down their noses, and make all kinds of assumptions about you. God hates all of that. But He allows it so we can learn to discern and value His voice above the noise. The great challenge during times of discipline is to *respond to God and refuse to react to your enemies and critics.* It takes both humility and grit to submit to God's correction while simultaneously rejecting any notion of insecurity, inferiority, scarcity, and condemnation. None of those are in the heart of God. He disciplines those He truly loves and intends to use. And once the season of correction and refinement are through, God will deal with your enemies and critics in ways that will make them tremble. Every time I see this dynamic, it not only assures me of God's great care for me when He corrects me, it also puts a fear in me to handle another's disciplinary season with great honor and respect. Gloating is never acceptable for the believer. God does His best work in and through His humblest saints.

LEARN Read Micah 7.

FLOURISH If God is disciplining you or someone you know, stay humble and hopeful.

PRAY

Precious Lord,
You're a good Father. I bow before You. Thank You for loving and defending me. Amen.

221

God Promises Peace

Look! A messenger is coming over the mountains with good news!
He is bringing a message of peace.

Nahum 1:15

*J*onah warned the city of Nineveh that God's judgment was coming. The people sincerely repented and received God's mercy instead. Over time, though, Nineveh lost the spiritual ground it had gained. Unfortunately, one hundred years later, God called Nineveh—the capital of Assyria—a city of murder and lies. And though Assyria was a military superpower and seemed impossible to defeat, God could reduce them to rubble in an instant. Why would a loving God want to destroy a whole city? When a city is so vile that it's known only for its wickedness, you can be sure that the weak and the vulnerable are the ones who pay the highest price. When lawlessness and corruption run rampant, the weak are exploited the most, suffer the greatest, and are most desperate for a defender. Here in the midst of this impossible situation, God proclaims good news and peace. *Peace* here translates this way: "Completeness, wholeness, peace, health, welfare, safety, soundness, tranquility, prosperity, perfectness, fullness, rest, harmony; the absence of agitation or discord."* Jesus brought the good news and brings the good news. He speaks peace to His people. And at the right time, He will deal with the wicked, defend the weak, and deliver His people.

LEARN Read Nahum 1–3.

FLOURISH Use your prayers, your gifts, or your presence to bring the message of God's *peace* to a vulnerable person or people group.

PRAY

Father,
Cut off the strength of the wicked and increase the power of the godly.†
Work wonders in our day. Amen.

New Spirit-Filled Life Bible (Nashville: Thomas Nelson, 2002), 1218.
†See Psalm 75:10.

Look Around and Be Amazed

The LORD replied,
"Look around at the nations;
    look and be amazed!
For I am doing something in your own day,
    something you wouldn't believe
    even if someone told you about it.
Habakkuk 1:5

*H*abakkuk looked around and felt utter dismay. His heart broke over the injustice and corruption around him. How long before God would intervene? He wasn't whining or complaining; he sincerely sought God for answers to heartfelt questions. Habakkuk's words could easily be declared today: "I am surrounded by people who love to argue and fight. The law has become paralyzed, and there is no justice in the courts. The wicked far outnumber the righteous . . ."* So how did God respond? Unbeknownst to Habakkuk, God was already working. "Look around and be amazed, for *I am doing something . . .*" In every generation, the godly lament over the wickedness in their midst. And in every generation, God's plan is *already in motion* before His people even know to ask for it. Your call today is to look around for the good and for God moving in your midst. In fact, grow expectant about what He's up to. May you see Him work in ways that utterly surprise and amaze you. You can be sure of this: He is working, moving, and arranging circumstances this very moment.

LEARN Read Habakkuk 1.

FLOURISH Look for God's movement in your life. Be amazed. Let that realization sink deep into your bones. (It'll put faith in your heart.)

PRAY

Lord,
Let me see Your miracles once again! I want to see Your glory at work.
Thank You for working in my day! Amen.

*Habakkuk 1:3–4

Habakkuk's Priorities

> I will climb up to my watchtower
>   and stand at my guardpost.
> There I will wait to see what the LORD says
>   and how he will answer my complaint.
> Habakkuk 2:1

*M*any have lamented to God over the years because of the wickedness in their day. Sometimes God responded; other times He seemed silent. So why did God respond to Habakkuk with such clarity and assurance? Habakkuk had a humble, earnest heart. It's been said that there are two opposite responses to living in sinful times: We either put our heads in the sand and entertain ourselves to death, or we shake our fists at the dark and blame God and everybody else for ruining our idea of what life should look like. But as this chapter says, *the righteous shall live by their faithfulness to God.* Habakkuk pursued God and positioned himself in such a way that he wouldn't miss Him. Habakkuk realized that he was appointed as one of the guardians of the kingdom and took his place at the guard post. There, he waited and listened for how the Lord would address the wickedness and decay around him. Habakkuk cared about righteousness and he longed for revival. He never demanded an answer from God; instead, he appealed to Him for one. What if we all did the same?

LEARN Read Habakkuk 2.

FLOURISH Find your high ground so you can hear what God is saying. See yourself as a guardian of the kingdom. Look and listen for God to address the times we're in. Share what He reveals with those who will listen.

PRAY

Mighty King,
You've made me a guardian of the kingdom. Speak to me about the times. Grant me opportunities to help others so that they may hear and be saved. Amen.

Yet I Will Rejoice

> Even though the fig trees have no blossoms,
> and there are no grapes on the vines . . .
> yet I will rejoice in the LORD!
> I will be joyful in the God of my salvation!
> Habakkuk 3:17–18

The word *yet* carries so much meaning, so much depth, such great faith. We all walk through times of testing, discipline, or even reduction, all of which are critical for developing our faith. Testing proves and strengthens our faith. Discipline corrects and refines our character. Reduction prepares us for growth and abundance. God continually draws us deeper so we'll be more firmly rooted in Him. We have an incredible propensity for shifting our weight onto the things that we want. We long for promotion, provision, and protection from hardship, and yet we so quickly put our hope in and draw our value from those very things. But when God allows us to go for a time without such gifts, we remember afresh that any gift from His hand pales in comparison to the treasure of knowing His heart. Furthermore, when we come to a place with God where we can look at our devastation, heartbreak, or not-yet, and then look to Him and sincerely say, "And yet . . ." we find Him to be everything we need and more. And when the season does change, we're less apt to be tempted by the very things we thought we needed in order to be okay. Our souls will be freer.

LEARN Read Habakkuk 3.

FLOURISH Write out your own "and yet" faith declaration.

PRAY

Father,
You withhold no good thing from me. I will trust You while I wait on You. You are better than any gift I long for. And I already have You. Thank You. Amen.

The Danger of Complacency

"I will search with lanterns in Jerusalem's darkest corners
to punish those who sit complacent in their sins.
They think the LORD will do nothing to them,
either good or bad."

Zephaniah 1:12

*I*t's been said that we become like the gods we worship. Whatever we continually behold, we consistently reflect. Some of God's own children had so lost sight of His majesty, power, and authority that they shrugged their shoulders and chose to live the way they so desired. They reduced God's influence to that of a lifeless idol. Furthermore, they projected their own indifference onto Him, thinking He cared very little as to whether people did right or wrong, as if He himself would never react to sin or respond to righteousness. The word *complacent* in this passage is akin to the process of curdling, thickening, or settling into. In other words, when we let go of our conviction, and when we stop caring about sin (and worse yet, when we somehow think that God is on the same page), something destructive settles within us. Our faith curdles; our sin becomes like quicksand, and we shrug our shoulders over the consequences of it all. God will have none of it. He is not indifferent about *anything*. Never confuse God's patience with complacency. Sin has its consequences and righteousness has its rewards. If you know someone who is complacent in their sin, pray and fast for them. It's no small thing to God. A day of reckoning *is* coming unless they wake up and repent.

LEARN ▸ Read Zephaniah 1.

FLOURISH ▸ Ask the Lord to show you if you've misjudged Him in any way.

PRAY ▸

> *Lord,*
> *I want to know You more. Show me Your heart, Your passion, and Your convictions. Awaken me. Amen.*

God Delights in You with Gladness

He will take delight in you with gladness.
With his love, he will calm all your fears.
He will rejoice over you with joyful songs.
Zephaniah 3:17

God is not indifferent about *anything*. He is passionate, kind, and true. He takes great delight in you and cares deeply about every nuance of your story. He's well aware of the lies you picked up when life let you down, and He's wholeheartedly committed to helping you sort through your story in a way that heals you and restores your perspective. Every delay, every denial, every pause in your story has a purpose to it. Every hardship, every steep hill, and every harrowing experience has served to shape you into the person you are today. Though at times it may have felt as though He looked away or lost your address, He never did. And never will. Though the world continually projects its painful perspectives onto His character, He remains who He is. He is the everlasting Father, God of all comfort, and lover of our souls. You know what will heal your heart? The thought of His smile when you come into His presence. Imagine Him fixing His eyes on you with great delight as He listens to what you have to say. He's not in a hurry. He has time for you. His heart *for* you will forever change you.

LEARN Read Zephaniah 3.

FLOURISH Picture God's delight in you. Imagine the kindness on His face as He listens to your prayers. Allow His song over you to reverberate in your heart.

PRAY

Father,
Sometimes I forget how much You love me. Help me to know and experience Your love in a way that changes me forever. Thank You, Lord. Amen.

When You Can't Seem to Get Ahead

"This is what the LORD of Heaven's Armies says: Look at what's happening to you! You have planted much but harvest little."

Haggai 1:5–6

The people had returned to their homeland to rebuild the temple after the armies of Babylon had destroyed it. They continually encountered opposition, delays, and frustrations, so they lost their zeal, focus, and sense of purpose. When this happens to God's people, we tend to lose sight of our identity and our purpose. We begin to operate out of a scarcity mindset instead of out of the abundance of our heir status. We grab for ourselves and forget about the greater call on our lives. Haggai came onto the scene and asked the leaders why they were more focused on their own personal comfort and gain than they were on their God-given task. He then called people back to their original task of rebuilding the temple. There's a message in this story for us. Oftentimes when we encounter roadblocks, setbacks, and delays, we lose heart, and then we lose focus. We forget our purpose. We start grabbing for ourselves, but we never get ahead. What's the answer? Return first and foremost to keeping God at the center of your life. Seek His kingdom first. Follow His lead. Everything else will fall into place.*

LEARN   Read Haggai 1.

FLOURISH   Have you abandoned a God-given task because you've lost heart? Reengage today.

PRAY

Mighty God,
Give me laser focus and fierce faith. Help me to stay the course and be about Your work on the earth today. I know You'll provide everything I need. Amen.

*See Matthew 6:33.

Be Strong, Get to Work

"Be strong, all you people still left in the land. And now get to work, for I am with you, says the LORD of Heaven's Armies."

Haggai 2:4

The people of Judah had returned to God and reengaged in His purposes. They stepped back into the powerful river of His provision. It's the same with us. When we dabble on the shoreline of His purposes, we'll never experience the power of His provision. We miss so much when we're out of sync with His will. The river of God runs wild; it's strong and powerful. And when we jump in, we're strong and powerful, and He takes us on a wild ride. Why do we work so hard to avoid the work He puts before us? Maybe it's fear of failure, anxiety over the cost, or our flesh's aversion to challenge. And yet, we're made for the river! If you're postponing obedience for self-preserving reasons, or for any other reason, don't waste another day. Be strong and get to work. You will experience the Lord's provision, presence, and empowering grace in ways you never otherwise would. Don't fear what the rest of the world fears. You're safest in the center of His will—not always safe from harm, but safe from destroying your influence by your own self-protection. Jump into the river of God. Your life will never be the same.

LEARN Read Haggai 2.

FLOURISH If your current assignment doesn't require faith of some kind, it's time to seek and trust God.

PRAY

Lord,

I want to live in the flow of Your power and provision when I work and when I rest. Give me faith and courage to jump into the river and go where You lead. Amen.

Not by Might, but By His Spirit

"This is what the LORD says to Zerubbabel: It is not by force nor by strength, but by my Spirit, says the LORD of Heaven's Armies."

Zechariah 4:6

God's people had a monumental task before them: rebuild the temple. Facing literal and spiritual opposition, the Lord reminded them that they would never accomplish their call in their own strength. Military reinforcement wouldn't get the job done either. Only by the *Spirit's power* would the mountains move, the enemies flee, and the way become clear for them to finish their task. It's the same with us. Our call is not an easy one. In fact, it's *impossible* apart from the grace of God and the empowering work of the Holy Spirit. Why does God invite us to partner with Him in a way that positions us to need Him every moment of every hour? Because we need Him that much whether we realize it or not. But when we're engaged in purposes that are beyond us, we learn something of God's character. We no longer fear our limits. We grow confident in *His* abilities, assured of *His* strength. We stop looking to our accomplishments to validate our worth. We instead look at every task, large or small, as an opportunity to trust God and see what He will do with a heart of faith. And then we offer it back to Him. It's the only way to live.

LEARN Read Zechariah 4.

FLOURISH If you're relying on your own strength in *any* way today, look to the Lord, invite His Spirit's intervention, and see what God will do.

PRAY

> *Precious Father,*
> *I look to You. My help comes from You. Intervene by Your great power.*
> *My soul waits for You. Amen.*

Seeds of Peace and Prosperity

"For I am planting seeds of peace and prosperity among you. The grapevines will be heavy with fruit. The earth will produce its crops, and the heavens will release the dew."

Zechariah 8:12

God's people wandered far away from His best for them. They sinned, practiced idolatry, cheated the poor, and exploited the weak. They looked more like the world than they did their Maker. Then their temple was destroyed, and they were carried off into captivity. After seventy years they returned to their homeland and began the work of rebuilding the temple. And yet they lost heart once they encountered opposition and delay. Their apathy led them to care more about their personal comfort than they did God's kingdom. This grieved the heart of God. But then they heeded the prophet's charge to get back to work. As a result, God pronounced blessing over their lives and their land for their obedience. Though we have to be careful not to always attribute blessing to obedience or poverty to disobedience, it is important to note that something changes in the land and in our lives when we sincerely seek the heart of God. He plants seeds of peace and prosperity in our midst. He offers us an otherworldly peace and He prospers our soul. Worldly treasures may come and go, but these treasures belong to *anyone* who sincerely seeks Him.

LEARN Read Zechariah 8:1–13.

FLOURISH Nurture the seeds God has planted in your life. Water them with His Word. Seek peace and pursue it. Trust God to prosper your mind, body, and spirit.

PRAY

Father,
With my whole heart, I will follow You. Show me how to nurture the seeds You plant in my soil. I want life to spring up all around me. Amen.

We Have Heard, God Is With You

"Please let us walk with you, for we have heard that God is with you."
Zechariah 8:23

Zechariah pronounced an end to the old and a declaration of the new. He prophesied about a day when Israel would no longer be the object of scorn; instead, she'd be a symbol of God's grace and power. Over the centuries, God's chosen people have loved Him, wandered from Him, rebelled against Him, and then repented before Him, only to wander again. But a day is coming when the Jewish people will recognize Christ as their Messiah and will seek Him wholeheartedly. "Jerusalem will be a holy place—highly respected throughout the world because its people will have a change of heart toward God. People from other nations will see how God has rewarded His people for their faithfulness and want to be included in their great blessings."* Though this is a prophecy for the nation of Israel, there's a potential promise here for us as well. Imagine walking so closely with the risen Lord, listening so intimately for His voice, and obeying Him so wholeheartedly that those around you run to catch up with you, long to walk with you, and seek to learn what you know about the great God of heaven. May your life reflect God's active and real presence on the earth today.

LEARN Read Zechariah 8:14–23.

FLOURISH Ask God to release fresh favor and power over your life. Steward it well.

PRAY

Lord,
I want my life to so reflect Your heart of grace and power that when others encounter me, they encounter You. Raise me up to reflect Your glory. Amen.

*Life Application Study Bible, 1959.

Righteous and Victorious, Yet Humble

> Look, your king is coming to you.
>   He is righteous and victorious,
> yet he is humble, riding on a donkey—
>   riding on a donkey's colt.
>
> Zechariah 9:9

Zechariah prophesied the coming Messiah five hundred years before His birth. The people of Jerusalem needed a victorious king, a warrior to defend them and protect them. But nobody expected Him to be the kind of King that He is. He's righteous, victorious, and *humble*. Though the prophecies described Him, much of the world missed Him. And so it goes today. Even the disciples who knew Jesus personally expected Him to use His miracle-working power to rise up and defeat Rome. But He wasn't that kind of king. He lived a righteous, humble life, and defeated sin and death *victoriously*. He turned the world upside down and started a kingdom movement that's still going strong today. One day He will gather His people together, He will overthrow wicked governments, unseat wicked leaders, confront evil forces, and disarm them all. He'll restore everything the enemy stole from us. The Israelites tried to get it right, but they couldn't. We try to get it right, but we can't. So our King came to us. He lived and died for us. Rose again for us. And now, finally, *we* can live righteous, victorious, humble lives, just like our King.

LEARN   Read Zechariah 9.

FLOURISH   Ponder these attributes today: *You are righteous.* You have a right standing before God because of Jesus. *You are victorious.* You will overcome every battle. *You are humble.* You know where your help comes from.

PRAY

Father,
   Thank You for sending Your Son. Jesus, thank You for coming to earth. Holy Spirit, thank You for empowering me to live like my King. I am forever blessed. Amen.

Testing God

"Bring all the tithes into the storehouse so there will be enough food in my Temple. If you do . . . I will open the windows of heaven for you. I will pour out a blessing so great you won't have enough room to take it in! Try it! Put me to the test!"

Malachi 3:10

*E*very time I read Malachi chapter 3, I cringe. I gasp when I read how God asks His children to return to Him and they respond with, "How can we return if we've never wandered away?" Wouldn't God know if you wandered away? And shouldn't you tremble at such an appeal? They go on to question if it even *pays* to obey Him. Pays? There's no fear of God. No sense that He's right about anything. They want their will, their way. Still, God asks them to bring in the tithe, to sow seeds into the kingdom. He even invites them to *test Him* and see if He doesn't unlock provision and blessing beyond their imagination. This passage has been misused as a license to use God for personal gain. But that's not the invitation here. Instead, He's saying, "If you will dare to see me as your provider, you will find me faithful to the point where you trust me with every other area of your life." It's still true today.

LEARN Read Malachi 3:1–14.

FLOURISH Approximately 95 percent of Christians today still refuse to trust God as their provider. Ministries are trying to function on 5 percent of the resources God intended. If you're in that 95 percent, I dare you to trust Him.

PRAY

Lord,
    Forgive us for trusting ourselves more than You! Forgive us for white-knuckling resources that ultimately come from and belong to You. Give me faith to sow generously. Amen.

The Lord Listened and Remembered

Then those who feared the LORD spoke with each other, and the LORD listened to what they said. In his presence, a scroll of remembrance was written to record the names of those who feared him and always thought about the honor of his name.

Malachi 3:16

*T*hat time you leaned across the table, grabbed your friend's hand, and encouraged her to hang in there and trust God, the Lord listened, and wrote it down. That time when you were on the phone crying your eyes out and your friend prayed for you. He was there. That moment when you anxiously shared your story of faith and resilience and of how God sustained you, He leaned in, listened, and opened His book. He's so taken by your faith that He remembers every faith conversation, every heartfelt moment of worship, every act prompted by your faith. When together as a family you bow and sincerely give thanks for food that blesses and sustains, God's right there. He is well aware of those who disregard Him. And He's intimately aware of those who honor Him. On earth the lines seem blurry between believers and unbelievers. Hard to tell them apart sometimes. But in heaven? There's perfect clarity. Absolute distinction. Make no mistake about it.

LEARN Read Malachi 3:16–18.

FLOURISH Ponder the very real presence and attentiveness of God the next time you offer words of encouragement to another.

PRAY

Lord,
I forget sometimes how much my faith matters to You. How much I matter to You. When I'm encouraging another in the faith, help me to be as attentive to You as You are to me. I love You, Lord. Amen.

The Sun of Righteousness
Will Rise

"But for you who fear my name, the Sun of Righteousness will rise with healing in his wings. And you will go free, leaping with joy like calves let out to pasture."

Malachi 4:2

*R*ight in the middle of my health relapse, I had a vivid dream. I walked through a large field with a fence surrounding its perimeter. Outside the fenced area were mountains and streams and wildflowers. It was beautiful enough inside the fence, but I longed for the freedom beyond the borders of my surroundings. When I approached the edge of the field, I saw a gate that was bolted and chained shut—like there was no way out. Suddenly, out of nowhere, the enemy unleashed a fury of creatures that swarmed and attacked and pushed me back, away from a gate that was impenetrable anyway. I woke up and realized afresh how desperately the enemy wants us to stay captive. Yet if we contend for our freedom and trust God's promises, we will experience a measure of freedom we never dreamed possible. And there's a day up ahead when the gates of hell will no longer prevail against us in *any* way. We will go free and leap with joy, like calves let out to pasture. Keep walking. Keep believing. The Sun of Righteousness *will* one day rise with healing, redemption, and restoration in His wings.

LEARN Read Malachi 4.

FLOURISH Ask God if there's a new measure of freedom that He wants you to appropriate in your life. *Imagine* a new level of freedom in your life.

PRAY

Lord Jesus,
It's for freedom that You've set me free. And one day, my soul will know a joy I never imagined. Show me what freedom looks like today. Amen.

He Will Save His People from Their Sins

"And she will have a son, and you are to name him Jesus, for he will save his people from their sins."

Matthew 1:21

I blew it the other day. I woke up full of condemnation and berating thoughts—though none of those things come from the Father's heart. I then remembered mercy, forgiveness, and grace. I relished afresh the precious gift of God's Son. Our flesh pulls us toward the very things that drain the life and purpose right out of us. Sin of any kind destroys the prospect of the new things God wants to do in and through us. Jesus stepped in to interrupt sin's curse and hold on us. He came to save us from the downward cycle that would ultimately destroy us. Consider what Jesus has done. He stepped down from His throne in heaven, came to earth, endured crucifixion, took our punishment, died our death, defeated our enemy, forgave us of our sins, gave us His Holy Spirit, grafted us into the royal family, offered us heir status along with Him, and made us active participants of His promises, and He ultimately secured our eternity. We won't fully grasp all we've inherited until we see Jesus face to face. But know this today: He will save you from your sin if you allow Him to. He wants life for you, wholeness for you, freedom for you.

LEARN Read Matthew 1.

FLOURISH Ask the Lord if there's a besetting sin that He wants to deal with in your life. No condemnation. Just a holy invitation.

PRAY

Precious Lord,
Thank You for all You've done for me! Set me free to worship You with everything in me! You are Lord. Amen.

Provision, Protection, and Promotion

Then Jesus was led by the Spirit into the wilderness to be tempted there by the devil.

Matthew 4:1

The Spirit led Jesus into the wilderness to be tempted by the devil. The wilderness is where we are tested and proven time and again. We're vulnerable in the wilderness, but it's where we must learn to resist temptation and remember what's true. People in recovery often use the HALT acronym to help them stay out of trouble. If you're hungry, angry, lonely, or tired, you're at risk, so be careful. In His wilderness, Jesus was no doubt hungry, possibly tired and lonely too. And when He was most vulnerable, the enemy went after God's faithfulness in three areas that he'll go after in us as well—provision, protection, and promotion. The enemy wanted Jesus to take matters into His own hands, to force an early outcome in hopes that He'd thwart His ultimate purposes for you and me. But Jesus saw right through the enemy's scheme and prevailed even in His weakest moments. Notice too how the devil attacked and questioned Jesus' identity with every temptation. It will be the same for you. Is God faithful? Will He really come through for you? Does He really love you? Are you really the heir He says you are? These are truths we must settle in our souls long before those wilderness seasons come.

LEARN Read Matthew 4.

FLOURISH Consider the questions above and go after the truths you know your soul needs.

PRAY

Lord,
You kept the big picture in mind in Your weakest moments. Help me to do that too. I want to believe You and prevail, even when my heart is faint. Thank You, Lord. Amen.

Congratulations,
the Kingdom Is Yours!

"God blesses those who are poor and realize their need for him,
for the Kingdom of Heaven is theirs."

Matthew 5:3

Oftentimes when we come to the edges of ourselves, we tend to despair. And our enemy wants it that way. When we notice our limits in our capacity to love another, or a limit to our patience, or a limit in our heart for faith, we must know, we have a place to go with those limits. Jesus says that blessed—most happy and to be envied—are those who finally grasp that they'll never be enough in themselves. Because now, finally, they can step forward and inherit more of the kingdom. We come to Christ for the first time through the low door of humility. We admit our need for a Savior. We grow in much the same way. If the enemy can't get you to strive in your own strength, he'll try and get you to despair over your lack of it. Either way, he wants you to keep your focus on yourself. But the day you come to the edges of yourself, manage a smile, look up, and wiggle your toes in the fresh grass of kingdom territory, you'll never again despair over your limits. You'll see yourself as blessed beyond measure. For every limit, God offers lavish grace and an endless landscape of kingdom territory just waiting to be apprehended.

LEARN   Read Matthew 5:1–16.

FLOURISH   Identify a limit that most troubles you. Now smile, look up, and apprehend God's limitless grace and provision just waiting for you!

PRAY

Father,
    I open my arms, put a smile on my face, and ask for more of You! Increase my capacity for all that You are. I am blessed beyond measure. Amen.

Send It On Ahead

Store your treasures in heaven, where moths and rust cannot destroy, and thieves do not break in and steal. Wherever your treasure is, there the desires of your heart will also be.

Matthew 6:20–21

God wants us to live with the end in mind. He's set eternity in our hearts. How we live here deeply impacts how we'll live there, when we're forever with Him. How we steward our time, treasure, and talents impacts what kind of stewardship awaits us on the other side. And when it comes to our desires, Jesus reminds us that they *start* with what we treasure. Whatever we hold closest to our hearts fuels our daily desires. Hold heaven close. Treasure Jesus most. Storing up treasures in heaven means to live like His promises are true, to remember what He values, and to tend to His concerns on the earth today. We lose our reward when we live out of our insecurities or when we misuse our time, treasure, and talents to prove something Jesus has already proven and paid for. But when we—out of loving response for all God has done—give a cup of water, offer a kind word, give a gift, forgive an enemy, move forward in faith, or pray a bold prayer, heaven takes note and Jesus rewards. This earth will pass away. Sin, self-ambition, and pride in our accomplishments will all pass away too. Whatever you do for Jesus will last.

LEARN Read Matthew 6.

FLOURISH Jesus instructed you to store up treasures in heaven. No one can do that for you. Think about eternity today. Live accordingly.

PRAY

Father,
Help me to live more for the next life than this one. Life on earth is short; eternity is long. Awaken the reality of eternity within me. Amen.

The Power of Persistence

"Keep on asking, and you will receive what you ask for. Keep on seeking, and you will find. Keep on knocking, and the door will be opened to you. For everyone who asks, receives. Everyone who seeks, finds. And to everyone who knocks, the door will be opened."

Matthew 7:7–8

I first read this passage as a new believer and took it literally—until more seasoned believers cautioned me with all sorts of qualifiers. Eventually, I returned to my original persistence. We don't dictate to God. And He's not a means to an end. He's the end as well as the beginning. However, Jesus himself charged us in this passage to persist and keep persisting. Why? Because we give up too soon. Our dreams are too small. And we often don't want to pay the price. Our hope isn't in an outcome—it's in Jesus, who invites us to persist in faith and to believe for the impossible. Life's twists and turns have left me breathless at times, but my persistence has changed me. I've either seen miraculous breakthroughs around me, or I've experienced personal breakthroughs within me. God knows what He's doing when He invites us to run hard after Him. It's interesting too that Jesus inserted this invitation amidst His caution around our tendency to judge others. What if we sought God for wisdom and perspective on those we're tempted to judge with the same passion we seek Him for His blessings in our lives?

LEARN Read Matthew 7.

FLOURISH Consider how God might be asking you to persist in prayer. Engage with Him today.

PRAY

Lord,
   Stir up a passion in my soul. Help me to persist in prayer in a way that honors You and changes me! Amen.

Rest for the Weary, and a Burden That's Light

Then Jesus said, "Come to me, all of you who are weary and carry heavy burdens, and I will give you rest. . . . For my yoke is easy to bear, and the burden I give you is light."

Matthew 11:28–30

*I*magine the Pharisees' dismay when Jesus confronted them and debunked the religious traditions and manmade laws that exhausted people and left them worn out with nothing to show for it. Jesus has incredible compassion for the weary soul. And He'll never ask us to grind our gears to the point of exhaustion. That's not to say we won't experience seasons of hard work, long hours, and exhausting opposition. But always, amidst such times, God offers provisions of grace, exit ramps for rest, and His shoulders to help carry the weight of our burden. No matter if you're exhausted because you've committed to more than God asked of you, or if you're in a battle through no fault of your own, bring your weary self to Jesus. *Find rest for your soul.* If the weight of your burden is more than you can bear, ask Him to hold it for you. He'll do the heavy lifting. It's not only possible to experience replenishment right in the midst of these trying seasons, *it's essential.* Take Jesus up on His offer to fill you back up again. Your need for rest is natural. God's provision for you is *super*natural.

LEARN Read Matthew 11.

FLOURISH Unplug and take some time to rest in God's presence. Give your burdens to Him. Ask for more of His empowering grace.

PRAY

> *Dear Jesus,*
> *Help me find rest in You. Here's the burden of my heart. Will You carry it for me? Flood my heart with peace and rest today. Amen.*

A Great Separation Awaits Us

"But when the Son of Man comes in his glory, and all the angels with him, then he will sit upon his glorious throne. All the nations will be gathered in his presence, and he will separate the people as a shepherd separates the sheep from the goats. He will place the sheep at his right hand and the goats at his left."

Matthew 25:31–33

What a sobering passage, no? Author John Burke shared this on my radio show: "Earth is like a compressed time capsule—tastes of heaven and tastes of hell. But one day, the two shall separate." For those who trust Christ for salvation, life on earth is as bad as it gets. A day is coming when we'll worship without distraction, serve without opposition, and live without that constant, nagging sense of not-enough-ness. For those who've rejected Jesus' precious gift of grace, life on earth is as good as it gets. Sorrow and terror will be their only friends. Scripture says that all of creation groans for the day when God reveals who His children really are.* There are plenty of posers—those acting the part. But God knows which souls belong to Him. May the reality of that important day fuel you to care about those who are lost. May God open your mouth and anoint your words to share the Good News with those who are headed for an eternity without Him.

LEARN Read Matthew 25.

FLOURISH Ponder that inevitable day of separation. Who comes to mind? Pray for them. Share the gospel.

PRAY

Lord,
Forgive me for being so wrapped up in my daily affairs that I forget about the day to come. Help me to live ready and to help others live ready too. Amen.

*See Romans 8:19.

True Story

The Roman officer and the other soldiers at the crucifixion were terrified by the earthquake and all that had happened. They said, "This man truly was the Son of God!"

Matthew 27:54

*J*esus was content to be misunderstood. He was on a mission to save all who would believe in Him. The King of Kings humbled himself so low as to die a criminal's death on the cross. He endured abhorrent dishonor and disrespect. He was mocked by fools and killed by religious leaders. He was abandoned by His friends and felt forsaken by His Father. At any moment He could have called the whole thing off and thousands of angels would have come to His aid. But He endured it all—all for love. Once He gave up His Spirit, the thick veil tore from the top to the bottom. The earth quaked. The sky turned black. The dead rose. It took all of these earthly phenomena for the guards and soldiers to finally declare, *"Truly, this was the Son of God."* John Eldredge said this on my show: "One day, your story will be told correctly." Eventually the truth will win. We waste so much precious energy and lose valuable perspective when we try to manage others' opinions of us. What if we just stayed on mission? What if we entrusted our story to the One who knows the whole truth? Like Jesus, we would become a force to reckon with.

LEARN Read Matthew 27–28.

FLOURISH Put a stop to *any* thoughts about what others might think about you. Renew your mind with thoughts of God's fierce love for you.

PRAY

Lord,
Help me to stay on mission. Give me fierce faith and courageous conviction. Just like You. Amen.

The Wonder of Good Soil

"Listen! A farmer went out to plant some seed."

Mark 4:3

*J*esus talked about four kinds of soil (heart conditions): not guarded; not grounded; not given to the things of God; and nurtured soil that produces thirty, sixty, and even one hundred times what was planted. These are metaphors for the condition of our heart. The first soil speaks of the person who lives in proximity to the Word but doesn't see its value. They may attend church or watch online, but it's really a side note in their lives. The second soil speaks of the person who values the Word, but only when it suits them. When life gets hard, they look for other solutions and forget what they already know. The third soil speaks of the person whose heart is divided and conquered. They're pulled in several directions between competing desires and worries about how to manage it all. But they love their faith too. It's just not their highest priority. The fourth soil speaks of the person who understands and embraces the wonder of the seed that's planted in good soil. They've experienced enough divine multiplication in their lives to see the value of tending their soil and guarding their heart. They treasure the Word, they love new growth, they pull the weeds, and they are continually receptive to the living, active Word of God. Theirs is a full life that nourishes many. Jesus wants this for all of us.

LEARN Read Mark 4:1–25.

FLOURISH Tend to the soil of your heart. Pay attention to and deal with anything that would disrupt your peace, flourishing, and hope.

PRAY

Lord,
   I want my heart to be healthy soil that nurtures and nourishes the Word You've planted in me. May what You've planted in me multiply one hundredfold. Amen.

Peace and Authority

When Jesus woke up, he rebuked the wind and said to the waves, "Silence! Be still!" Suddenly the wind stopped, and there was a great calm.

Mark 4:39

I once followed Jesus right into a storm. I stepped out in faith thinking Jesus was about to take me to a place of peace and rest, when in fact, He led me right into a storm because He had a few things to teach me. Jesus did the same for the disciples. He knew that once they got into the boat and sailed for a while, these seasoned fishermen would encounter such fierce winds and overpowering waves that they'd fear for their lives. Did Jesus brace for impact? No. He fell asleep! The disciples actually had to wake Him up (this was no light nap). Jesus got up and rebuked the wind and the waves. He called for peace and stillness. The disciples watched in awe. While the storm raged, they questioned Him, "Lord, don't You care?" Once He spoke peace over the storm, He questioned them, "Where's your faith?" Given the ministry opportunities that awaited the disciples on the other side of the lake, they needed to learn how to access peace and rest when chaos swirled around them. We do too. Don't wait for the storm to learn this lesson. Cultivate a heart of peace and rest today. Stand in your authority today. And when the storm hits, you'll be able to stand strong. God is always preparing you for your next phase of the journey.

LEARN Read Mark 4:35–41.

FLOURISH Actively cultivate a heart of both peaceful rest and bold authority.

PRAY

Lord,
I marvel at Your ways. Grant me a peaceful heart that rests in You and help me to stand in the authority You've entrusted to me! Amen.

Optimistic Resilience

She replied, "That's true, Lord, but even the dogs under the table are allowed to eat the scraps from the children's plates."

Mark 7:28

*T*he Jewish people once considered Gentiles scavengers. Dogs. And not the cuddly, house-pet kind. One day a Syrian-Phoenician woman approached Jesus, fell at His feet, and begged Him to deliver her little girl who was possessed by a demon. At first it seemed as though Jesus refused to help her and insulted her in the process. I used to struggle with Jesus' response to this situation until I looked a little deeper into it. John Eldredge once shared on my show, "Picture a glint in Jesus' eye as He spoke to her. He knew she was up for this banter. He was trying to teach the disciples a lesson." The study note in my Bible says it this way: "On the surface, Jesus' words may seem harsh and unsympathetic, but the woman recognized them as a wide-open door to God's throne. Jesus did not use the negative term for 'dogs' that referred to scavengers; instead, He used the term for a household pet. The woman took the cue and added to his analogy of pets under a family dining table. Her attitude was expectant and hopeful, not prickly and hypersensitive. . . . We could learn from this woman's singular purpose and optimistic resilience. Jesus really does want to meet our needs. When we pray, we're talking to a friend."*

LEARN Read Mark 7.

FLOURISH Determine not to take things personally even if they're intended that way. And pray earnestly with joy and optimistic resilience.

PRAY

Lord,
I desire more faith! More confidence. More resilience. Do a miraculous work in me! Amen.

*Life Application Study Bible, 2124–25.

Practicing the Art of Remembering

> "'You have eyes—can't you see? You have ears—can't you hear?' Don't you remember anything at all?"
>
> Mark 8:18

Our brains hold on to negative experiences more readily than they do the positive ones. We remember fear, trauma, pain, and betrayal because we feel it all the way down to our bones. But positive memories can actually play a part in healing our hearts, and redemptive memories remind us of God's faithfulness (and that we actually have a history with Him). Imagine the toll on our souls when we carry painful memories with us wherever we go. We end up living in continual reaction to our painful present. Jesus wants us to travel light. He wants to redeem our perspective. He was trying to warn the disciples about the influence of ungodly leaders. But the disciples were still stuck on the small issue of who forgot the bread, and they were arguing about it. They'd completely forgotten about His ability to multiply the loaves! That's the other thing. We'll never see ourselves in the bigger story until we allow God to change our most repetitive thoughts. Determine to practice the art of remembering a few minutes every day. It'll open your ears and eyes to the presence of God in your midst. You have a history with God. You have a future with Him too. And He's very much at work in your present moment.

LEARN Read Mark 8.

FLOURISH Practice remembering your favorite moments in life—times when you laughed, felt loved, and sensed God's nearness. It'll do wonders for you.

PRAY

Lord,
Bring truth to my most painful memories. Help me to remember that which glorifies You and heals me. Amen.

People Just Like Us

John said to Jesus, "Teacher, we saw someone using your name to cast out demons, but we told him to stop because he wasn't in our group."

Mark 9:38

I had a friend whose little ones loved to play at her feet. One day her son wrapped his arms around her leg and said, "I love my mommy." My friend smiled until her son gripped her leg tighter, looked at his sister, and declared, "*My* mommy!" To which her daughter replied, "*I* love my mommy. She's *my* mommy!" They went back and forth until they were in an all-out brawl. My friend went from delight to despair in a matter of moments. This frequently happens within the church. Different denominations claim to have cornered the market on truth, or a special relationship with God and His Word. But Scripture tells us that there are many tribes and tongues that will gather together for the Marriage Supper of the Lamb. We must not confuse a narrow mind with the narrow way. Oswald Chambers once wrote, "Let God be as original with others as He is with you." My Bible study note reads, "(Jesus') followers will not all resemble each other or belong to the same groups. . . . People don't have to be just like us to be following Jesus with us."* Jesus promised we'd *all* be tested to prove our faith. He asked us to live at peace with one another.

LEARN Read Mark 9.

FLOURISH Read a blog or a book from a Christian who travels outside your lane.

PRAY

Lord,
   Give me a grander picture of what Your kingdom looks like! Forgive my narrow-minded insistence that everyone walk and talk like me! Amen.

*Life Application Study Bible, 2132.

Let God Direct the Conversation

They were now on the way up to Jerusalem, and Jesus was walking ahead of them. The disciples were filled with awe, and the people following behind were overwhelmed with fear. Taking the twelve disciples aside, Jesus once more began to describe everything that was about to happen to him.

Mark 10:32

The disciples were filled with awe. The people were filled with fear. Jesus wanted His followers prepared. He opened His mouth and led with this important word: *Listen*. But apparently they weren't listening. Jesus went on to describe the horrific events that awaited Him in Jerusalem, down to the details that He'd be mocked, spit upon, flogged, whipped, and then killed. Why didn't this jarring news suddenly stop them in their tracks? Somehow, James's and John's minds had wandered elsewhere. They were thinking about status and position. Jesus spoke about suffering. They wanted to talk about promotion. We must discern the conversation God wants to have with us. He always loves us—always wants what's best for us. So we must *listen* when He cautions, corrects, or redirects. He wanted the disciples prepared so that when the unthinkable happened, they'd remember the rest of the story—that He would rise again. Amazingly, God promoted the disciples to places of honor that they could never imagine during their time on earth. He answered their prayer, and then some. But the prize never comes without the process of preparation. Don't get ahead of God. He's always watching out for you.

LEARN ▶ Read Mark 10.

FLOURISH ▶ Spend some quiet time listening for God's voice. Open His Word. Let Him speak.

PRAY ▶

Father,
You are always watching out for me. Help me to discern the conversation You want to have with me today. Amen.

People Used to Say . . .

"What's more, your relative Elizabeth has become pregnant in her old age! People used to say she was barren, but she has conceived a son and is now in her sixth month. For the word of God will never fail."

Luke 1:36–37

*W*hat disparaging things have people said about you? What berating things have you said about yourself? What if God moved in such a way that those things were *no longer true*? And what if the lies no longer felt true? Can you picture it? There was such shame attached to barrenness in Elizabeth's day. But as He often does, God called Elizabeth to wait longer than most to see her dream fulfilled, because the answer to her prayers served a greater purpose than she could imagine. God is always redeeming stories. People used to say I was insecure. That's no longer the case. People used to say that I was weak and fragile. That's no longer true. I used to berate myself because my short-term memory was messed up from Lyme disease. That's not an issue for me any longer. What about you? Do you believe God can change the narrative of your story? Are you remaining hopeful and expectant? People will say what they say and think what they think. But may their limited perspectives have zero impact on your faith. For *nothing* is impossible with God.

LEARN Read Luke 1.

FLOURISH Identify a few areas in your life you want God to redeem. Add some faith to your prayers. And expectancy too.

PRAY

Lord,
I refuse to be bound by my past limitations or by others' perspectives of me. You are the God who saves, redeems, and restores. Change my story for Your glory. Amen.

The Power
of the Good News

"The Spirit of the Lord is upon me,
    for he has anointed me to bring Good News to the poor.
He has sent me to proclaim that captives will be released,
    that the blind will see,
that the oppressed will be set free. . . ."

Luke 4:18

*J*esus first stepped on to the ministry stage when He was baptized in the Jordan River. When He came up out of the water, the Holy Spirit descended upon Him like a dove. The heavens opened and His Father declared His affection for Him. Then Jesus, full of the Holy Spirit, went into the wilderness to be tempted and tested by the devil. He emerged from that spiritual battle victorious and, in the power of the Holy Spirit, went to the synagogue, stood up, and read a prophecy from Isaiah that was being fulfilled before their very eyes. He proclaimed Good News to the poor, freedom for captives, and sight to the blind. *He is the Good News.* Love came down to rescue us! The gospel of Jesus Christ is more than a four-step prayer to secure our eternity. It's the very power and the presence of God to radically change a life—from hell-bent to heaven destined; from lost to found; from blind to sighted; from captive to totally, completely free. As the Father sent Jesus, and with the same power, so He also sends you.

LEARN Read Luke 4.

FLOURISH Ponder the power the gospel has to radically save a life. Ask God to send you to those who are desperate for this good news.

PRAY

Father,
*   Here am I; send me! Lead me to those who would love You if they knew You. Open their eyes, prepare their hearts, and speak mightily through me. Set them free, Lord. Amen.*

When Increase Comes

And this time their nets were so full of fish they began to tear!

Luke 5:6

*W*hen Jesus had finished speaking from their fishing boat, He instructed the disciples to go out to the deep and let down their nets to catch some fish. Simon replied, "We worked hard all last night and didn't catch a thing, but if you say so, I'll try again." This time their nets were so full they began to tear. They needed help to bring in all of the fish. The abundant catch almost sunk their boat! When Simon Peter witnessed the Lord's great power, he also realized his own sinful state and begged Jesus to leave his presence. When the Lord takes you deeper, several things happen almost at once. The increase that you prayed for will likely stretch you beyond your capacity. Things may pull apart at the seams. You may feel like you're sinking. And in the midst of increase, growth, and the stress that goes along with it all, you'll be acutely aware of your own humanity and sinfulness. The enemy will spew in your ear that you're in over your head. Do not fear these growing pains. Instead, grow in grace. Grow your team. And grow in your dependence on Jesus. You're made for this.

LEARN ▶ Read Luke 5.

FLOURISH ▶ If you long for increase, ask for it. If you're managing much now, don't lose perspective. He's only answering your prayers.

PRAY ▶

Lord,
Lead me to the deep places with You! Increase Your work in and through me. Multiply my offering and give me grace to manage all You've entrusted to me. Amen.

Judging Others

> "Do not judge others, and you will not be judged. Do not condemn others, or it will all come back against you. Forgive others, and you will be forgiven. Give, and you will receive. Your gift will return to you in full—pressed down, shaken together to make room for more. . . ."
>
> Luke 6:37–38

*I*f you've ever been on the receiving end of someone's critical assessments, you know how painful it is. We live in a ready-*shoot*-aim culture, where people are quick to believe the worst, not the best. People are pronounced guilty even if they're proven innocent. We *must not* get caught up in the groupthink so prevalent in our day. Jesus wants His followers to live and love a different way. Though Scripture calls us to rightly discern good from evil, right from wrong, and life from death, the word *judge* in this passage refers to our tendency to separate, pick apart, and put ourselves above another. And the word *condemn* is to determine a verdict against someone else. Honestly, our opinions don't matter as much as we think they do. Unless we're directly involved and impacted by someone, we're best to hold our thoughts and pray about what we think we see. In this passage, I love how Jesus turned on a dime from judgment to generosity. When we're gracious, generous, and forgiving like our Savior, we will walk in a fullness that the world desperately needs.

LEARN Read Luke 6.

FLOURISH Pray earnestly for the person you're most tempted to judge. It'll bless God's heart and change your perspective.

PRAY

Lord,

Give me eyes to see others the way You do. Help me love them and pray for them even when I don't know the whole story. You do. And that's enough. Amen.

Today Might Be the Day

"Daughter," he said to her, "your faith has made you well. Go in peace."
Luke 8:48

I wish I knew her name. We know her as the woman with the issue of blood. Her story moves me to tears and inspires me to courage. She hemorrhaged for twelve years. If she lived in our day, she would have at least received compassion. She not only endured chronic illness, body odor, fatigue, and financial brokenness, but she was also painfully shunned by society. She had to yell, "Unclean!" when others were nearby so that no one would defile themselves by touching her. Imagine. How does a person keep their hope alive under such circumstances? I'm sure she had many days of discouragement and defeat. But one day, she heard Jesus was in town. And that day, she tossed aside her labels and social stigmas. She pressed through the crowd with persistence and faith. The throng of people pressed up against her and jostled her. But then she grabbed a fistful of Jesus' robe and everything changed. Sheer power surged down her arm, throughout her body, and no doubt made her cheeks flush. She was instantly healed. Jesus stopped in His tracks to find out who had touched Him with that kind of faith. He wanted her to know that she hadn't taken healing from Him. He'd freely given it to her. Don't give up hope. Keep pressing in. Today might be the day.

LEARN Read Luke 8.

FLOURISH Tell your soul, "My breakthrough is on its way. Today might be the day."

PRAY

Lord,
Give me faith and persistence to lay hold of Your promise. Break through for me. My soul waits for You. Amen.

Authority and Awe

"Look, I have given you authority over all the power of the enemy, and you can walk among snakes and scorpions and crush them. Nothing will injure you."

Luke 10:19

Years ago as a young mom, I stood in my living room one day, overwhelmed by fear and anxiety. Lyme disease raged in my body. Neurological symptoms surged in my face, head, and down my arms. Bill collectors called every day about our medical debt; we were in over our head. I thought the whole battle might swallow me whole. There, in that moment, the Lord's voice thundered in my soul, "Susie, are you a believer simply because you've secured your eternity? Or do you actually *believe* this stuff? When are you going to shift your weight off your fears and on to my promises? Fear and faith are opposing forces. You have to turn your back on one to behold the other. I've given you authority. Now's your time to *take authority*." That was a game-changing moment for me. The disciples marveled that the demons obeyed them. Jesus wanted them to walk in their authority but with humility. The devil's pride and lust for power were his downfall. Jesus said, "Don't marvel that the demons obey you. Marvel that your name is written in the Book of Life." Take authority. Marvel that He saved you. What a mighty God we serve!

LEARN Read Luke 10.

FLOURISH Put any enemy harassment in its place today. And marvel at the miracle of your salvation.

PRAY

Lord,
Help me to stand in authority and to stay in a place of awe. What You've entrusted to me, what You've accomplished for me, is miraculous. Help me to walk accordingly. Amen.

He Rewards Those Who Are Ready

"He may come in the middle of the night or just before dawn. But whenever he comes, he will reward the servants who are ready."

Luke 12:38

When Jesus talked about the parable of the soils, He addressed distraction, immaturity, and divided affections. Here He similarly addresses how the worries of this life pull us away from the kingdom life and power to which our souls are heir. Jesus wants us to remove every distraction, to shut every door that offers the enemy access, and to fan the flame within us so we will not only discern the times, we'll be ready for His return. That posture of holy readiness means so much to God that He promises to *greatly reward* anyone who lives this way. Jesus' heart will be so overwhelmed by your faith that He will put on an apron, serve you at a banqueting table, and then pull up a chair and share a meal with you! Imagine it. If holy readiness blesses Jesus' heart that much, don't you think it should occupy our hearts as much? Though Jesus said it's unwise to try and guess the date of His return, it is wise to discern the times and seasons. Moments before Christ's return, some—including Christians—will be partying, indulging, and shrugging their shoulders at everything that matters to God. But may *you* live ready.

LEARN Read Luke 12.

FLOURISH Deal with your worries. Shut down any access you've given the enemy. Imagine sharing a celebratory meal with your friend Jesus.

PRAY

Jesus,
  You deserve my highest praise and my holiest life! I can't wait to see You face to face. Stir up a passion in my soul. Help me to cultivate a life of holy readiness. Amen.

Communion

> He took some bread and gave thanks to God for it. Then he broke it in pieces
> and gave it to the disciples, saying, "This is my body, which is given for you.
> Do this in remembrance of me."
>
> Luke 22:19

*T*hough His betrayal was *in motion*, Jesus served *communion*. Jesus knew that in a few short hours He would face rejection, torture, and execution. Before His followers had a chance to be traumatized by the devil's evil schemes, Jesus, in so many words, said to them, "*Remember this. Remember us. The enemy hasn't taken my life. I have freely given it. Though your badness once disqualified you, the Father's goodness has saved you. This is the new covenant. Though I am well aware of what lies ahead of me on that cross, my deepest desire beforehand is to be with you, break bread with you, and remind you that my promises are true. Though schemes are being devised behind my back, I want you, my beloved ones, to see my face.*" How many times do you suppose the disciples replayed that night in their minds? Did Jesus' actions impact them in greater measures as they grew in their faith over the years?* When we come to the table, we honor the memory of Christ's sacrifice. We embrace the power of His transforming love. And we believe in His ability to heal, restore, and redeem every aspect of our lives.

LEARN Read Luke 22.

FLOURISH The next time you have communion, slow down, be still, and ponder Jesus' heart for all who call Him Lord.

PRAY

Lord,
You were broken that I might be whole. Bring healing and redemption to me and through me. Amen.

*Adapted from Susie's book *The Uncommon Woman* (Chicago: Moody Publishers, 2008), 134–135.

The Prayer of Salvation

And Jesus replied, "I assure you, today you will be with me in paradise."

Luke 23:43

One day on my radio show, a man called in to ask about eternity. His voice quaked as he searched for answers. I had only a few minutes left of my show before I needed to hop on another channel to co-host a different show. I didn't want to miss an opportunity to pray with the man, but I didn't want to put him on the spot either. I whispered a prayer for wisdom. My clock counted down with two minutes to spare. I asked, "Sir, would you like to follow Jesus and trust Him with your eternity?" He immediately said yes. I led him in prayer of confession, repentance, trust, and declaration that Jesus is Lord. It was beautiful. Listeners emailed afterward and said they had to pull to the side of the road because they had too many tears in their eyes to drive. We stood in awe of God's faithfulness. Then I received a jarring email from an angry listener telling me they were pulling their funding because I hadn't prayed the "Romans Road" prayer with the individual. She added a few exclamation points to make sure I felt her angst. Plenty have prayed the "right" prayer with the wrong heart. Jesus saved the thief on the cross because of a simple yet heartfelt prayer. Trusting in Jesus is so much more about a surrendered heart than it is about the perfect words. Thank You, Jesus.

LEARN Read Luke 23.

FLOURISH God always cares more about the heart than He does the form. Consider your heart condition today. Trust Jesus.

PRAY

Lord,
Turn the hearts of the multitudes toward You! Use me to show them the way. Amen.

Light Always Wins over Darkness

The light shines in the darkness,
and the darkness can never extinguish it.
John 1:5

*D*r. Jim Wilder is a Christian counselor and a neuropsychological expert. One day during an interview I asked him, "If someone battles fear, do you tell them to face it head on?" He gently said, "No. Not at all. Imagine a child afraid of the dark. A loving father would pick up his little one, embrace him, and assure him of his father's love. Once the child is at home in his father's love, together, they walk into the dark room and turn on the light. Everything starts and ends with the Father's love. From there, you start to heal."* A thick darkness covers the earth, and it's only getting darker. But the glory of the Lord shines upon us.† We don't have to fear the darkness, and we won't, as long as we're at home in the Father's love. God's love heals the heart and will heal the world. The more you allow His love to impact you, the brighter your light will shine. Jesus gives life to everything and everyone. May His life—mightily at work within you—heal your soul, make you whole, and shine brightly through you so the world will know Him too.

LEARN Read John 1.

FLOURISH Consider the aspects of society that frighten you. Take some time in God's presence and reflect on God's fatherly love. Stay there until your heart is at rest once again.

PRAY

Lord,
The more I understand Your love, the less I fear the darkness. I am with You and You are with me. I have everything I need. Amen.

*My paraphrase of Dr. Wilder's answer.
†See Isaiah 60:2.

You Will *See* the Kingdom

Jesus replied, "I tell you the truth, unless you are born again, you cannot see the Kingdom of God."

John 3:3

*N*icodemus met Jesus in the dark of night most likely to avoid the suspicion of his colleagues, who were continually antagonistic toward Jesus. And he sincerely wanted answers. He'd heard about Jesus' many miracles. Jesus told Nicodemus that unless he was willing to be born again, he wouldn't *see* the kingdom of God. We walk by faith, not by sight. We come to Jesus by faith, but then He opens our eyes to a spiritual dimension, and we begin to really see. The word *see* in the passage above translates this way: to perceive, experience, or discern. In other words, those of us who *have* been born again get to *see*, *perceive*, and *experience* the kingdom of God! When you're born again, God's Spirit takes up residence in your soul. Suddenly your tastes change. Your values are rearranged and your spiritual eyes open up. You begin to see things differently. You see status as little more than a house of cards. You see humility as a sign of high-ranking honor. You see and embrace as treasured souls that bear the image of God those the world overlooks. In a world of overindulgence and selfish hoarding, you experience the outrageous joy of radical generosity. You discern the importance of faithfulness over achievement and true and lasting joy over fleeting sinful pleasure. Once you've been born again, you're a part of a living, active, powerful kingdom.

LEARN Read John 3.

FLOURISH Ask God to show you the sacred amidst the familiar. May your eyes open to the kingdom all around you.

PRAY

> *Father,*
> *Open my eyes to see Your kingdom. I want more of You. Amen.*

Saving Face
or Saving Grace

"Come and see a man who told me everything I ever did! Could he possibly be the Messiah?"

John 4:29

She went to the well in the midday to draw water, most likely to avoid the gossip and the glares from the other women. Jesus, tired from a long walk, sat down by the well. He asked for a drink of water. This woman had three strikes against her. She was a Samaritan (considered an inferior race), a woman (considered an inferior gender), and known to be living in sin. No "respectable" Jew would ever consider talking to someone in public under even one of those conditions. But Jesus will cross every social barrier to get to us. He is full of grace and truth. He treated her with honor and respect, but He also addressed the sin that He knew would destroy her. She soon realized her path to freedom. She left her water jar and ran back to face the people she'd worked so hard to avoid. The townspeople got one look at this woman and realized that their opinions held no more sway over her. Saving face had been swallowed up by saving grace. Because one woman was willing to be known as someone who needed saving, nearly a whole town decided to follow Jesus. Imagine the impact in the world today if more of God's people dropped the façade and truly celebrated what Jesus saved them from.

LEARN   Read John 4.

FLOURISH   Note those places in your life where you try too hard to present well. How might God's grace heal you there?

PRAY

Jesus,
    Help me to be honest and real about my need for Your everyday grace.
May people be drawn to You because of the way You saved me. Amen.

Jesus' Tough Love

When Jesus saw him and knew he had been ill for a long time, he asked him,
"Would you like to get well?"

John 5:6

*J*esus had such compassion for the hurting and the broken. And He was tough on the religious leaders who made impossible demands of the weak yet refused to lift a finger to help them. Jesus had spine and heart. This story in John chapter five takes an interesting turn. Jesus approached a man who'd been stuck on a mat for thirty-eight years. Jesus spoke to the heart of the matter, as He always did. Follow Him through the gospels and you'll marvel at how He addresses the heart issue with every encounter. In this instance, He asks the man, "Do you *want* to get well?" When you suffer a long time, you get used to it, identify with it, and lose any sense of hope or expectancy. The first three words out of the man's mouth were "I can't, sir." Sometimes Jesus heals instantly. But some of us need a healing journey more than an instantaneous miracle. Jesus wanted this man to participate in his own healing process, so He told him to stand up, pick up his mat, and walk. Later on, when he saw the man again, Jesus added, "Now you are well. Stop sinning, or something worse may happen to you." This was a rare instance where Jesus was tough on the sufferer. Sometimes we need comfort. Other times correction.

LEARN Read John 5.

FLOURISH Have you settled for something that Jesus wants you to address? Ask Him to speak to you.

PRAY

Lord,
Search my heart. Bring comfort to my soul and correction to my heart where I need it. Thank You for loving me as You do. Amen.

Making God in Our Image

Jesus told them, "If God were your Father, you would love me, because I have come to you from God. I am not here on my own, but he sent me."

John 8:42

*I*n every generation, there's a remnant that fears God and honors His Name. Unfortunately, the Pharisees had fallen in love with their power, they believed their own press, and they used their position to manipulate systems and exploit the vulnerable. They'd fallen so far from the heart of God that they didn't recognize Him when He came to earth. Everything they accused Jesus of, they themselves were guilty of. Jesus finally replied to them, "If God were your Father, you would love Me." The same is true today. When we manipulate our faith to match our lives, when we pick and choose what we want to be true about God, we will find the Jesus of the Bible hard to understand, and even offensive at times. But when we discern God's heart for righteousness, holiness, redemption, and deliverance, we will see Jesus as the much-needed Savior of the world. All wisdom comes from above. All Truth originates from the Holy One. He's the only uncreated One. Think about it: All other religions are counterfeit. All other paths to God actually lead away from Him. Jesus is the Way, the Truth, and the Life. Once we've seen Him for who He is, we've seen God for who He is.

LEARN Read John 8.

FLOURISH Read the gospels back to back. Ask God for a fresh revelation of himself as you read.

PRAY

Jesus,
You and the Father are one. Help me to see and know You as You are—
not as I think You should be. I will follow Your terms, not mine. Amen.

A More-Than-Enough Life

"The thief does not come except to steal, and to kill, and to destroy. I have come that they may have life, and that they may have it more abundantly."

John 10:10 NKJV

*W*e have to contend for some of the things God has promised us. Our enemy searches and looks for every opportunity to disrupt our lives, destroy our influence, and kill any hint of new life that springs up within us. Thankfully, we can know that every time the devil makes a move, God already has a plan. Jesus came not only to destroy the devil's influence in your life, but also to give you life—*abundant* life, which translates this way: "Superabundance, excessive, overflowing, surplus, over and above, more than enough, profuse, extraordinary, above the ordinary, more than sufficient."* How many of us can honestly say that we live in the overflow and surplus of God's blessings for us? This is not a prosperity gospel message. It's not even about material blessings, which come and go. The truly abundant life is a life healed and whole; restored and redeemed; free and secure; full of faith, hope, and love. Those are the things the devil wants to destroy. But if we allow enemy influence more than we contend for eternal blessings, we'll miss the fullness Jesus offers here. The happiest people on the planet are those who wholeheartedly follow Jesus and live like His promises are true.

LEARN Read John 10.

FLOURISH Ask God for a vision of what a spilling-over, flourishing life might look like for you.

PRAY

Jesus,
I don't want to settle for less than Your best for me! Show me what abundance looks like in my life. Amen.

*New Spirit-Filled Life Bible, 1461.

Remain in His Love

"I have loved you even as the Father has loved me. Remain in my love."

John 15:9

I've noticed that whenever my spiritual disciplines start to feel like ought-to's and should-do's (instead of get-to's), I've lost sight of God's love. When I take beautiful practices and turn them into efforts to prove my worth, I fall down every time. I lose heart too. It's the Father's love that changes us, keeps us, and renews us each day. We have an aversion to grace, and we default to performance. This takes a toll on the soul. But Jesus' victory settled all that for us. He wants us to live wholly in response to His great love for us. And though Scripture says that nothing can ever separate us from God's love,* Jesus still instructs us to *remain* in His love. What does that mean, exactly? The Word translates *remain* this way: to be held, kept continually, to continue to be present with.† Isn't that just beautiful? When Jesus tells you to remain in His love, He's inviting you to be continually present with Him; continually reminded of His affection for you and consistently aware of His righteousness through you. We lose our way when we lose sight of His love. This is Jesus' great gift to us—this invitation to be continually present with the One who loved us first and loves us most.

LEARN Read John 15.

FLOURISH Spend fifteen minutes a day pondering Jesus' deep affection for you. It will change your life.

PRAY

Jesus,
   Help me to remain continually aware of Your nearness, Your patience, and Your love. I'm held. I'm loved. I'm blessed. Thank You, Lord. Amen.

*See Romans 8:31–39.
†Strong's Interlinear Bible Search, StudyLight.org, John 15:9.

Make Us One, Lord

"I pray that they will all be one, just as you and I are one—as you are in me, Father, and I am in you. And may they be in us so that the world will believe you sent me."

John 17:21

Some of the most powerful events I've ever been involved with include multiple Bible-believing denominations working together for the sake of their community. They refused to divide along denominational, racial, or even economic lines. They *joined together* on the basis of biblical Christianity for the sake of their community. Together they prayed for businesses and families and children and the hurting and the broken. Together they served tirelessly to plan an event in order to communicate the love of a Savior who is accessible to all who would call on His name. God promises that when He sees that kind of unity He cannot help but *command a blessing.** When we identify more with our divisions than we do with our Savior's deepest desire for unity, we've lost our way. When we answer the call to walk in biblical unity, *God's power becomes tangible*. When Jesus was on His way to the cross to suffer for our sins, one of the last things He prayed was that we would be one, that the world might actually believe and embrace His reason for living, dying, and defeating sin and death. If unity matters so much to Him, shouldn't it matter as much to us?

LEARN Read John 17.

FLOURISH Reach out to someone from a different denomination and build a friendship. Learn to walk in unity.

PRAY

Jesus,
Forgive us for so easily dismissing Your heart's desire. Start with me, Lord. Show me what to do. My eyes are on You. Amen.

*See Psalm 133:3.

Harnessed Power

As Jesus said, "I am he," they all drew back and fell to the ground!

John 18:6

*J*esus gathered with His disciples in an olive grove, a place where He'd be pressed, and His will surrendered, for our sakes. The guards arrived with blazing torches and weapons at the ready. Jesus knew precisely why they'd come, so He stepped forward to meet them. Nobody took His life. He freely gave it. Imagine the scene in the heavenly realm: The angels held their breath with their swords drawn, watched every move, waited for the slightest signal from the King they loved so much. Yet He never exerted His will. He surrendered it. He asked the guards who they were looking for. They replied, "Jesus the Nazarene." As soon as He uttered the words "I am He," the power of the Godhead burst forth from Him and knocked the soldiers off their feet! It's estimated that as many as six hundred soldiers were on the scene that night to arrest Jesus. Imagine Him stepping forth in surrender and then opening His mouth in power. We in our finite minds cannot fathom what we've gained because we have Jesus, but this we know: He is our King. And there is *none* like Him.

LEARN Read John 18.

FLOURISH Ponder the scene in the garden. Picture Jesus' temperament. Imagine the force that knocked six hundred soldiers to the ground. Write out a prayer of thanksgiving.

PRAY

Jesus,

There is no one like You. Since I have You, I have everything. I want to know You more. I want to reflect Your humility, pray from a place of intimacy, and walk in Your power. Lead me onward, Lord. Amen.

Power, Not Preference

He replied, "The Father alone has the authority to set those dates and times, and they are not for you to know. But you will receive power when the Holy Spirit comes upon you. And you will be my witnesses, telling people about me everywhere—in Jerusalem, throughout Judea, in Samaria, and to the ends of the earth."

Acts 1:7–8

*D*uring the forty days after His crucifixion, Jesus appeared to His disciples from time to time to prove that He was alive and to talk with them about the kingdom of God. The disciples asked, "Has the time come for You to free Israel and restore our kingdom?" A fair question considering they'd walked through the trauma of watching their Savior's execution. They experienced the elation of seeing Him resurrected. Wouldn't the obvious next step be to overthrow Rome and liberate the Israelites? But Jesus didn't give them the answer they were hoping for. If He had, you and I would not be part of the kingdom today. Jesus had a much bigger mission on His mind: salvation for those who would trust Him in every generation to come. He didn't placate to their preferences, as understandable as they were. Instead, He promised power—a power that would give sight to the blind, strength to the weary, healing to the broken, and salvation to the lost. A power that is still changing the world today. If God's not giving you what you want at the moment, perhaps His plan is bigger than you can imagine.

LEARN Read Acts 1.

FLOURISH Remind your soul today that God's story for you is always greater than you imagine.

PRAY

Lord,
Help me to think, pray, speak, and live in proportion to Your power and love. Increase my capacity for You. Amen.

Death Could Not Hold Him

"But God released him from the horrors of death and raised him back to life, for death could not keep him in its grip."

Acts 2:24

*W*hen Jesus surrendered himself to die for our sins, death grabbed Him in its clutches. The devil thought he'd won. But death could not hold Him in its grip. And since Jesus destroyed the devil's claim on us, death and destruction will not have the final say in our lives. Consider Peter. Before Jesus' resurrection, he was impetuous and inconsistent. He even denied knowing Jesus! After the resurrection, Peter became bold as a lion, consistent in faith, and powerful in speech. He spoke with such authority that when people heard him, they were cut right to the heart. Whatever weaknesses, insecurities, or inconsistences have been a reproach to you, know this: The reality of Christ's resurrection is great news for you! Since death could not hold Jesus down, nothing can hold you down. You now have a High Priest, sitting at the right hand of the Father, constantly interceding for you.* Can you picture it? Jesus sits next to the Father and continually prays for you, intervenes on your behalf, and makes a way where there is no way. What's holding you back today? It's no match for the resurrection power Christ has made available to you.

LEARN Read Acts 2.

FLOURISH Ask the Lord to show you how He's interceding for you these days. Pray along with Him.

PRAY

Lord,
I sometimes forget that You are always for me. Show me what You see and how You're praying for me. I want to live in step with You. Amen.

*See Romans 8:34.

Embrace Expectancy

But Peter said, "I don't have any silver or gold for you. But I'll give you what I have. In the name of Jesus Christ the Nazarene, get up and walk!"

Acts 3:6

A man who was lame from birth was brought to the temple gate each day *so he could beg*. When Peter and John entered the temple, the man did what he had done every other time: He asked for money. I imagine he kept his head down and just went through the motions of his spiel, hoping for a few coins. Peter refused to help this man remain a beggar. In his fierce, powerful way, Peter charged him, "Look at us!" Repetition makes us look down. Expectancy compels us to look up. One day on my show when I spoke with author and pastor Jeff Manion, he said, "It's one thing to stick with something for a long time. It's another thing altogether to keep your heart in it." So true. We so often settle without even realizing it. And as a result, the people around us adjust to and begin to accommodate our settled-for life. Much like the men who brought the lame man to the temple *to beg*. Peter raised the standard that day. He offered what God had entrusted to him: resurrection power. Before everyone's eyes, the man's feet and ankles were instantly *healed and strengthened*. Refuse to settle. Don't just go through the motions. Embrace expectancy. Resurrection power is available to you today.

LEARN Read Acts 3.

FLOURISH Ask God to show you where He wants your sense of expectancy to make a comeback.

PRAY

Jesus,
I don't want to settle for less than Your best for me! Raise up a new standard of faith and expectancy within me. Amen.

Unschooled and Ordinary

When they saw the courage of Peter and John and realized that they were unschooled, ordinary men, they were astonished and they took note that these men had been with Jesus.

Acts 4:13 NIV

I owe most of what I know to the school of suffering. Even so, I admire those with multiple degrees. Several times over the past few years, I've applied and been accepted to a university to further my education. Each time I prepared to return to the fray of textbooks, tests, and hours of study, I was offered a new book contract. The timing was never right for me to go back to school. Truth is, I wanted to go back to school for validation, but validation is never a good reason for a believer to do *anything*. Education is wonderful and important. But after seeking the Lord for my story, I realized He wanted me to move forward in faith, trusting that He's more than enough validation for me. Scripture says that He's given us *everything* we need for life and godliness. The *very power* that raised Jesus from the grave is alive in us. The people who watched Peter and John were astonished because they were unschooled, ordinary men whose lives were marked by an otherworldly power, boldness, and wisdom. Clearly, they'd been with Jesus. Whether you're educated or not, *there's no substitute for the power of God* that comes through intimate oneness with Jesus.

LEARN Read Acts 4.

FLOURISH Ask God if you've allowed *anything* to disqualify you from serving Him powerfully.

PRAY

Jesus,
You have a different plan for each of us. Help me to follow where You lead. When I look to anything but You, I miss the resurrection power that comes from You. You're more than enough for me. Amen.

The Danger of Facade

He brought part of the money to the apostles, claiming it was the full amount. With his wife's consent, he kept the rest.

Acts 5:2

*T*he church had begun. People, filled with the Holy Spirit, worshiped and shared meals together. The wealthy even sold their possessions so the poor would have enough to eat. There were no needy people among them. In come Ananias and Sapphira. With one foot in the kingdom and one foot out, they sold some property and *pretended* to give all of the money to the church. While others had given as freely as they'd received, these two lied about their offering. Nobody forced them to sell their property, and nobody demanded that they give a certain amount to the cause of Christ. So what were their sins? Dishonesty. Greed. And certainly trying to appear more spiritual than they actually were. When we put on a facade, we open the door to the enemy's influence in our lives. The enemy is the father of lies. Jesus is the Truth that sets us free. Whenever there's a big gap between how we act and how we truly are, it's an opportunity for the enemy to steal our joy, destroy our influence, and cause us to sin in ways we'll regret later. Scripture calls us to live up to what we've already attained.* God doesn't have unrealistic expectations of us, but He does expect us to be honest and real about where we are so we can grow from there.

LEARN Read Acts 5.

FLOURISH Be honest and real. Close any gaps. Do away with any facades. Jesus intends to redeem the real person. Not the pretend one.

PRAY

Lord,
Here I am. All of me. Change me from the inside out. Amen.

*See Philippians 3:16.

If God Has Made It Clean

> Peter told them, "You know it is against our laws for a Jewish man to enter a Gentile home like this or to associate with you. But God has shown me that I should no longer think of anyone as impure or unclean."
>
> Acts 10:28

I once walked away from a conversation I so wished I'd handled differently. A woman shared about someone's redemption story, but instead of celebrating the new things God had done, she wrinkled her nose and spoke of the sordid details from this redeemed woman's past. So many prickly barbs in a single conversation. Repeatedly, I tried to move the conversation to the positive, but to no avail. I wish I would have stopped the flow completely and reminded this precious tribe that if Jesus has chosen to forget her sins and ours, we should too. After Jesus' resurrection, the Holy Spirit empowered the disciples to turn the world upside down. He also blew to smithereens many of their preconceived ideas. One day during a time of prayer, the Lord showed Peter that the Gentiles were not unclean or inferior people. They were ones Jesus loved and came to save. Your journey and mine—with all of its twists and turns, highs and lows—is sacred, holy ground to our Father. We'd be wise to treat one another's story with the kind of love, honor, and consideration our Father has shown us.

LEARN Read Acts 10.

FLOURISH If you're hanging on to salacious parts of your story or another's that Jesus has already washed in His blood, give those to Him. Don't call something unclean that Jesus has declared clean, precious, forgiven, and free.

PRAY

Lord,
I tend to remember all of the wrong things. Purify my heart so I see every story through Your eyes. Amen.

When Prison Walls Shake

Suddenly, there was a massive earthquake, and the prison was shaken to its foundations. All the doors immediately flew open, and the chains of every prisoner fell off!

Acts 16:26

*P*aul and Silas were severely beaten and thrown into a deep dungeon, but something happened in that dark dungeon that thwarted the enemy's plans. Paul and Silas *prayed* and *worshiped*, and the other prisoners *heard them*. The earth quaked, the prison walls shook, and the chains of *every* prisoner fell off! Paul even had the opportunity to lead the jailer and his household to faith in Jesus. When life circumstances throw us into a pit and we're at the end of ourselves, the most powerful, strategic thing we can do is to pray and worship. After all, we have access to the inner throne room of the Most High God. And He inhabits (makes His home among) the praises of His dear people. People are always watching how we respond to hardship; our response to our trials has the potential to set many captives free. I remember one dark night of the soul when I felt bloodied and beat up by my battle, because God seemed silent and I felt abandoned. In the dark of my bedroom, I dropped to my knees, lifted my hands, and worshiped. I could feel the oppression lift and I knew I was gaining ground in my battle. We worship because He's worth it. And He promises to strengthen those whose hearts are turned toward Him.*

LEARN Read Acts 16.

FLOURISH No matter what season you're in, pray with persistence and worship with passion.

PRAY

Father,
You are the one true God and I worship You. Break these chains and set captives free! Amen.

*See 2 Chronicles 16:9.

Face the Facts, Yet Still Believe

And Abraham's faith did not weaken, even though, at about 100 years of age, he figured his body was as good as dead. . . . Abraham never wavered in believing God's promise. In fact, his faith grew stronger, and in this he brought glory to God.

Romans 4:19–20

I once heard a story about a woman who, when her husband served her divorce papers, held the papers up and laughed at them as an act of faith. My heart broke for this dear woman. Though it should go without saying, faith isn't about denial. It's about deliverance. Faith faces the facts head on and declares, "While you may be true, truer still is God's Word and His promise to me. I will err on the side of faith (not fear) until my own eyes see how the Lord will come through for me." I once wrote a paraphrased prayer after studying Abraham's faith in Romans chapter four. Here it is: Without weakening in my faith, I will face the fact that there are many reasons I should not be able to fulfill the call of God in my life. But I will not waver in unbelief regarding the promises of God. No, I will be strengthened in my faith, giving glory to God because I am fully persuaded that God has the power and is able to do what He's promised. Therefore, I put no confidence in my weaknesses or obstacles. I put all of my confidence in the faithfulness of almighty God, who daily establishes His purposes for me!

LEARN Read Romans 4.

FLOURISH Personalize the prayer above and make it your own.

PRAY

Lord,
Give me faith to see mountains move, waters part, hearts restored, and lives forever changed. Amen.

A Place
of Undeserved Privilege

Because of our faith, Christ has brought us into this place of undeserved privilege where we now stand, and we confidently and joyfully look forward to sharing God's glory.

Romans 5:2

Several times in my life, I've been invited to a place at the table among notable leaders. Each time, I looked around and couldn't help but hum that old *Sesame Street* tune, "One of these things is not like the other." I felt utterly in over my head and completely dependent on the Lord. *Prayed* I wouldn't make a fool of myself. The sense of undeserved privilege will never be lost on me. In Christ Jesus, we have a place at the table of grace. In fact, we have the *same* right standing before the Father as Jesus does. *Righteous. Holy. Redeemed. Without fault.* We've not earned our way there. We don't deserve such status and advantage. Yet we now have the rights of an heir. We have the privileges of royalty. We have access to God himself and heavenly help. We are no longer earthbound travelers. We are citizens of heaven. We've placed all of our trust in Christ and in His death and victory over *our* sin. God will never look at us the same way again. He'll never see you through the filter of your sins or wandering ways. He's not hung up on your weaknesses. When He looks at you, He sees pure, spotless righteousness. What a blessing to stand in this place!

LEARN Reads Romans 5.

FLOURISH See yourself as God sees you. Let it in. Walk accordingly.

PRAY

Father,
  I am Yours. I stand before You in a place of divine privilege. I'm speechless. Help me to grasp it and live in a manner worthy of Your Name. Amen.

Shut the Door, Live Fully Alive

When he died, he died once to break the power of sin. But now that he lives, he lives for the glory of God. So you also should consider yourselves to be dead to the power of sin and alive to God through Christ Jesus.

Romans 6:10–11

*O*ftentimes after major output, we're tired, weary, and especially susceptible to enemy attack. The recovery community uses the acronym HALT to remind them when to guard their heart and their steps. *Hungry. Angry. Lonely. Tired.* These apply to us too. One day after a big event, I sensed the enemy waiting for me to stumble and fall. I felt weak and vulnerable, so I alerted my intercessors and asked them to pray. One friend shared about a dream she'd had the night before. In the middle of the night, a man tried to break in the front door. She ran to the door to find his arm reaching through, trying to pull down the chain lock. She slammed the door shut and called the police. She said, "We have the spiritual reinforcements we need but sometimes we need to build a stronger door." We all leave certain doors open—or unlocked—which grants the enemy easy access to our lives at just the wrong time. Maybe you need to shut the door on fear, unforgiveness, worry, or self-pity. Or maybe your struggle is with overindulgence of some kind. Remember, the enemy's intent is to destroy you, so shut the door on him. Live the full, rich life Christ died to give you.

LEARN Read Romans 6.

FLOURISH Ask God to show you any open doors in your life. Shut them. ☺

PRAY

Jesus,
Show me where I'm vulnerable. Help me to build a stronger door.
Amen.

Life to Your Body

The Spirit of God, who raised Jesus from the dead, lives in you. And just as God raised Christ Jesus from the dead, he will give life to your mortal bodies by this same Spirit living within you.

Romans 8:11

When we trust Jesus for salvation, His Spirit takes up residence in our soul. Jesus was buried under the heap of the world's sin. And the *very power* that raised Him from the grave is now *alive* in us. The phrase *lives in us* translates "dwells." His Spirit actually abides—finds its home—within us. And the phrase *gives life to your mortal bodies* means, "spiritual power that invigorates, restores life, endues with new and greater power in life."* Is God's Word true? Yes! Is His power alive within you? Yes! Is it possible that the same Spirit that raised Christ from the grave is able to quicken your mortal body, give strength to your bones, and add fresh energy to your steps? Yes, yes, it is. As someone who has fought illness and contended for health my whole adult life, I've learned how important it is to actively engage our faith by doing what we *can* do, and then trusting God to do what only He can do. *Every* step we take toward healing and wholeness matters. We all have next steps to take. May Jesus show you your next steps.

LEARN Read Romans 8:1–17.

FLOURISH Make some healthy adjustments to your life. Engage your faith and declare that God's invigorating power is mightily at work in your life!

PRAY

Lord Jesus,
Your Spirit is alive and at work in me! Show me what needs to change in my life. And quicken my mortal body with the power of Your Spirit. Amen.

*Strong's Interlinear Bible Search, StudyLight.org, Romans 8:11.

A Foretaste of Glory

And we believers also groan, even though we have the Holy Spirit within us as a foretaste of future glory. . . .

Romans 8:23

*T*he time I was facedown on the floor, devastated by a friendship betrayal, I felt the Lord's comfort and peace. The Holy Spirit whispered to me to rise up and pray for my enemies. There have been countless moments when God's love has flooded my soul and swallowed up my insufficiency: the time I felt prompted to call a friend with a precise and powerful word of encouragement, or the time I stepped up to speak, feeling fragile and weak, only to have His power rise up within me with great clarity and boldness. There's nothing like the movement of God's Holy Spirit within us; this is how we know we belong to Him.* Those profound otherworldly moments are just a *taste* of things to come. Jesus gave us His Holy Spirit as a promise to us that He's coming for us. And when He does, He'll redeem every aspect of our stories. We'll see with new eyes. And what we see will take our breath away. We'll hear new songs. We'll have new bodies, and nothing will hurt, break down, or fall apart. Never minimize or underestimate the power and the presence of the Holy Spirit in your life. He offers peace, comfort, correction, and direction. He empowers and awakens. The more deeply you know God's Word, the more clearly you'll discern His voice.

LEARN Read Romans 8:18–39.

FLOURISH Recall the Holy Spirit's recent activity in your life. Thank the Lord.

PRAY

Father,
Thank You for Your presence in my life. Fine-tune my ears to hear Your voice above all others. Amen.

*See Romans 8:16.

Everything

For everything comes from him and exists by his power and is intended for his glory. All glory to him forever! Amen.

Romans 11:36

*H*ave you ever walked through a long battle, fought valiantly, taken ground inch by inch, only to wonder if and when God might step in? I've had to fight hard for my health. One day my attitude ventured into dangerous territory. I went from crying out to God to questioning when He would do His part. I shudder to remember or even admit this now. In His fatherly, authoritative way, He questioned me, "Susie, who provided you with the funds to go to the doctor and to purchase the medicine and supplements?" Immediately, I buckled. "You, Lord." He wasn't finished with me. "Who keeps your heart beating and puts breath in your lungs without fail? Who has offered you a support system to weather this battle? And who has promised that you'd emerge stronger and wiser than you were when you started?" Again, I could barely speak. "It's You, Lord. Only You." The next morning, this passage from Romans absolutely arrested me. Everything comes from Him, is sustained by His power, and exists for His glory. Even our faith is a gift from Him, to be offered back to Him. We own nothing that didn't come from His hand. Our very life-breath is His intentional gift to us. May we never forget it.

LEARN Read Romans 11.

FLOURISH Thank *God* for the gifts that you've either taken credit for or taken for granted.

PRAY

Lord,
You've given me Your life and breath and purpose and promises. Help me not to forget that everything comes from You and is sustained by You, for Your glory. Amen.

Surrender and Be Revived

And so, dear brothers and sisters, I plead with you to give your bodies to God because of all he has done for you.

Romans 12:1

One day on my show, Chip Ingram shared some interesting insight with me. He said, "Susie, people often ask me how to get unstuck. They long for a personal revival but don't know how to get there. My answer always surprises them. I say, 'Surrender. Let go of whatever you're white-knuckling right now. Let it go and offer your whole self to God with a heart of surrender. I believe personal revival will come.'"* We lose power when we cling to our own way. We lose heart when we strive to force an outcome. And we lose perspective when our thoughts get stuck on our own will. Revival comes when we simultaneously release our cares and cling more firmly to Jesus. We then reset our gaze and renew our mind with thoughts of God's goodness, His faithfulness, and His sovereignty in our lives. When we walk in step with Him, He leads us even when we're unaware. A mind conformed to the world is obsessed and occupied with the small story, with things that will burn up and pass away. When your mind is transformed by God, you see redemption possibilities all around you. You're occupied with God's presence and His profound affection for you. You trust Him because you *know* Him.

LEARN Read Romans 12.

FLOURISH Open your hands and release whatever comes to mind. And then rehearse His promises.

PRAY

Lord Jesus,
I surrender my whole life to You! Forgive me for clinging to things I cannot control. I trust You, Lord. Revive my heart once again. Amen.

*My paraphrase of Chip's insight.

An Accumulative Spiritual Wealth

Through him, God has enriched your church in every way—with all of your eloquent words and all of your knowledge.

1 Corinthians 1:5

*W*e so often measure God's ability and our capacity in small increments. I remember a time when I was heading into a big weekend of ministry, yet I'd felt so drained from sick kids, sleepless nights, and a glaring sense of my own humanity. I didn't own any bootstraps and didn't have the strength to hike them up even if I did. I went to my knees and asked the Lord for strength. He reminded me that He'd forged a deep well within me over the years. We have a history together. He's not limited by a bad week, so I don't have to be either. In his devotional *Sparkling Gems from the Greek*, Rick Renner writes about the word *enriched* in the passage above; it's *ploutizo*, where we get the word *plutocrat*—someone who is so wealthy that his handlers cannot give him a definitive number on his wealth because it's accruing at such a fast rate. When we walk with the Lord day in and day out, we accrue a spiritual wealth that multiplies faster than we can imagine. We gather a lifetime of wisdom, experiences, and insights from walking with our Savior. Don't let a bad day or a bad week throw you off. You're richer than you know.

LEARN Read 1 Corinthians 1:1–9.

FLOURISH When you have an off day, step back and remind yourself how rich you are in Christ Jesus. Tell your soul what's true.

PRAY

Father,
I can be so shortsighted at times. I'm supremely wealthy in You! When my well feels dry, help me to draw from Your endless supply. Thank You, Lord. Amen.

God Chooses the Weak

God chose things despised by the world, things counted as nothing at all, and used them to bring to nothing what the world considers important.

1 Corinthians 1:28

Mine was an impossible situation. Or so it seemed. How could God possibly take a terminally insecure girl, full of self-contempt and fear, and deliver her from all of those things? I feared trauma. I feared rejection. I feared others' opinions. I was my own worst enemy; I didn't have the faintest idea of how to cut myself some slack. Yet somehow, by the miracle of God's grace, He first saved my soul, and then over the years has made me whole. People who see me now think of me as strong, feisty, and bold, and maybe parts of me really are, but I have more healing to go. And I remember so well who I was when He found me. I've met many Christians along the way who'd say the same thing. They operate at high levels even by the world's standards, but there's no hint of pride or self-importance in them—only humility and gratitude. They do excellent work with grace and joy. They remember where they came from and how God saved them. God specializes in taking nobodies and making them somebodies. The world can't figure it out because it makes no sense. God gets the most glory when He's the one who writes our story.

LEARN Read 1 Corinthians 1:10–31.

FLOURISH Spend some time pondering who you'd be without God's grace. Thank Him for His miraculous work in your life.

PRAY

Lord,
I was an orphan and You adopted me! I was lost and You found me. I was nobody and You made me a somebody. I'm forever grateful. Amen.

What God Has
Freely Given You

We have received God's Spirit (not the world's spirit), so we can know the wonderful things God has freely given us.

1 Corinthians 2:12

A dear listener who called in to my radio show struggled to get her words out. She'd had an abortion several years prior and could not get out from underneath the dark cloud of shame and guilt. My heart broke for her. I felt nudged to ask, "Dear one, have you ever prayed and asked Jesus to forgive your sins, heal your soul, and save you for all eternity?" Through her tears, she said, "No. That's why I called in." My heart beat in my chest as I led her through the prayer of salvation. Together we declared Jesus as Lord and asked God to forgive her, cleanse her, and fill her to overflowing. I pictured the Holy Spirit taking up residence in her soul and guiding her all the days of her life. She cried tears of joy as we said good-bye. Life is so painful, yet we're not meant to sort it all out on our own. We need Jesus. We need our heavenly Father. We're desperate for the Holy Spirit's influence. One of the reasons God gave us the Holy Spirit is *so we can know* the things He has freely given us. Access. Grace. Forgiveness. Mercy. Grace. Power. Insight. Direction. Grace. Wisdom. Freedom. Redemption. Grace. What has God given us? Oceans and oceans of grace. A life redeemed. Promises fulfilled. Praise His Name.

LEARN Read 1 Corinthians 2.

FLOURISH Search the Scriptures to better grasp all God has *freely* given you.

PRAY

Father,
You've given me everything. Help me to discern all You've offered me and let it change me forever. Amen.

What You Think of Me

As for me, it matters very little how I might be evaluated by you or by any human authority. I don't even trust my own judgment on this point. My conscience is clear, but that doesn't prove I'm right. It is the Lord himself who will examine me and decide.

1 Corinthians 4:3–4

*I*f you catch yourself worried and flurried over what others might be thinking of you, stop in your tracks and say out loud (in private might be best ☺), "It matters very little what you think of me. It doesn't even matter what *I* think of me. I think I know my own heart, but I might be wrong about myself. Why put weight on the opinions of mere humans when we all see as through a cloudy mirror? I will not elevate you above me, nor me above you. Our stories are in progress and no one knows every detail except for God himself. He's asked us not to judge things ahead of time, before we know what's what. When will we finally see with clarity? When Christ returns! So I refuse to waste any more brain space wondering or worrying about your ever-changing thoughts about me or anyone else. In fact, I've decided to trust my own perceptions less and trust God's opinion more. From this day forward, I will fill my thoughts with God's amazing grace and abundant love toward sinners just like me. What a joy to be fully known and deeply loved!"

LEARN ▸ Read 1 Corinthians 4.

FLOURISH ▸ Practice a zero-tolerance policy when it comes to thoughts about others' opinions.

PRAY

Father,
I've allowed the enemy to steal my joy one too many times. I'm done with that! Fill my heart and mind with thoughts of You. Amen.

Purpose in Every Step

So I run with purpose in every step. I am not just shadowboxing.
1 Corinthians 9:26

*W*e were out to dinner with our retired pastor and his wife. He leaned across the table and said, "I want you two to go home and interview each other. Find out what most brings each of you *rest*, *joy*, and *fulfillment*. If you put these off until retirement, you'll enter that season feeling dead upon arrival." We were only in our forties, yet we knew this was a word straight from the Lord. Kev and I processed the next day for three hours, and as a result, made some major, God-ordained life changes. Disciplined athletes know this, and we should too. There's a distinct purpose for every season in our lives. Training will look different from one season to the next. People who do the same thing in every season rarely gain momentum and often lack vision. There's a time to gain ground, to hold your ground, and to recover lost ground. There's a time to learn new skills, to reaffirm timeless truths, and to receive fresh input. There's a time to pull back and recover and a time to step out and take risks. To run your race with purpose in every step, you need to discern the season God has you in right now. And remember, wisdom's path is always peace.

LEARN Read 1 Corinthians 9.

FLOURISH Spend time with a loved one or spouse and talk through the season you're in right now. Prayerfully discern where your focus should be.

PRAY

Father,
Help me to discern where You have me right now. Help me run this race to win the prize. Show me the wisdom in my disciplines and the weight of my choices. Amen.

The Four I-Sins

These things happened as a warning to us, so that we would not crave evil things as they did. . . .

1 Corinthians 10:6

*T*he Israelites had experienced God in miraculous ways, yet their history with Him was never compelling enough to keep them from repeatedly wandering toward self-destruction. Paul reminds us in this passage that though God was *good to* the Israelites, He wasn't *good with* everything they did. Their painful journey serves as a cautionary tale for us. Consider their four I-sins: *Idolatry, Immorality, Irreverence*, and *Irritation*. The first two say to God, "I want more!" while the second two shout, "I am more!" *Idolatry* is born out of discontentment. When we loosen our grip on God's goodness, our eyes start to wander. Once our spiritual amnesia kicks in, we try lesser gods to see if they might satisfy. *Immorality* is so often born out of unhealed brokenness, and sometimes out of just plain decadent sinfulness. Yet we destroy our bodies and our souls when we walk through this door. *Irreverence* comes from pride and ignorance. We value our opinion above God's and before we realize it, honor falls by the wayside. *Irritation* springs from entitlement. We think we deserve more than God or others are giving us at the moment. If we rehearse those thoughts long enough, they'll spew out of us. What's the answer? Identify which I-sin you're most drawn to. Shut the door. Strengthen your walk with the Lord. Remember His love. Rely on His goodness.

LEARN Read 1 Corinthians 10.

FLOURISH Rid your life of these I-sins. Rehearse God's goodness today. Remind your soul that everything you need is found in Him.

PRAY

Lord,
I'm prone to wander. Bind my heart to Yours. You are good. I love You. Amen.

Love Heals and Redeems

Three things will last forever—faith, hope, and love—and the greatest of these is love.

1 Corinthians 13:13

Curled up in a ball in my bed, I held fistfuls of my bedsheets and blinked back my tears. Just back from the ER, doctors had told Kev they thought I had MS.* I could barely look at my husband. We were so young, with three little boys, and he'd already endured so much with me. Fear put a chokehold on my perspective. I asked my husband to divorce me. Sobbing, I begged, "Please. Marry someone who loves Jesus, who will love and play with our boys. I'll go live with my parents. I'm so sorry things turned out like this." Clearly, I wasn't thinking. My pain was speaking. Kneeling at my bedside, my husband put his finger over my lips and said, "You stop that right now. You are my bride and you always will be. If I have to kneel down and kiss you because you're in a wheelchair, then that's what I'll do." I was shocked. I'll never forget that tangible display of the Father's love. Unconditional love heals the heart like nothing ever could. We self-sabotage because of fear and insecurity. Every heart needs those who will go the distance with them. Every heart is desperate to be loved amidst their brokenness. May you know and experience the kind of love that heals and redeems.

LEARN Read 1 Corinthians 13.

FLOURISH Ask God to love through you in a way that's beyond you. May you experience such love as well.

PRAY

Father,
Thank You for the countless ways You love me. Heal me completely so I can love that way too. Amen.

*My diagnosis turned out to be Lyme disease.

Strong and Steadfast

So, my dear brothers and sisters, be strong and immovable. Always work enthusiastically for the Lord, for you know that nothing you do for the Lord is ever useless.

1 Corinthians 15:58

I've spoken to many ministry leaders over the years who've gone through painful seasons when they've been easily dismissed or replaced. They poured their hearts into serving the Lord, only to be tossed aside as if none of it meant anything to anybody. They're not the only ones. Husbands and wives have fought hard for marriage only to be left single because the other walked away. They wonder if all of the effort is wasted in God's eyes. Brokenhearted parents raised their kids to love Jesus, only to end up with prodigal children. If only life involved a predictable formula that guaranteed predictable results. Only God knows why things shake out the way they do. But one thing He promises: your work for Him, your faith steps, your heartfelt prayers, your selfless love and service are *never* wasted. Never for naught. Every time a believer serves God in any capacity, heaven takes note. Records are kept for a future reward. And the current atmosphere is changed because you—as a faith-filled person—are part of it. You won't know this side of heaven how profoundly your service impacted the greater kingdom story, but someday you will. Let it be enough for now to know that nothing you do for Jesus is *ever* wasted.

LEARN Read 1 Corinthians 15.

FLOURISH Add faith to every one of your deeds. Picture the eternal impact. Leave the results to God.

PRAY

Father,
You are so good to me. You've collected my tears of sorrow and frustration and remembered my service for future reward. My delight is in You. Amen.

Comforted Comforters

He comforts us in all our troubles so that we can comfort others. When they
are troubled, we will be able to give them the same comfort God has given us.

2 Corinthians 1:4

I once attended a ministry event with quite a few other authors and speakers. I ran into an author friend whose son is in prison. This woman has taken a parent's worst nightmare and turned it into a mighty ministry for those whose lives have been turned upside down by crime. She's someone who is very present and looks deep into your eyes when you speak. When I saw her and she saw me, her compassion undid me. I couldn't hide it anymore. I broke down and told her about my son who'd lost his way. She wrapped me up in a hug and cried with me. My trial was akin to a mud puddle if hers was a tsunami. Yet she'd received such comfort from the Lord, she had more than enough comfort for me when I needed it. God comforts us in our pain and sends messengers when we need them most. And as we arise out of the ashes of our pain, we're wiser and braver so we can truly help those God puts in our path. My son returned to the faith and is now a godly husband and father. I'm a grateful momma who has endless compassion for parents of prodigals. Christlike comfort changes us.

LEARN Read 2 Corinthians 1.

FLOURISH Comfort others with the comfort you've received. Watch God grow your compassion before your very eyes.

PRAY

God of all comfort,
  Hold me close and heal my heart. Use me for those who need what You've imparted to me. Amen.

Where the Spirit
of the Lord Is

For the Lord is the Spirit, and wherever the Spirit of the Lord is, there is freedom.

2 Corinthians 3:17

*W*hen the Holy Spirit is given free rein in our lives, He gives us the desire to do the very things that bring Him glory, allow us to flourish, and move His purposes forward.* It's the precious Spirit of God that winces within us when we say something we shouldn't, do something we ought not do, or consider something that would ultimately destroy us. It's that same Spirit who fills us with peace when we're on the right track, about to make the right decision or take a faith risk that makes no sense. The word *freedom* in this passage isn't a freedom to live as we want; it's the freedom to be everything God intended us to be. When the Spirit moves in our midst, He moves obstacles out of our way, and sometimes those obstacles are within us. When we set our minds on the things above, on the things of the Spirit, we experience *life* and *peace*.† When we come to Christ for the first time, He fills us with His Holy Spirit and does so continually as we walk with Him and stay sensitive to His guidance in our lives. Is it possible to walk in the flesh and be filled with the Spirit? Yes. Christians do so every day. But at great cost. God gets the glory and we are set free when we're continually in step with the Spirit of God.

LEARN Read 2 Corinthians 3.

FLOURISH Walk intimately, continually in the Spirit even more so today than yesterday.

PRAY

> *Holy Spirit,*
> *Fall afresh on me. Lead me onward. Amen.*

*See Philippians 2:13.
†See Romans 8:6–8.

We Carry This Treasure

But this beautiful treasure is contained in us—cracked pots made of earth and clay—so that the transcendent character of this power will be clearly seen as coming from God and not from us.

2 Corinthians 4:7 VOICE

I have a nephew who, when he was little, was the clumsiest little fellow I knew. Yet his momma still allowed him to carry the breakables from the car to the house whenever we gathered as a family. One day as I watched him carry a glass casserole dish, I cheered him on, but in a matter of moments, I heard him holler from outside, "Whoooaaa!" and I knew he'd landed in the shrubs. Which he did. The squirrels were thrilled. I think of that moment every time I ponder the idea that Jesus lives in me—someone who all too often falls in the shrubs and drops the dinner. It's like He's entrusted the family heirloom to a toddler. More so, He has made us a kingdom of priests, a holy nation, His prized possession. We carry this treasure—the presence and the power of the living God—in these earthen vessels so that we'll constantly remember that this power comes from *Him*. We lose heart when we're more surprised by our badness than we are His goodness. God knew who He was getting when He saved us. He's thrilled to count us as His own. With our mistakes and missteps, we're still His treasure, where He dwells.

LEARN Read 2 Corinthians 4.

FLOURISH Ponder the treasure within. Walk in power. Remember the Source.

PRAY

Father,
I'm so honored that You dwell with me. All glory and honor belong to You. Amen.

Live by Believing, Not by Seeing

For we live by believing and not by seeing.
2 Corinthians 5:7

*W*hy do we need to live by faith and not by sight? Because often-times, what our eyes see contradicts what God's Word says. We'd like to place God's promises over every moment of our lives and see a perfect alignment at all times, but that will never be our experience this side of heaven. God's promises come to pass over time, much like His prophecies. We will experience times and seasons when it looks, feels, and seems like God's promises aren't true at all. But they are. That's what faith is for. If we tether ourselves to a specific outcome, we'll be disappointed. If we expect God to operate on our timeline, we will be disappointed. "Paul reminds us that though we may think we are at the end of our rope, we are never at the end of our hope."* Where do you need to engage your faith today? What circumstances are holding your gaze and stealing your joy? Remember, faith is for the long journey, and promises take time to come to fruition. But ask any serious praying believer and they'll tell you this: The answers do come. Once you've learned the secret of abiding in Christ, relying on His Word, praying His promises, and staying in it for the long haul, you'll never rely on anything else like you rely on God. Live by faith today.

LEARN   Read 2 Corinthians 5.

FLOURISH   Switch your gaze to God's promises and live by faith.

PRAY

> *Father,*
>   *I look to You. I believe You. I will wait for You. Your promises are true, and You are faithful to Your Word. Amen.*

*Life Application Study Bible, 2569.

We Serve God
No Matter What

We serve God whether people honor us or despise us, whether they slander us or praise us. We are honest, but they call us impostors. We are ignored, even though we are well known.

2 Corinthians 6:8–9

*T*his faith journey isn't for sissies. We endure hardship, betrayal, accusation, and slander. But we also see miracles and lives changed, and we get to partner with God in a way that transforms us. The tricky thing is that when you live in a developed country where Christian service can quickly turn to status and even celebrity, your motives may falter. You may develop an attachment to your position, to the power or status that comes with it, and to the idea that your worth is somehow tied up in it all. That's why God sometimes allows our house of cards to come crashing down. It's not good for us, and it doesn't glorify God when we serve Him in a way that mostly serves us. Paul modeled this better than anyone. He determined to serve God no matter what. If you've been dissed, dismissed, or overlooked, don't squander your influence by taking offense and taking it out on God. Determine that you will serve your King no matter who's looking. He's the ultimate authority and the One who rewards your faith. When it's all about His kingdom and not yours, you'll not only survive your battles, you'll thrive in spite of them.

LEARN Read 2 Corinthians 6.

FLOURISH Take some time to consider your motives today. Seek first His kingdom. He'll take care of you.

PRAY

Heavenly Father,
I bow before You this day. I'm at Your service. Show me what obedience looks like in this season. Amen.

Waves of Increase

You will be made rich in everything so that your generosity will spill over in every direction. Through us your generosity is at work inspiring praise and thanksgiving to God.

2 Corinthians 9:11 VOICE

Our finances were a mess, yet we longed to live freely and generously. When God brought us to this passage, it jumped off the page and into our hearts. He whispered to us His truth: *"I will provide seed for you as you begin to sow. I will supply and increase your store of seed and enlarge the harvest of your righteousness. You'll be made rich in every way <u>so that</u> you can be generous on every occasion, causing many to thank me because you dared to trust me as your provider."* Suddenly I had a vision of being generous not just with our finances, but also with our time, our prayers, our kindness, and our compassion. We were fearful financial sowers at the time. In other words, we sowed sparsely, not generously. But we began to apply biblical principles to our finances, then we added generous sowing, and we literally saw the enemy's plan for our finances *fall apart*. Standing here now I look out over the landscape of God's faithfulness to this word He gave to us so long ago, and I am awestruck. The more we sowed, the more waves rippled back to us *so that* we could become even more generous than before. I have a dream to see every believer walk in the flourishing generosity God offers them.

LEARN Read 2 Corinthians 9.

FLOURISH Sow more seeds than you're used to. Start in small increments if need be. But grow in your sowing.

PRAY

Lord,
I claim this promise as my own. Lead me onward. Amen.

God's Mighty Weapons

For though we walk in the world, we do not fight according to this world's rules of warfare. The weapons of the war we're fighting are not of this world but are powered by God. . . .

2 Corinthians 10:3–4 VOICE

Given the vitriol we see on social media today, even among Christians, you'd think that our hope lies in government, right leaders, and our rights being hailed as most important. Of course, we long for righteous leaders and a healthy government. And our freedoms are precious. But these aren't necessary for Christianity to thrive. The opposite is actually true. The kingdom is bursting at the seams in the world today where Christianity is most vehemently opposed. We hope because of Calvary's Hill—where Jesus died and rose again. Now, you who believe on His name and are filled with His Spirit have the power and the authority to take out the spiritual forces that not only oppose you, but that oppose the truth about God and His kingdom. You don't and won't win the war with clever arguments or savvy talking points. Overexposure to angry media, no matter which side of the aisle you're on, will only fuel your fear and empower your angst. Refuse to fight your battles as the world does. Determine to get on your knees and in Christ's authority, pull down every stronghold and every arrogant thought that exalts itself above the knowledge of God. Unless you fight your battles in the spiritual realm, you'll lose your battles in the earthly realm.

LEARN Read 2 Corinthians 10.

FLOURISH Take your angst to your prayer closet and fight valiantly there.

PRAY

Father,
You've positioned me to fight my battles from a place of victory. Give me faith to believe. Amen.

Where Power Is Perfected

"My grace is sufficient for you, for my power is made perfect in weakness."

2 Corinthians 12:9 NIV

*P*aul said something very interesting in this chapter. He opted not to share too much about his experiences so that others wouldn't think more highly of him than they ought. He wanted his life to speak for itself. Most of us are the opposite: We prefer that others think more highly of us than we deserve. But Paul was so confident in his identity in Christ that he determined not to manipulate the opinions of others. God kept Paul humble so He could use Paul greatly. Paul begged for relief from his thorn in the flesh, some limitation that no doubt slowed him down and made him more dependent on God. God said no to that request. He promised that through Paul's continual, humble dependence, he'd come to know a power he'd know no other way. Think about the juxtaposition of these two desires at war within us. We strive to manage others' opinions of us, and we beg for relief from our weaknesses. And yet when we cease striving and let our lives speak for themselves, we'll settle into a holy sense of identity. And when, in our weakness, we look for God's power to be perfected in us, we'll settle into a holy sense of contentment amidst our limitations. God's grace is all about His presence, His power, and His enough-ness. And we *have* His grace.

LEARN　　Read 2 Corinthians 12.

FLOURISH　　If you strive for appearance's sake or berate yourself for your weaknesses, settle into God's grace and watch His power work wonders in you.

PRAY

Holy God,
I am empowered by Your grace. I'm covered, assured, secure, and equipped. My weaknesses will always be upstaged by Your strength. Yes, Lord. Amen.

Setting Aside
God's Unmerited Favor

I do not set aside the grace of God, for if righteousness could be gained through the law, Christ died for nothing!

Galatians 2:21 NIV

very year, on the night before Christmas Eve, we gather around the table with our family. We take our time answering these three questions: 1) What did God teach you this past year? 2) What life lesson will you take with you into the coming year? 3) What do you want from the Lord in the year to come (e.g., wisdom, faith, understanding, etc.)? One of our sons shared this with raw eloquence: "Launching into adulthood challenged me. Though you raised me to believe that my identity is rooted in Christ, I realized there were places of unbelief in my own soul. I looked inward at myself to try and reason with my sense of not-enough-ness, but that only left me in greater despair. Then one day the Lord impressed upon my heart that He actually likes my presence, likes to be with me. And that I bring value to the places where He leads me. He reminded me that as much as my earthly father loves me, He loves me that much more. I really do believe I have value because Jesus said so." We're surrounded by His favor, yet too often we set it aside to strive our way out of a hole that we're not actually in. May God give you a fresh revelation of your intrinsic value in Him.

LEARN Read Galatians 2.

FLOURISH Sit with God. Ask for a deeper understanding of how much you're worth.

PRAY

Lord,
Help this to sink in for me! I want to revel in Your unmerited favor and swim in oceans of grace. I want to live like I'm free. Amen.

Do We Earn Our Miracles?

I ask you again, does God give you the Holy Spirit and work miracles among you because you obey the law? Of course not! It is because you believe the message you heard about Christ.

Galatians 3:5

I once gave the commencement address at a university. I marveled at the sea of students who worked so hard to earn their degree. They deserved the pomp and circumstance! Isn't it something that God reached down from on high to save the lowest, most needy of humanity? None of us can proudly line up and move our tassel from right to left because we've fulfilled the requirements of the law. With wide-eyed wonder, we stand amazed that we have a status we did not earn. God gave us the Holy Spirit as a sign of our future inheritance and a gift of His grace. There's not one single righteous act that prompted God to do such a thing for us. Even our faith is a gift from His heart to ours. It's the same with miracles. My son was miraculously healed from a serious back injury. He didn't earn it, but he did believe for it. I long to see more miracles. I once interviewed Lee Strobel about his book *A Case for Miracles*, in which he researched indisputable, documented cases of miracles that cannot be explained away. I said to Lee, "It's a mystery as to why God heals some and not others. Have you noticed any common denominators?" He replied, "Only that everyone He healed believed that He could and embraced a humble, expectant posture before Him."

LEARN Read Galatians 3.

FLOURISH Ask for a gift of faith. Believe that miracles still happen in our day.

PRAY

Lord,
Move in power through me! Amen.

How You Fall from Grace

For if you are trying to make yourselves right with God by keeping the law, you have been cut off from Christ! You have fallen away from God's grace.

Galatians 5:4

I've worked in media for over a decade, and I've seen plenty of leaders rise and fall. But then I read Paul's words above and realize that though they may have fallen, they haven't fallen from grace. How do you fall from grace? By trying to earn your own way. The Jewish Christians tried to impose their Jewish laws and traditions onto the Gentiles who had recently come to Christ, as if to say, "You're a substandard Christian unless you add these elements to your faith walk." Paul stepped in and said that the opposite is actually true. He went on to say, "*I am a sinner if* I rebuild the old system of the law I already tore down."* Dallas Willard once asked John Ortberg, "Who uses up more grace? Believers or unbelievers?" John guessed the unbelievers. Dallas replied, "No, John. Believers burn up more grace than a 747 burns up jet fuel!"† Of course our choices matter, and they'll always have consequences. But grace is another matter altogether. When we try to earn our way, we've lost our way. When we rely wholeheartedly on the saving, empowering grace of Jesus Christ, we find ourselves freer and happier than we had ever imagined. Amazing grace.

LEARN Read Galatians 5.

FLOURISH Live wholeheartedly by the Spirit and you'll enjoy the empowering grace Jesus offers.

PRAY

Lord,
I marvel at Your grace. May Your Spirit constantly and continually awaken me! Amen.

---

*See Galatians 2:18.
†John Ortberg shared this story on my show one day.

Don't Grow Weary, the Harvest Will Come

So let's not get tired of doing what is good. At just the right time we will reap a harvest of blessing if we don't give up.

Galatians 6:9

Seattle Seahawks staffer Ben Malcolmson joined me on my show one day. He told a story about a time when he was in college and tried reaching out to his fellow football players for Jesus. He held prayer meetings, but no one showed. He offered to teach a Bible study, but no one showed. He fasted and prayed. One day he had an idea. He put a Bible in every player's locker. He arrived at practice expectantly the next day, hoping for a break-through. The guys had torn their Bibles to shreds and thrown the pieces on the locker room floor. He was devastated and felt like a fool. Years later he ran into a teammate who told him a story that blew Ben away. This guy was raised in a Christian home but had wandered from the faith. He partied a lot in college. That day in the locker room, another player asked this guy about the Bible. The fallen-away Christian sat down and explained the gospel. The guy came to Christ, but sadly, died suddenly not too long after. Ben found out way after the fact that God had used his efforts to save one soul for eternity and bring another back to the faith. Never doubt God's faithfulness. Keep on keeping on. One day you'll hear stories that will take your breath away.

LEARN Read Galatians 6.

FLOURISH Keep sowing seeds into the lives of others. Live expectantly. The harvest will come.

PRAY

Lord,
Give me faith to keep sowing and believing, knowing that You are up to something good. Amen.

Every Spiritual Blessing

All praise to God, the Father of our Lord Jesus Christ, who has blessed us with every spiritual blessing in the heavenly realms because we are united with Christ.

Ephesians 1:3

*W*hen we crossed over from 1999 to the year 2000, people braced for impact. News media reports predicted doom and gloom. Some sold their homes and bought farms. Others purchased generators. People waited in long lines to purchase candles, water, and dried foods. A scarcity mindset had taken over. I tended toward fear. But then I read this passage from Ephesians and went facedown. *Help me grasp what You're saying here, Lord.* I suddenly sensed that there were countless untapped storehouses in heaven, provisions that had never been claimed, virtues that had never been pursued. I longed to see people set free, yet I knew my own limitations only too well. I sensed the invitation to reach up by faith and lay hold of the things I longed for. I've prayed this prayer almost every day for the past twenty years: *Thank You, Lord, that I have the tongue of the learned, a tongue of the wise. I know the Word that sustains the weary; I speak, and captives are set free, the depressed are delivered, and the sick are made well; the rejected realize they're accepted, the lost are found, and the righteous are mobilized. I am an anointed, appointed woman of God, and Your Word is alive in me!* I wonder what heavenly realm blessings you might lay hold of.

LEARN Read Ephesians 1.

FLOURISH Prayerfully read Ephesians chapter 1. Ponder His promises. Boldly ask for what you need to bring His kingdom to earth.

PRAY

Father,
Grant me the audacity to ask You for everything You long to impart to me. Amen.

God's Work of Art

For we are the product of His hand, heaven's poetry etched on lives, created in the Anointed, Jesus, to accomplish the good works God arranged long ago.

Ephesians 2:10 VOICE

We watch our grandson every Saturday because his parents both work that day. Our son drops him off at 6:30 am and picks him up at about 1:30 pm. Before they leave, we all have lunch together and spend an hour or two on the floor thoroughly enjoying our little treasure. I know others thoroughly enjoy their grandkids too, but I'm completely smitten by our little guy. I see parts of his mom and his dad in him. He is a true masterpiece. I whisper in his ear that he is mighty in God, and I tell him regularly how much his family loves him. I'm *always* happy to see him. I'm human and yet I love him with an otherworldly love. God is divine and yet loves you with the same passion I've described times a million. He's *completely* taken with you. He loves what makes you smile. He aches over what breaks your heart. He hears the silent whispers in the night. And He's right now, arranging good work for you to do. God created you. You are His masterpiece, His work of art. And He didn't create you so you can sit on a shelf as wall art. He created you to change the world.

LEARN Read Ephesians 2.

FLOURISH Imagine God's joy in creating you. Linger with that thought. Ask Him what good work He has assigned you in this season of your life.

PRAY

Lord,
I want to grasp this truth. Show me how You feel about me. Give me faith and clarity to fulfill my God-given call in this season. Amen.

Above and Beyond

Now all glory to God, who is able, through his mighty power at work within us, to accomplish infinitely more than we might ask or think.

Ephesians 3:20

My health relapse lasted about three years. I'm on the other side now—about 95 percent recovered. Quite honestly, that journey felt like a walk through hell. When surges of symptoms overtook me, so did fear and anxiety. I wrote about this in my book *Fully Alive*. As I mentioned in an earlier devotion, God whispered to my heart one day, *"The storms reveal the lies we believe and the truths we need."* That began a battle to uproot the lies I believed and replace them with the truths I needed. I fasted, prayed, cried out to God. I meticulously followed doctors' orders. I curled up in a ball in my dark bedroom and watched sermon after sermon. I hung on for dear life because I know God, and I knew He'd come for me. And He did. I stand here now redeemed, set free, and utterly amazed at the inner work God accomplished in me. Above and beyond what I could have imagined. God can only do through us what He's first done in us. This is a promise packed with meaning. We like to dream about the big things God might do through us. And we should. But dare to believe that God will use every enemy attack on your life to transform you into a warrior you never dreamed you could be.

LEARN   Read Ephesians 3.

FLOURISH   Identify what God is working on in you. Imagine your freedom and transformation. Keep marching.

PRAY

Father,
I don't like to suffer! I'm not fond of battles. But I know they'll come. So have Your way in me! Do the impossible in and through me. Amen.

Live a Life Worthy of Your Calling

Therefore I, a prisoner for serving the Lord, beg you to lead a life worthy of your calling, for you have been called by God.

Ephesians 4:1

*U*ntil Jesus returns for His Bride, our two natures will constantly be at war within us. Our carnal nature bids us come, take the bait, eat the fruit, justify sin, hide from God. And our soul shrivels. Our spiritual nature calls us upward, into His presence, to walk in His way, taste His goodness, tremble in His presence, and experience redemption. And our soul flourishes. William MacDonald writes, "From heaven the angels are compelled to admire His unsearchable ways past finding out. They see how God triumphed over sin to His own glory. They see how He has sent heaven's Best for earth's worst. They see how He has redeemed His enemies at enormous cost, conquered them by His love, and prepared them as a Bride for His Son. . . . They see that through the work of the Lord Jesus on the cross, more glory has come to God and more blessing has come to [believers] than if sin had never been allowed to enter. God has been vindicated; Christ has been exalted; Satan has been defeated; and the church has been enthroned in Christ to share His glory."* Oh, the victory He has won! Be done with lesser things. Rise up and live in a manner worthy of your calling.

LEARN Read Ephesians 4.

FLOURISH Refuse to allow pettiness, drama, or distractions to keep you from the best of what God has for you.

PRAY

Father,
You are high and lifted up. Glorify Your Name in me. Call me higher, Lord. Amen.

---

*William MacDonald, *Believer's Bible Commentary* (Nashville: Thomas Nelson, 1989), 1928.

Make the Most of Every Opportunity

Make the most of every opportunity in these evil days.
Ephesians 5:16

*O*nce a month, my husband and I go on Facebook Live to share a few devotional thoughts and to pray for those in need. The prayer requests come in so fast, we can barely keep up with them all. We love standing in the gap with those who suffer. Recently I sensed God wanted some extra time with me prior to our session. I love spending time with Him. But for some reason, this particular night, I could hear myself *repeatedly* saying, "Just one more minute" as I worked to gather some Bible verses for an upcoming event at our radio station. A good use of time, right? But not the *best* use of time. Though we had a great time praying for others, I felt a spiritual oppression throughout the session. Then, wouldn't you know, a troll hopped on and repeatedly called us false teachers, urging folks to stop listening to us. It was unnerving. I felt deeply convicted by God after the fact. He was only calling me to himself to prepare me ahead of time. To make the most of every opportunity is to discern God's highest and best will for you at every given moment. It translates this way: *to make wise and sacred use of every opportunity.** These are evil days. Trolls are everywhere. Listen to the Lord.

LEARN Read Ephesians 5.

FLOURISH Slow your pace and turn your face to the One who loves you most.

PRAY

> *Lord,*
> *You're always watching out for me. Help me to take my every cue from You—to redeem my moments and to live a listening kind of life. Amen.*

*Strong's Interlinear Bible Search, StudyLight.org, Ephesians 5:16.

Spiritual Warfare, Explosive Power

> Above all, taking the shield of faith with which you will be able to quench all the fiery darts of the wicked one.
>
> Ephesians 6:16 NKJV

*Y*ears ago I read the book *This Present Darkness*, and it forever changed my prayer life. Author Frank Peretti paints a graphic picture of the spiritual world, of the battle between demonic influences and spiritual forces. I remember one scene where a beaten-down pastor of a small congregation cried out to the Lord for help. From outside the church, you watch as a spirit of despair zeroes in on the church window, going in for the kill. Your heart skips a beat as you watch this vulnerable, discouraged pastor, unknowingly about to take another hit. At precisely the right moment, a white-winged angelic warrior swoops down and hurls the leathery winged creature into space. I literally dropped the book and cheered when I read that line. In the book of Ephesians, we read about the shield of faith, with which we are equipped to extinguish *every* fiery dart the enemy sends our way. "The Greek word used here is the word *dunamis* which denotes *explosive power or dynamic power* and is where we get the word 'dynamite.'"* We need to get better at using our NO. *No, you can't have my children, my marriage, my calling, my community!* When you raise your shield of faith, explosive things happen in the spiritual realm.

LEARN Read Ephesians 6.

FLOURISH Start saying NO to the enemy. Raise your shield.

PRAY

Father,
You've equipped me to win in battle. Teach me to stand in faith. Amen.

*Rick Renner, *Sparkling Gems from the Greek* (Tulsa, OK: Teach All Nations, 2003), 659.

He'll Finish What He Started

And I am certain that God, who began the good work within you, will continue his work until it is finally finished on the day when Christ Jesus returns.

Philippians 1:6

*W*henever we try to rush maturity, or sprint through grief, or blow past our weaknesses, we actually slow down our spiritual development. We'll bend toward sin management, self-editing, and fear responses, all of which turn us inward instead of upward. God started this work, and He's the one who will finish it. I have a unique vantage point now that my sons are grown. We were purposeful in teaching our sons to know God's love, to treasure His voice, and to understand that His ways are best. But as a friend once said, "Life has a way of life-ing you." Each of them walked through their share of hurts, missteps, and trials that left me unnerved and wondering what would happen to the precious faith we'd nurtured deeply when they lived under our roof. Two of our three sons actually wandered for a season. But as I've learned to entrust the middle story and the final outcome to God, I've watched His guiding hand gently move them back to the center of His will. He's not in a hurry. He's okay with the process. He's not worried about their missteps. He loves and leads, guards and guides, protects and provides. He'll do the same for you and for those you love. He *will* finish what He started.

LEARN Read Philippians 1.

FLOURISH Remember that God not only has a 30,000-foot view of the story, He has intimate knowledge of every nuance. He is faithful.

PRAY

Father,
Your patience with our process takes my breath away. Help me to trust You more. Amen.

Leveraging Your Power

> Though he was God,
>> he did not think of equality with God
>> as something to cling to.
>>> Philippians 2:6

One day I stood a mother's-distance away while Jordan, age four at the time, stood in line for an order of fries. After the fourth person butted in front of him, I stepped up and asked him about it. He shrugged his shoulders like he was unsure of himself. I realized that though our son was kind, he was also insecure. We began to pump him full of truth. "Jordan, when God looks at you, His heart beats out of His chest because He loves you so much. You're no better than others, but you're not less than, either. Your opinion matters and God made you for a purpose." Over time we saw him rise up with a newfound confidence. One day Jordan was back in line, this time for an ice-cream cone. And just like before, people stepped in front of him, and he did nothing to hold his spot. When I approached him, he said, "Oh, don't worry, Mom. I know I could keep my place in line if I wanted; it's just that all these people look hungrier than me!" Suddenly, Philippians 2:6 passed through my mind. Jesus didn't consider equality with God something to leverage for His benefit. In fact, He leveraged it for ours, and in a way that cost Him everything. You have power for a purpose. Wield your influence for the sake of others.

LEARN Read Philippians 2.

FLOURISH God has entrusted you with a sphere of influence. May everyone around you benefit because of you.

PRAY

Lord,
Forgive me for trying to prove I'm somebody, when You've already proven it for me. Live valiantly through me. Amen.

Eyes Upward, Press On

I focus on this one thing: Forgetting the past and looking forward to what lies ahead, I press on to reach the end of the race and receive the heavenly prize for which God, through Christ Jesus, is calling us.

Philippians 3:13–14

*I*f anybody had bragging rights, it was Paul. Yet he considered all of his achievements, all of his accomplishments, pure rubbish compared to the surpassing greatness of knowing Jesus. It's premature to *forget about your past* if God hasn't healed you of your past. Paul spoke here of past laurels, past missteps, and past sins as things to leave with Christ Jesus. If we try to rush past our pain, it will catch up with us. If we try to rest on past laurels, they'll trip us up. "Paul's desire to know Christ sprang from no other motive but to enjoy Him. He wanted Christ for Christ's sake, not his own. He was a lover of God, not a user of God. And whether he moved in Christ's resurrection power or was stretched to his last ounce of endurance, it mattered little. For Paul, it was all a part of the most fulfilling journey of all: truly knowing God."* There *is* a heavenly prize waiting for you on the other side. Your current status, your past sins carry no weight when you're under grace. *Jesus* cleanses, calls, and qualifies you. Treasure the prize and run to win.

LEARN Read Philippians 3.

FLOURISH Give your sin and your need for status to Jesus. Embrace His all-empowering grace instead.

PRAY

Jesus,
You are my prize, my most treasured possession. Help me to run my race until I see You face to face. Can't wait. Amen.

*New Spirit-Filled Life Bible, 1664.

Fix Your Thoughts

Fix your thoughts on what is true, and honorable, and right, and pure, and lovely, and admirable. Think about things that are excellent and worthy of praise.

Philippians 4:8

*D*r. Troy joins me on my radio show once a month. One day before the show we were chatting about the physiological consequences of insecurity. He said the most amazing thing: "I don't think we fully comprehend how important our thought process is. Insecurity has its consequences. It fosters unhealthy thought patterns, which lead to unbelief, which then lead to poor choices—anything from eating terrible food to making destructive life-altering choices. But it doesn't stop there. When you harbor thoughts of insecurity, you are creating a divided kingdom within you, which cannot stand, let alone thrive. Your brain is wired to help you survive. God made it that way. When you embrace thoughts that are contrary to life, it's like putting one foot on the gas pedal and one foot on the brake. Imagine what that would do to your motor. Your brain wants you to survive and heal and to move forward. And yet the insecure person consistently feeds the brain a contrary message. Insecurity is bad for our system. We're made for more." Indeed, we are.* God has wired us to thrive. Any thoughts contrary to that which is pure, right, lovely, and excellent are destructive for your system and your soul. It takes both grit and grace to contend for a renewed mind, but it will change your life.

LEARN Read Philippians 4.

FLOURISH Up your game. Refuse thoughts that diminish. Fix your thoughts on what is good.

PRAY

Lord,
  Call me higher. Give me a vision for what a renewed mind looks like.
Amen.

*Excerpt taken from *Fully Alive* (Minneapolis: Bethany House Publishers, 2018), 174.

Rescued from a Kingdom

For he has rescued us from the kingdom of darkness and transferred us into
the Kingdom of his dear Son.

Colossians 1:13

*W*e were born into a kingdom of darkness. Stuck there. Unable to
rescue ourselves. Destined for ever-increasing levels of depravity
and captivity. Without hope apart from divine intervention. The word *darkness* translates this way: "ignorance of respecting divine things; accompanying
ungodliness; consequent misery in hell; persons in whom darkness becomes
visible and holds sway."* You've no doubt seen people so steeped in evil that the
darkness is actually visible on them. We were once darkness's captives—until
Jesus came. He died our death and paid our ransom. He broke our chains.
He embraced us with great passion and transferred us into His family, the
kingdom of Light. There, He bestowed upon us royalty, dignity, power, and
authority. We now walk in love, boldness, kindness, and truth. The old kingdom can no longer claim us. We now work with God to help set other captives
free. Paul opened this chapter with prayers for grace and peace. These are
ours as well. *Grace* translates this way: "joy, pleasure, delight, sweetness; favor,
merciful kindness; exerting holy influence upon the soul that keeps, increases,
and strengthens." *Peace* translates, "fearing nothing from God and content
with its earthly lot."† Do you see what we've inherited here? An unshakable
kingdom. We have *every* reason for joy, thanksgiving, and holy confidence.

LEARN Read Colossians 1.

FLOURISH Ponder the distinction between the two kingdoms. Worship
the One who rescued you!

PRAY

Father,
I cannot fully grasp what You've done for me. I bow low, raise my
hands high, and worship You. Amen.

*Strong's Interlinear Bible Search, StudyLight.org, Colossians 1:13.
†Strong's Interlinear Bible Search, StudyLight.org, Colossians 1:2.

Continue the Way
You Started

And now, just as you accepted Christ Jesus as your Lord, you must continue to follow him.

Colossians 2:6

I was in eighth grade when I first turned my heart toward God. I sat out on a picnic table, looked up into the night sky, and prayed, "God, I know You're real. If there's more to You than what I know, please make Yourself real to me. I'll start to read the Bible, though I think it's kind of boring. But if You can help me out with that, we have a deal." I had no idea what I was saying. But God did. I found a Bible, began to read, and absolutely fell in love with Jesus. I asked Him to save me a thousand times. My salvation was more of a process, not a definitive moment I can recall. We all have different salvation stories, but we have this in common: We came through the low door of humility. We admitted our need and confessed our sin. We decided to believe that what Jesus did, He did *for us*. We asked Him to forgive us, cleanse us, and fill us. Then we reoriented our whole lives to follow Him. Salvation isn't about checking a box and praying the right prayer. It's about radical transformation from the inside out because Jesus becomes Lord of your life. Just as you embraced Him wholeheartedly when you came to Him, follow Him in that same way. Stay on His heels. Listen for His voice. Do what He says. He is a Good Shepherd. You can trust Him.

LEARN ▶ Read Colossians 2.

FLOURISH ▶ Draw closer to Him. Stay deeply rooted in Him.

PRAY ▶

Jesus,
    Bind my heart to Yours. Keep me close to You. Draw me nearer still.
Amen.

Let Peace Decide

And let the peace that comes from Christ rule in your hearts. For as members of one body you are called to live in peace. And always be thankful.

Colossians 3:15

When I was a fairly new believer, I was looking to buy a car. A friend suggested I buy his car because he wanted an upgrade and he promised a good price. He showed me the car, took me for a ride, and asked what I thought. I smiled and said, "I'll have to pray about it." He looked a bit perturbed but nodded okay. After praying, I felt very unsettled in my spirit. I let him know I wouldn't be buying his car. He got angry because he didn't understand it at all. He ignored me after that. And the car died within a month. I felt grateful I listened to the Holy Spirit's leading. The word *peace* in this verse translates "umpire; to decide, direct, control, to rule."* When you are in Christ, *Christ is in you.* The Prince of Peace has taken up residence in your soul. His peace should always be your guide. Not man's opinion. Not your own reasoning. Not the pressure of the moment. If His peace is present, move forward. If there's no peace, stay put. And find your way back to peace again. Let God's peace be your constant companion throughout your day. Wisdom's path is always peace.

LEARN   Read Colossians 3.

FLOURISH   Cultivate and prioritize the peace of God in your life.

PRAY

Prince of Peace,
    Fill me afresh with a sense of Your presence. I treasure Your direction in my life. Lead me on. Amen.

*Strong's Interlinear Bible Search, StudyLight.org, Colossians 3:15.

Mature and Fully Assured

Epaphras, who is one of you and a servant of Christ Jesus, sends greetings. He is always wrestling in prayer for you, that you may stand firm in all the will of God, mature and fully assured.

Colossians 4:12 NIV

I'm mentoring a young woman who is a gifted writer, full of insight, rich in character. She's walking through the fires of betrayal, abandonment, and rejection. I encouraged her to start a blog and a podcast. She smiled thinly. "How does that feel?" I asked. She replied, "I'd love to. But every time I start, the enemy rails in my ear, 'Who do you think you are?'" I smiled and said, "Well, there's your assignment. Figure out the answer to that question. Who *do* you think you are? I see who you are. God loves who you are. But you need to know who you are. Next time the enemy spews that question, I want you ready with a feisty, faith-filled answer: *'I'll tell you who I am!'* First discern God's heart for you, then discern His will; and then move forward with a face like flint." Epaphras told Paul about the ungodly influences infiltrating the Colossian church. He wrestled fervently in prayer that Christians there might stand firm in the will of God, mature in the faith, and live fully assured of their place because of grace. You face the same battles. Live assured. Persevere. Stand firm in His will. Know His ways.

LEARN Read Colossians 4.

FLOURISH Craft an answer for this question: Who do you think you are?

PRAY

Lord,
   You love me. You've called me. And You invite me to persevere and stand firm in spite of enemy opposition and ungodly influence. Strengthen me to that end today. Amen.

A Holy Momentum

As we pray to our God and Father about you, we think of your faithful work, your loving deeds, and the enduring hope you have because of our Lord Jesus Christ.

1 Thessalonians 1:3

*E*xperts say that you find momentum in your life's calling when you combine your passions, your gifting, and your people. You'll become a force to reckon with. Paul commended the Thessalonians for their *faithful work*, their *loving deeds*, and their *enduring hope*. Passion, gifting, and people are extremely important. But without faith, hope, and love, you will lean away from God's best, not toward it. What's the *faithful work* God has assigned to you? Have you signed up for more than God has asked of you? Research shows that work is actually good for us. It's taking on more than God asked that slows us down and wears us out. Have you found a healthy rhythm in your work? An ebb to your flow? It's a worthy pursuit. And how about *loving deeds*? Are you going through the motions? Easy to do. Much harder to keep your heart in it. But oh, the power and the momentum when our hearts are engaged! And then there's *enduring hope*. Did you know that hope actually propels you forward? "Hope is never inferior to faith but is an extension of faith. Faith is present possession of grace; hope is confidence in grace's future accomplishment."* Want to be a triple threat? Master these: faithful work, loving deeds, enduring hope.

LEARN Read 1 Thessalonians 1.

FLOURISH Identify what you need to adjust to have a healthy, powerful rhythm.

PRAY

Lord,
Empower my faith, inspire my deeds, and awaken new hope within me. Amen.

New Spirit-Filled Life Bible, 1684.

Your Proud Reward

After all, what gives us hope and joy, and what will be our proud reward and crown as we stand before our Lord Jesus when he returns? It is you!

1 Thessalonians 2:19

We hear so much bad news through the media that we sometimes forget that good news is thriving all over the world. Countless Christians are living out their faith in their everyday lives. Communities are changed, people are restored. God is good! Paul was overjoyed for the way the Thessalonians loved and followed Jesus in spite of intense persecution. He looked ahead to heaven, and he imagined these redeemed lives as his crowning achievement. Two things may surprise us on Judgment Day. First, we'll be undone by the things God remembers and rewards. We'll gasp and our heart will skip a beat when Jesus rewards us for the ways we loved when it didn't suit us, prayed when we didn't feel like it, and pointed someone to Jesus though we felt ill-equipped or unworthy. But the second equally surprising reality is that some will arrive empty-handed—nothing to show for it. They may have had flashy ministries on earth, but they built them on earthly fame, not kingdom passion. And there are those who lived practically like atheists. They sincerely trusted Christ for salvation but lived much of their lives for themselves. A sobering question to ask ourselves before Jesus returns is this: *Do I have people and fruit to show for my labors? Or are my efforts just for show?*

LEARN Read 1 Thessalonians 2.

FLOURISH Note which efforts are fruitless, a distraction, or a drain. Live fully engaged, for the kingdom of God.

PRAY

God,
Help me to live a faithful, fruitful life. You are my great reward. Amen.

Filling in the Gaps
of Your Faith

Night and day we pray earnestly for you, asking God to let us see you again to fill the gaps in your faith.

1 Thessalonians 3:10

*A*s I've mentioned before, I'm almost fully recovered from my health battle. My most recent lab report revealed strong progress with just a few weak spots. My doctor likens it to plugging up holes so health can prevail. In the same way, we all have gaps in our faith, places where God wants to shore us up, strengthen us with truth, and establish us in freedom. For instance, because of my history with God, I have confidence that He is the one who will establish me. I don't need to posture or position for opportunities. But there are other places in my life where my gaps become evident. When pressure comes at me from all sides, I feel fear rising up within me. I fear the toll it will take on my health. I fear that it will disrupt my sleep. I fear that I'll make a mistake. Jesus modeled faith. He slept through the storm. He wants to shore up our faith and teach us how to embrace peace amidst great pressure. When we experience wholeness and freedom, we're able to fill in the gaps for others. God is working even now. Don't fear your weaknesses. Embrace the process. Respond in faith. You're on your way to freedom. And many will benefit as a result.

LEARN Read 1 Thessalonians 3.

FLOURISH Teach others what you know. Identify your gaps and ask Jesus to fill them.

PRAY

Lord,
I want to be mature, whole, and free. Strengthen and establish me, I pray. Amen.

A Quiet Life

Make it your goal to live a quiet life, minding your own business and working with your hands, just as we instructed you before. Then people who are not believers will respect the way you live, and you will not need to depend on others.

1 Thessalonians 4:11–12

*W*e live in a day when everyone, it seems, wants their five minutes of fame, no matter the cost or reason. Paul's words carry even more weight today than they did when he first delivered them. To *lead a quiet life* means to be secure in your lot, to fill your space and run your race, not whipping here and there, overcommitted, over-striving, over-proving that you're something you're not. People are watching our lives more than we probably realize. I once received a scathing email from a listener letting me know that my guest was actually her neighbor. She said, "He has this big platform and looks so spiritual on social media, but he's a terrible neighbor. His dog poops in everybody's yard, and we watch him watching the pup from his window. He's unapproachable and acts better than everyone else. Like his goal is to be famous." Ouch. Now, maybe there's more to the story, but the point is, our lives send a message. Paul charges us to live so honorably that even those who don't share our faith will respect us. It's the only way we'll earn the right to share God's love when the time is right. Your life is a living, breathing gospel message.

LEARN Read 1 Thessalonians 4:1–14.

FLOURISH How might you more fully fill your space and more honorably run your race?

PRAY

Lord,
Sometimes I forget that people are watching how I live. Call me higher, call me deeper. Amen.

We'll Meet Him in the Air

Then, together with them, we who are still alive and remain on the earth will be caught up in the clouds to meet the Lord in the air. Then we will be with the Lord forever.

1 Thessalonians 4:17

Scripture teaches us that Satan is the prince of the power of the air.* The enemy has authority where Christ's authority is not enforced. He has the power (and has used it strategically) to influence media, entertainment, education, and science. The prince of the air has clearly occupied his space in a way that has shaped our culture. One might despair if thoughts stayed there. But did you know that it's in *this* space where Jesus will gather us to meet Him in the air? We will be glorified where the enemy has been magnified. "The air is Satan's sphere, so this is a triumphal gathering in open defiance of the devil right in his own stronghold."† Think about it. We will meet Jesus in the air! We will behold Him, be like Him, and be restored because of Him. That day *is* coming! "God will turn tragedy into triumph, poverty to riches, pain to glory, and defeat to victory. All believers throughout history will stand reunited in God's very presence, safe and secure."‡ Turn your eyes upward today. Live as one who is spoken for. Be joyful and expectant.

LEARN Read 1 Thessalonians 4:17–18; 5.

FLOURISH Be encouraged. The enemy's doom is sure. And so is your victory.

PRAY

Father,
What You have done for me. What You have won for me. Thank You.
Amen.

*See Ephesians 2:2.
†*Believer's Bible Commentary*, 2038.
‡*Life Application Study Bible*, 2673.

What Faith Prompts You to Do

So we keep on praying for you, asking our God to enable you to live a life worthy of his call. May he give you the power to accomplish all the good things your faith prompts you to do.

2 Thessalonians 1:11

Some of the Thessalonians misinterpreted Paul's first letter and needed to be redirected. He charged them to live ready for Christ's imminent return. So they quit their jobs, lived idly, and waited around to be snatched up into the air. Paul followed up with a second letter, urging them to live ready while living responsibly. There were tasks to complete, needs to meet, people to love, and a God to serve. We have work to do. And how we steward our lives and our God-given assignments here directly impacts how we'll live out our eternity. Paul prayed they'd not only fully engage their faith and live robust lives, but that God would give them the power to accomplish everything their faith prompts them to do. The *power to accomplish* translates this way: "miracle power, moral power, excellence of soul, power resting upon forces; to abound, furnish supply, render complete, filled to the brim."* My faith prompted me to attend a writers conference, to go on several mission trips in spite of my fears, and to sow generous amounts of money back into the kingdom. With each faith step, I've experienced God's power and provision. I've developed an appetite for faith. How about you? What is your faith prompting you to do?

LEARN ▶ Read 2 Thessalonians 1:11.

FLOURISH ▶ Engage your faith and take some risks.

PRAY ▶

Father,
Lead me out onto the water. Prompt me over and over again to live by faith. Amen.

*Strong's Interlinear Bible Search, StudyLight.org, 2 Thessalonians 1:11.

Your Life Prevents Evil

For this lawlessness is already at work secretly, and it will remain secret until the one who is holding it back steps out of the way.

2 Thessalonians 2:7

A Bible scholar suggested on my show one day that the enemy has an antichrist waiting in the wings in every generation because he doesn't know the day or the time of the Lord's return. This verse definitely speaks of the evil lurking in the shadows, of how lawlessness is already at work. So what's holding back this evil force, bent on annihilating mankind? Opinions vary on this. One thought is that the Holy Spirit, at work in the lives of believers, is the resistance that stops the enemy from unleashing pure evil on the earth. Once we're gone, taken up, the firewall is removed and lawlessness will abound. Think of how God has used believers to stand in between the wicked and the weak. Consider the ministries that run to the battle line in times of need. How much evil is held at bay because a grandma prays for her grandchildren, or a pastor stands in the gap for his community, or a godly mentor loves on fatherless children? Why do you suppose the godliest saints endure the greatest opposition? They pose a threat to the dominion of darkness. What if you're a part of God's resistance army? How might your life shut down an enemy scheme?

LEARN Read 2 Thessalonians 2.

FLOURISH Stand in faith and move in your God-given authority today.

PRAY

Father,
I have nothing to fear, for You are with me. Help me to stand in the gap against the enemy schemes in our day. Victory belongs to me because I belong to You. Amen.

What's a False Teacher?

They set themselves up as experts on religious issues, but haven't the remotest idea of what they're holding forth with such imposing eloquence.

1 Timothy 1:7 MSG

*I*t breaks my heart how freely some wield the "false teacher" label against sincere Bible-believing Christians simply because they hold different opinions on secondary doctrine. I purposely cross denominational lines both in my show and with my speaking events. I love people in many Bible-believing denominations. We'll be in heaven together. Is it possible to love and respect our fellow Christians while holding to our convictions? Not one of us sees with perfect clarity.* We're all works in progress. Yet God is patient with us, so why are we not with one another? What is a false teacher? "They teach what is contrary to the truth found in Scripture (1:3, 1:6–7; 4:1–3). They promote trivial and divisive controversies instead of helping people come to Jesus (1:4). They aren't concerned about personal evidence of God's presence in their lives, spending their time on 'meaningless discussions' instead (1:6). Their motivation is to make a name for themselves (1:7)."† "Some will accomplish great things for God and preach gospel truth effectively but will depart from the faith and gradually turn to seducing spirits and false doctrines. Because of their former anointing and zeal for God, they will mislead many."‡ Pray for grace and discernment.

LEARN Read 1 Timothy 1.

FLOURISH Ask God to help you discern the difference between a difference of opinion and a departure from His Word.

PRAY

> *O Lord,*
> *Fill me with discernment and grace. I need both in increasing measures. Amen.*

*See 1 Corinthians 13:12.
†*Life Application Study Bible*, 2687.
‡*Life in the Spirit Study Bible*, 1915.

Pray for Everyone, Leaders Too

I urge you, first of all, to pray for all people. Ask God to help them; intercede on their behalf, and give thanks for them. Pray this way for kings and all who are in authority so that we can live peaceful and quiet lives marked by godliness and dignity.

1 Timothy 2:1–2

One day on my radio show I said, "We live in a highly polarized culture; even Christians stand on opposite sides of the political aisle. However, if you call yourself a Christian, you're called to pray for your leaders whether you like them or not." Trust me, I said this with great care and gentleness. Many appreciated it. But one listener did not. She wrote me a letter with many capital letters and exclamation points, telling me how thoroughly uninformed I am on the issues of our day. I could definitely be more informed, I'm sure, but I know what Scripture says. And when it comes to the leaders you most despise, don't you think they'll be better off if they get more of Jesus? We're to pray for everyone, ask God to help them, intercede on their behalf. What if every Christian prayed for *everyone* with that kind of passion and sincerity? The answer? We'd live peaceful, quiet lives, marked by godliness and dignity. God wants this for us. May we do what He says and see what He will do.

LEARN Read 1 Timothy 2.

FLOURISH Take a few minutes of your prayer time each day and pray for whomever God brings to mind. Pray for leaders too.

PRAY

Lord,
I forget the power of my prayers. Give me a passion for intercession.
Burden my heart with what burdens Yours. Amen.

Do Not Neglect
Your Spiritual Gift

Do not neglect the spiritual gift you received through the prophecy spoken
over you when the elders of the church laid their hands on you.

1 Timothy 4:14

Once upon a time there was an accountant. He was gifted with spreadsheets, numbers, and financial projections. But he didn't appreciate the value of his gifts, so he became a pastor. He wrestled to find joy and attributed his struggle to the self-denying nature of the ministry. He led a few people to Christ over the years, but not many. He saw some growth in his people, but not what he'd hoped for. Then he died and went to heaven. Jesus rewarded him for his faith and thanked him for his heartfelt service. Then He lovingly said, "I never asked you to become a pastor. I appointed you to become an accountant so you could help manage a large organization. I gifted you with numbers for a reason." God has gifted you in special ways for a special purpose. Don't fall for the trap of spiritualizing some gifts over others. God has an important role for you to fill. Don't neglect your spiritual gifts. Spiritual atrophy is a real thing. If you're called to speak, speak with precision and power. If you're called to serve, do so with all of the enthusiasm and gusto you have in you. If you're called to teach, teach with excellence and joy. Your gifts are meant to be some of God's great gifts to the world.

LEARN Read 1 Timothy 4.

FLOURISH Talk with a friend today about how you're both stewarding your spiritual gifts. Inspire each other.

PRAY

Lord Jesus,
Fan the flame within me! Stir up a new passion within me! Work mightily through me! Amen.

Godliness with Contentment

But godliness with contentment is great gain.
1 Timothy 6:6 NIV

I once knew a young woman who battled perpetual discontentment. She missed out on her beautiful life completely because she anxiously looked ahead to all of the next-things she wanted but didn't yet have. One day she asked me why she was always so miserable. I gently answered, "Discontentment. It blinds us to our current blessings and hinders us from forward-moving faith." I went on to explain the passage above. Godliness is a reverent, holy pursuit of God. It's what compels us to lean in and listen for that still, small voice. It's what allows us fresh revelation around our next place of promise. It's what positions us for wisdom about what our next steps should be. And contentment? We're all in the not-yet in some ways. It takes great maturity to have forward-moving faith and vision while embracing your current lot and assignment. Most people leave before they actually leave. They abandon their current assignment before God has released them. If you want forward-moving faith that propels you to great maturity, don't run after the next shiny thing. Run after God. With all your might. And thank Him for your lot, right here, right now. Look around and thank Him for the blessings you'd miss if they went away tomorrow. Godliness *with* contentment *is* great gain.

LEARN Read 1 Timothy 6.

FLOURISH Run hard after God. Thank Him passionately for your current assignment.

PRAY

Lord,
Thank You for the life You've given me. Show me how to live here and dream with You about my future. Amen.

Enough with the Fear!

For God has not given us a spirit of fear, but of power and of love and of a sound mind.

2 Timothy 1:7 NKJV

I've battled fear on varying levels my whole life. But it wasn't until my most recent health battle that I learned of fear's toxic effect on my physiology. When your fears go rogue, they actually cause a cascade of inflammation inside your body. Did you know that inflammation is the soil where sickness and disease grow? My doctors firmly told me, "Susie, you cannot afford to allow fear in your life right now. Your body is already too inflamed." That's when I declared war on my fears. The spirit God has given us compels us to walk in power, to love sacrificially, and to keep our wits about us in a world gone mad. God has wired us to live and thrive in love. Fear has to do with punishment. Love has everything to do with redemption, wholeness, and restoration. Fear makes us cower, pull inward, and forget who we are. Love makes us open up, look up, and remember again that we're someone God loves. When fear drives us, nothing good comes of it. Fear affects our brain's ability to process information and to make sound decisions. Fear diminishes our body's ability to rightly absorb and use the nutrients we ingest. Fear compels us to make self-sabotaging decisions. Can you see why fear is such a tool of the enemy? Fear is a spirit, and it's not from God.*

LEARN Read 2 Timothy 1.

FLOURISH Deal with your fears. Deepen your understanding of God's love.

PRAY

Father,
You've given me a spirit of power, love, and sound mind. Help me to walk accordingly. Amen.

*Adapted from *Fully Alive*, 61.

A Soldier, a Farmer, and an Athlete

Endure suffering along with me, as a good soldier of Christ Jesus.
2 Timothy 2:3

We as God's people need to learn how to suffer well. We hear much about prosperity and promises and not enough about endurance and perseverance. Those who've suffered and emerged from the ashes have much to teach the world. I owe some of my greatest lessons to the school of suffering. Paul not only calls us to suffer well, he charges us to think like soldiers, farmers, and athletes. What do they have in common? They know discipline, patience, and focus. They're not idle, they're engaged with an end-goal in mind. They know how to endure hardship when opposition comes. Soldiers don't get tangled up in affairs that distract and derail them from their calling. Farmers know how to sow seeds and wait patiently for the harvest. And athletes discipline their bodies, practice their drills, and master their skills. You and I are called to see ourselves as citizens of heaven, part of the Lord's army. We're called to sow the gospel, with ample seeds of faith, kindness, generosity, hope, and love. We're to live expectantly as we wait for the promised harvest. Finally, we're to get into the habit of saying no to ourselves, of denying fleshly indulgences that only weaken us and make us vulnerable. None of this is for salvation or to gain the Father's love. All of it is to make our lives count when so many live distracted lives.

LEARN Read 2 Timothy 2.

FLOURISH Refuse obligation. But consider God's invitation. What is He asking of you in this season?

PRAY

Father,
I want to be a good soldier for You! Train me, teach me, lead me onward. Amen.

A Form of Religion Yet Without Power

They will act religious, but they will reject the power that could make them godly. Stay away from people like that!

2 Timothy 3:5

*I*n this sobering chapter, Paul warns Timothy of the perilous times ahead: "For people will love only themselves and their money. They will be boastful and proud, scoffing at God, disobedient to their parents, and ungrateful. They will consider nothing sacred. They will be unloving and unforgiving; they will slander others and have no self-control. They will be cruel and hate what is good. They will betray their friends, be reckless, be puffed up with pride, and love pleasure rather than God" (2 Timothy 3:2–4). What will it look like for us to stand in the opposite spirit? We, by God's grace and by the empowering work of the Holy Spirit, will determine to be lovers of God, generous givers, humbly gracious, God-fearing, parent-honoring, and continually grateful. We'll cherish the sacred and see the holy amidst the common. We'll catch glimpses of heaven impacting the earth. We'll love *and* forgive. We'll generously bless others and be models of self-restraint. We'll be kind. We will cherish what is good. We'll be faithful to our friends, careful with their pain, and humble about our own stories. We'll forsake momentary pleasures for the greater glory that comes with deeply knowing God. "Religious imposters will steadily denigrate."* But we who fear God's name will shine ever brighter till the full light of day.

LEARN   Read 2 Timothy 3.

FLOURISH   Press in to God. Ask Him to make you more like Him.

PRAY

Lord,
   I refuse to take my cues from the culture. I look to You! Purify and empower me. Amen.

---

*New Spirit-Filled Life Bible, 1714.

Pure Heart, Pure Perspective

Everything is pure to those whose hearts are pure. But nothing is pure to those who are corrupt and unbelieving, because their minds and consciences are corrupted.

Titus 1:15

Brain science has proven what the Bible has always said: What you look for, you will find; where your thoughts go, your life goes. Interestingly, when you rehearse certain thoughts, even if they're not true, your brain will begin to look for evidence to back up your mindset, even if it's all a farce. If you're convinced no one likes you, your brain becomes hypersensitive, picking up on any nuance to confirm your bias. When someone fills their mind with vile images, sexual exploitation, and depravity, they impair their perspective and actually damage their brain. Conversely, a pure heart and mind brings peace to the soul and life to the body.* When you renew your mind by reading and memorizing Scripture and guarding against toxic thoughts, when you guard against bitterness, unforgiveness, and offense, and when you believe the best about others and refuse to read between the lines, your whole life will be transformed. Your heart and mind are treasured gifts. Guard them with diligence. Life flows from those places. In due time, it'll be almost instinctive for you to think right thoughts, to believe the best about others, to see with redeemed eyes, and to enjoy freedoms that don't corrupt.

LEARN   Read Titus 1.

FLOURISH   Spend significant time and earnest effort keeping your heart pure and your mind renewed.

PRAY

Lord,
Purify my heart. I want to see You! Show me the hidden places within me that muddy the waters of my perspective. Help me think rightly and see redemptively. Amen.

*See Proverbs 14:30.

Minister from Mercy

When God our Savior revealed his kindness and love, he saved us, not because of the righteous things we had done, but because of his mercy.

Titus 3:4–5

I have a sister who has the spiritual gift of helps. I don't know anyone who has more capacity to help others in a variety of ways than my younger sister. One minute she'll be cleaning out someone's gutter, and the next, mowing their lawn or cleaning their house or taking pictures for their family Christmas card. I have different gifts that I seek to steward well, but I constantly feel like a substandard Christian when I measure my life against hers. Of course, it's not a competition, and one should never compare gifts with another. Paul reminds us here that we don't work our way into salvation. Praise God. I'd be in trouble otherwise. By His mercy He saved us. But out of the overflow of God's grace, Paul also charges us to help those in need, do excellent work, and steward well the call set before us. We get nowhere when we compare our service to another. But we do well when we spur one another on to love and do good deeds.* When we strive to prove, we've forgotten mercy. When we serve for love, we remember it again. Life in the Spirit leaves us clean, fresh, redeemed, and restored. We have nothing to prove, but much good work to do.

LEARN   Read Titus 3.

FLOURISH   Move out of your comfort zone and help someone in need.

PRAY

> Lord,
>   *I want to grow in good deeds because You've done so much for me. Increase my capacity to love and serve. Amen.*

*See Hebrews 10:25.

How to Energize Your Faith

[I pray] that the sharing of your faith may become effective by the acknowledgment of every good thing which is in you in Christ Jesus.

Philemon 1:6 NKJV

I was in eighth grade when I became a Christian. I understood that I was saved but didn't grasp that I was loved. It would take years for that truth to sink down into my soul. One day while in college, two beautiful, identical twin sisters approached me and asked about the twinkle in my eye. I told them about Jesus and His love for us. They were so filled with wide-eyed wonder, they grabbed other girls from their floor and brought them to me as well. The more I shared what I'd learned from God's Word, the more my faith quickened within me. I felt my spirit come alive. The word *effective* in the passage above is *enereges*, where we get the word *energy*. Paul prayed that Philemon would be increasingly activated and energized in his faith *as he acknowledged* the riches Christ had deposited within him. I eventually grew to understand that I was not only saved, I was loved and called and equipped and grafted into a royal family line. The more I learned, the more I had to share with others. This is why it matters that we not only share our faith, but that we understand what we possess. The deeper your well, the more you'll have to draw from, and the more energized you'll be as you share with others.

LEARN Read Philemon 1:1–7.

FLOURISH Consider all God has done in you and share accordingly.

PRAY

Lord,
Energize me as I share who You are and what You've done. I am rich beyond measure and You are good beyond comprehension. Amen!

When God Calls You to Return

It seems you lost Onesimus for a little while so that you could have him back forever.

Philemon 1:15

*P*hilemon's slave, Onesimus, ran away, but then he met Paul, who introduced him to Jesus, who radically transformed his life. Paul discipled Onesimus and became a dear friend and brother in the faith. Because Paul was such a man of integrity, he instructed Onesimus to return to Philemon. "When God finds runaways, he often sends them back to the very places and people from which they ran in the first place. As God has become real in your life, how has your past come into new perspective? Are there still situations from your past that need to be resolved? In what ways has your relationship with Christ given you new opportunities and resources to face what you used to run away from?"* What might this look like in today's world? Maybe you ditched a relationship at the first sign of conflict. Or left a job when you didn't experience the affirmation you were looking for. Or abandoned a ministry when it started to cost you. Or left a church because you viewed your experience through a consumer lens. God offers grace, redemption, and forgiveness for all of these. Sometimes you can't go back and pick up where you left off. But you can go back and rebuild some bridges. Sometimes God calls us back for a short season so He can launch us out into the next season.

LEARN Read Philemon 1:8–25.

FLOURISH Ask the Lord if you need to go back so you can go forward.

PRAY

Jesus,
   Forgive me for my self-sabotaging ways. Lead me to life and life abundant. Amen.

Life Application Study Bible, 2725.

He Cleansed Us,
Then Sat Down

When he had cleansed us from our sins, he sat down in the place of honor at the right hand of the majestic God in heaven.

Hebrews 1:3

After He defeated death and cleansed us from sin's power to destroy us, Jesus sat down in the place of honor at God's right hand. If we could peel back the sky, we'd see the angels singing *Holy, holy, holy is the Lord!* We'd see power and light emanating from the throne. We'd be so undone by God's power and majesty that our knees would buckle right underneath us. Oh, to get a glimpse of the reality of heaven! We'd stop our striving and posturing, and we'd worship instead. We'd see the power of our prayers and the sacredness of our obedience. Jesus finished the work necessary to set us free. It's finished. Imagine if you started each day by telling yourself, *It is finished. Jesus already sat down. He's at His Father's right hand, ruling with power and majesty and authority. I am cleansed, forgiven, and free.* My pastor used to say that he wanted to live his life under the glory spout—the place from which God's power flows and empowers us. How do we so often miss what God offers us? We forget about the finished work of Christ. We strive to validate ourselves, to manage outcomes, and to control circumstances. If there is a glory spout, it's the place where we surrender our circumstances, entrust outcomes, and rest in the finished work of Christ. We're in good hands. The best hands.

LEARN Read Hebrews 1.

FLOURISH Rest. Entrust. Surrender. Remember, He sat down. It's finished.

PRAY

Jesus,
I want to live the powerful life You've made available to me. Lead me, Lord. Amen.

Be Careful Not to Drift

So we must listen very carefully to the truth we have heard, or we may drift away from it.

Hebrews 2:1

My brother was on a downward spiral, addicted to alcohol and drugs, thoroughly depressed. My brother-in-law asked him several times, "Are you ready to trust Jesus yet?" He never was. Rich gave him a piece of paper with his number and a Bible verse. He said, "Call me before you decide to take your life." One day, Jeff had hit bottom. He was down in his shop with a gun in his hand, ready to end it all. But then he remembered that piece of paper he'd tacked to the wall. Romans 8:28 stared back at him. He called Rich, who came right away, wrapped him in an embrace, and led him to the Lord. Jeff was radically, beautifully saved that day. He was miraculously delivered from his addiction too. Years later, the enemy taunted, depression surfaced, and shame put a chokehold on him. He began to wander back into his old ways. He was drifting because he'd stopped listening to the truth that sets men free. Thankfully, he didn't drift far before he came back to faith again. Some drift doctrinally; they lose their way. Others drift from their sense of identity and look for love in all the wrong places. Still others drift into trying to earn their way because grace seems too good to be true. We're drifters by nature. We need to inhale truth and exhale lies every single moment of our lives. Truth sets us free. Truth keeps us grounded.

LEARN Read Hebrews 2.

FLOURISH Rehearse the truths that your soul needs today.

PRAY

Lord,
Show me where I'm vulnerable to drift. Impart to me the truth that I need.

Think Carefully About This Jesus

Think carefully about this Jesus whom we declare to be God's messenger and High Priest.

Hebrews 3:1

Some of the Israelites idolized Moses and yet completely missed Jesus. Whenever we drift from a deep and intimate walk with God, we construct a savior that fits our preferences. But the author of Hebrews charges us to think carefully about this Jesus, the One who actually came to save us. At every turn, He frustrated people. They expected one thing and He delivered another. His own disciples wanted Him to overthrow Rome, but He came to save the world. Religious camps wanted Him to pick sides, but He picked sinners instead, because He knew they needed Him. He's not soft on sin, but He's full of compassion for the sinner. He says, "Follow me and live," and yet He also bids us come and die—die to our imagined rights, our self-preservation, our self-promoting ways. He wants us to live free, secure, and whole. He calls us to love ourselves and to love our enemies. He offers us no leniency for grudges, unforgiveness, or dishonor. He's not impressed with passionate worship if the life behind it is secretly living in sin. You can't earn His favor or bribe Him to look the other way. He sees all, knows all, and continually calls us higher, to be more like Him. Do you really want to follow Jesus? Because He'll ask for everything. But what He offers is beyond your wildest dreams.

LEARN Read Hebrews 3.

FLOURISH Ponder the aspects of Jesus' character that challenge you. Lean in and listen to Him.

PRAY

Jesus,
Forgive me for trying to fit You into my idea of what I think You should be. Reveal Yourself to me. Amen.

Rest Is an Act of Faith

God's promise of entering his rest still stands, so we ought to tremble with fear that some of you might fail to experience it.

Hebrews 4:1

*M*y husband has this Calvin Miller quote on his desk: "Lord, help me to remember that I can make more bricks in six days than I can in seven." When the Israelites wandered in the wilderness, they groaned and complained when they should have persevered and believed. Their faith would have been so precious to God. He provided for them, performed miracles for them, and made a way for them—many times in spite of them. We exhaust ourselves in similar ways. We commit to more than God asks of us, and we fall apart. We strive to prove our worth and we're left with either pride or humiliation, neither of which come from God's heart. We forget about the sacred, eternal rest that awaits us, and thus live like this life is all there is, and we forfeit an eternal reward.* Rest is an act of faith. It can even be an act of war on the enemy of your soul. When the devil tries to bait you into striving, take your place under the shadow of God's wing and rest awhile. The enemy will hate it and you will be restored. Rest from your labors. Rest from your striving. Rest even while you work because you know your eternity is secure. True rest requires perseverance, vision, and faith. We cannot mature until we learn how to rest.

LEARN Read Hebrews 4:1–11.

FLOURISH Find rest in God for the restless parts of you (identity, future, finances, etc.).

PRAY

Lord,
Lead me to deeper places of rest and assurance. I trust You. Amen.

*See 2 Corinthians 5:10.

God's Word, Alive and Powerful

For the word of God is alive and powerful. It is sharper than the sharpest two-edged sword, cutting between soul and spirit, between joint and marrow. It exposes our innermost thoughts and desires.

Hebrews 4:12

I knelt down, bowed my head, and rested my forearms on the couch. I couldn't help but notice the worn fabric from my many months on bedrest. I cried out to God, "O Lord, You promised to supply all of our needs. We're dying financially. I'm sick. But I'm holding on to Your promise." Moments later, I spoke my fears to my husband. "We'll never get out of this. We have more medical debt than income. I don't see a way out." Instantly I felt pierced by the Holy Spirit. *You don't "see" a way out? Do you need to see for there to be a way? Your own words defy the promises of God. Bring your words into agreement with the Word of God and then you'll pray with power.* I was praying one thing and saying another. "So why would the Bible refer to the Word of God repeatedly as a 'two-edged sword' or literally a 'two-mouthed sword'? The Word of God is like a sword that has two edges, cutting both ways and doing terrible damage to an aggressor."* We're like a divided kingdom when our words conflict with God's Word. Want to walk in power? Say and pray God's Word.

LEARN Read Hebrews 4.

FLOURISH Check your words. Do they line up with God's Word?

PRAY

Father,
Show me the inconsistencies in my thoughts and words. Call me higher.
I want to speak with precision and pray with power. Amen.

*Sparkling Gems from the Greek, 109.

Obedience through Suffering

Even though Jesus was God's Son, he learned obedience from the things he suffered.

Hebrews 5:8

*M*y legs were all tangled up in the bedsheets. My T-shirt was soaked with sweat. Kev slept peacefully next to me. Awash in fear and anxiety, I was too young to be so sick. I had three little boys to raise. I begged God, "Heal me, Lord. Please, heal me. My little ones need me. My husband needs a helpmate. Please, Lord." Every night my prayers seemed to bounce off the ceiling. Did God lose my address? *Where are You, God?* One night He broke His silence. His question forever changed the way I walk with Him. He whispered into the dark of my night, *"If I healed you, would you praise me?"* I replied, "Oh, yes, Lord! I'll shout it from the mountaintops!" He continued, *"Why is that? Would you praise Me because I'm God, the One who put the stars in place and sent My only Son to die for you? Or would you praise Me simply because you got your way?"* I was undone. I literally tore my shirt in repentance and went facedown on the floor. My life flashed before my eyes and I realized how much of it was about me, not about Him. He'd been my Savior. But that night He became my Lord. Even Jesus learned submission through the things He suffered. Don't waste your suffering. It'll purify your heart like nothing else can.

LEARN Read Hebrews 5.

FLOURISH Consider the conditions you've placed on your relationship with God. Open your hands and trust Him with *everything*.

PRAY

Jesus,
You modeled holy submission in a way that takes my breath away. I offer my whole self to You. Have Your way in me. Amen.

An Anchor for Your Soul

This hope is a strong and trustworthy anchor for our souls. It leads us through the curtain into God's inner sanctuary.

Hebrews 6:19

*Y*ou and I are anchored *upward* to God, where He sits on His throne in His inner sanctuary. Imagine! Though the storms rage and the winds about knock us over, we're *anchored* to God Almighty. Picture your soul's anchor leading upward. Remember that God's hold on you is stronger than your hold on Him. He's relying on himself (not you) to get you safely home. God wants you to partner with Him to accomplish His purposes on earth. You'll have to fight for some of the things God has promised you. You'll have to stand on His Word even when it doesn't feel true. But the battle will be worth it. And when it's all over but the shouting, you can be assured that Jesus will get you safely home because that's what He promised He'd do. Having to contend for the things God puts on my heart while the enemy works to steal my joy, kill my dreams, and destroy my sense of purpose—well, this fight has made me a fiercer woman of prayer. Anything worth having is worth praying for. The thing about an anchor is that it's built to withstand the fiercest storms. An anchor that's worth its weight will hold no matter which way the wind is blowing.* God's got you. Live by faith. Pray with power. You're secure.

LEARN Read Hebrews 6.

FLOURISH Remind your soul just how secure you are. Be bold in faith. Be confident in prayer.

PRAY

Lord,
I am tethered to a good God! Help me to believe that I'm as secure as I truly am and live accordingly. Amen.

*Adapted from Susie's book *Your Powerful Prayers* (Minneapolis: Bethany House Publishers, 2016), 110.

Don't Throw Away
Your Confidence

So do not throw away this confident trust in the Lord. Remember the great reward it brings you!

Hebrews 10:35

Two steps forward. Three steps back. I fought and fought to come back from this most recent health relapse. One day I'd gain ground and the next I'd lose it. My options? Give up and throw away my confidence, or rise up, grab a firmer hold on God's promises, and keep marching. My health battle was nothing compared to what persecuted Christians endured in the first century, or what they endure today. The writer of Hebrews charged believers to remember God's promises. Remember His love. He's worth it. And our faith matters. The word *confidence* in the verse above translates "cheerful courage, boldness, and assurance."* This speaks of both a steadfast spirit *and* a bold confession of God's faithfulness. It's amazing to think that our faith is so precious to God that He actually stores up a reward for us when we hold on to His promises. He gives us faith, encourages our faith, and then rewards us for our faith. How do we persevere when we feel like giving up? Verse 36 tells us, "Patient endurance is what you need now." Consider a long-distance runner, focused, paced, purposeful. Don't lose heart when the way gets long, and definitely don't make big life decisions when you're running uphill. Stay the course. God *will* reward you.

LEARN ▶ Read Hebrews 10.

FLOURISH ▶ Take a firm grip with your tired hands, and make a straight path for your feet.†

PRAY ▶

Lord,
This journey isn't for sissies. Help me to stand strong, stay the course, and remember Your promises. Amen.

*Strong's Interlinear Bible Search, StudyLight.org, Hebrews 10:35.
†See Hebrews 12:12–14.

Faith Is Your Substance

Faith shows the reality of what we hope for; it is the evidence of things we cannot see.

Hebrews 11:1

Miracles happen every day. The sick are healed. The lost are found. The barren have children. Prodigals come home. But what about those who pray and fast and stand on God's promises, and still their loved one dies? What did faith accomplish in that case? What *is* faith, anyway? Faith is the strong conviction that God is who He says He is and that He will do just as He promised. We get tangled up in doubt when we determine God's intended outcome before He even reveals it to us. We zero in on one possibility and miss all of the ways God is working in and around us. If God doesn't give us what we hope for in this life, it's because His answers to our desires are far and away better than we ever imagined, and those answers are meant to be ours throughout eternity. Furthermore, when we engage our faith and we place our hope firmly in God (and not in our expected outcome), something changes within us. We're so deeply connected to the life-force that flows from God, it can't help but shore us up and change us from the inside out. Our faith is never wasted on us, nor is it ever tossed aside by God. It is wise, though, to discern God's voice before we decide on what we think our outcome should reveal. His peace always confirms His ways.

LEARN Read Hebrews 11.

FLOURISH First discern God's voice, then engage your faith.

PRAY

Father,
You are faithful, kind, and true. And You never waver in being so. Let me hear Your voice that I might stand in faith. Amen.

When the Lord Disciplines

Don't make light of the LORD's discipline,
and don't give up when he corrects you.
Hebrews 12:5

*W*hen our boys were young and made choices they shouldn't, we'd get down on their level, look them in the eyes, and say, "You are too important to be making decisions like that." They'd stand up straighter even while they received correction. We tend to fall to two extremes when God's discipline comes: insecurity or ignorance. We fall into a heap and berate ourselves for messing up, or we shrug our shoulders and dismiss what's meant to stop us in our tracks. When God brings correction, we either crumble like we're nothing, or we refuse to change like it's nothing. God is a good, good Father, and He disciplines those He deeply loves. So when you've stepped out of the bounds God intends for you, God will come for you. One Bible scholar on my show said, "He'll first turn on the light and if you don't respond, He'll turn up the heat." I've heard far too many stories of folks who've either lost heart because they allowed God's correction to bring condemnation (which is not from Him), or they tossed aside their convictions and walked straight into a trap that destroyed their reputation. That's why the writer of Hebrews opens this chapter by telling us to get rid of anything that will trip us up and slow us down. God wants us to last long and finish strong.

LEARN ▶ Read Hebrews 12.

FLOURISH ▶ Have you allowed anything to remain in your life that gives the devil opportunity to dismantle your influence? Get rid of it.

PRAY ▶

Lord,
  Give me the desire to live a powerful and pure life. Show me the importance of my influence. Amen.

The Best-Kept Secret in the Bible

If you need wisdom, ask our generous God, and he will give it to you. He will not rebuke you for asking.

James 1:5

Suppose you received a letter from your local bank. There's an account with your name on it. An anonymous donor pledged to continually replenish the account as you withdraw the funds you need. What will you do? Leave it alone? Or draw from the generous provision offered you? I remember stumbling upon this passage in James as a young mom, desperate for wisdom on how to navigate sickness, medical bills, and motherhood. God highlighted it before me, and I realized that I never have to go without the wisdom I need. From that day forward I stretched out my arms and unabashedly asked for more and more God-given insight. To this day, I shamelessly run into God's presence and draw from His heavenly promise of wisdom. Amazingly, He's promised not only to give wisdom, but to *lavish* it upon us. The word *wisdom* translates this way: "knowledge of things human and divine; the act of interpreting dreams and always giving the sagest advice; supreme intelligence such as belongs to God."* Imagine—God wants to impart His supreme intelligence to you. God's wisdom will keep you out of trouble, help you to rightly interpret your trials, and keep God at the center of your life. Wisdom points others to Him. You have a wealthy, loving heavenly Father. Draw on the provision He's so freely offered you.

LEARN   Read James 1.

FLOURISH   Boldly, humbly ask for more and more wisdom.

PRAY

Lord,
    Pour out fresh wisdom on me today! Give sight to my eyes, clarity to my ears, and discernment to my heart. Amen.

*Strong's Interlinear Bible Search, StudyLight.org, James 1:5.

Favor, Not Favoritism

My dear brothers and sisters, how can you claim to have faith in our glorious
Lord Jesus Christ if you favor some people over others?

James 2:1

Favoritism creates inequity. It shows partiality toward one at the expense of the other. I've been on the receiving end of favoritism, and there's something insidious about it. You know you're in an unjust system; you just happen to be on the upside of it. You're set up to succeed, but you don't really thrive because it contradicts God's order of things. You have to posture to maintain favoritism and live in fear that you may lose it. Favoritism holds you captive to man's opinion and tempts you to overlook how others are treated. God hates favoritism. But He's all about favor. What's the difference? The word *favor* in the passage above speaks of showing preference due to outward circumstances. But look at the word *favor* in this passage: "Surely, LORD, you bless the righteous; you surround them with favor as with a shield" (Psalm 5:12 NIV). It translates this way: "pleasure, delight, good will."* God *indiscriminately lavishes love* on people. He is not impressed with wealth, status, or appearance. He is God, after all. But He's deeply moved by faith, humility, and love. He will never look at a convicted felon as worth less than a CEO of a Fortune 500 company. He looks at the heart. And if the heart is humble and receptive, He moves in and moves mightily.

LEARN Read James 2.

FLOURISH Allow God to challenge your prejudices that you might see everyone as He does.

PRAY

> *Lord,*
> *Forgive me for misreading situations and misjudging others. Give me*
> *Your heart so I can love the way You do. Amen.*

*Strong's Interlinear Bible Search, StudyLight.org, Psalm 5:12.

Gateway Sins That Destroy

For wherever there is jealousy and selfish ambition, there you will find disorder and evil of every kind.

James 3:16

*W*hen God awakens a fresh sense of purpose in us, we feel excitement, hope, and anticipation for what God might do. Other motivations awaken within us as well. Envy, impatience, comparisons, and ambition. We're all a pile of contradictions. God first ignites a sense of purpose in us, and then He takes us through a training process. I write extensively about this in my book *Your Beautiful Purpose.* As soon as a fresh sense of purpose arises within us, we have a choice to make: We either trust God and lean in to His purifying, preparatory work in us, or we run ahead, try to manipulate outcomes, and posture for promotion. If you're tempted toward the latter, I pray that the passage above stops you in your tracks. Where jealousy and selfish ambition are left unchecked, the enemy is given legal access to drive a wedge between us and our God-given purpose. Note the progression described in this chapter. These sins go from being earthly, to unspiritual, to demonic. God wants to preserve His dream for you in its purest form. And the enemy wants to pervert that dream so he can dismantle your influence. Settle it in your heart that God makes you wait because He's making you ready. When the time is right, He'll put you into position in an instant, and no enemy or obstacle can stop him!

LEARN Read James 3.

FLOURISH Ruthlessly deal with the sins of jealousy, comparison, and selfish ambition.

PRAY

Lord,
Use me! Prepare me for promotion. I trust Your timing. Amen.

Battle-Ready

Submit yourselves, then, to God. Resist the devil, and he will flee from you.

James 4:7 NIV

*S*ometimes the devil comes after you because you're about to break through. He sees your potential, is threatened by it, and aims to stop you. Other times he attacks because your progress in the faith obstructs his destructive schemes. Still other times he attacks because he sees an opening and he takes it. How do we give the devil permission to attack us? By our attitudes and sinful disobedience, like when we undermine authority, refuse to forgive, or embrace pride. The word *submit* in the passage above is a military term and means to get back in rank. We'll never have authority until we're under authority. On our own, we're no match for the enemy. But when we stand in Christ's authority, he's no match for us! If you're dealing with enemy opposition, first search your heart. Check your attitudes and get back in rank if you've stepped out from under God's protective authority. Now you're positioned to send the enemy packing. Resist the devil and he *has* to flee from you. The word *flee* expresses the idea that he literally runs for his life! If we could see into the spiritual realm, we'd see some Christians cowering in fear because of enemy opposition. And in other cases, we'd see the enemy running for cover because of the Christians who've learned to stand in their authority. Stay in rank. Stand in faith. Send the enemy packing.

LEARN　　Read James 4.

FLOURISH　　Keep a close watch on your heart and attitudes. Stay in rank. Pray with power.

PRAY

Lord,
　Quickly alert me the second I step out of rank. I want to live under Your authority. Amen.

Confession, Healing, and Freedom

Confess your sins to each other and pray for each other so that you may be healed. The earnest prayer of a righteous person has great power and produces wonderful results.

James 5:16

My producer and I did an onsite interview with author and pastor Bob Merritt. He pastors one of the largest churches in America. In his book *Done with That*, he openly writes about his struggle with wielding his words in a sometimes-hurtful way. He's one of the most humble, honest leaders I've ever met. In his relaxed way, he asked, "So what's your signature sin?" My answer? "I'm very present when I'm with others. I listen well. But when I'm in task mode, I'm in a hurry. I'll rush right past people and miss them completely." Pastor Bob asked the question in such a nonassuming way—because we all have signature sins—that I felt something lift as soon as I admitted my need for more of Jesus. The word *confess* in this passage means "to acknowledge openly and joyfully." Have you ever thought of confession that way? You would if you knew how loved and forgiven you already are. You'll never be delivered from a sin that you refuse to acknowledge. Things kept in the dark keep us captive. Determine to be free. Be honest about your shortcomings. Be joyful. You have a Savior. Stay in community. Healing and freedom are yours for the taking.

LEARN   Read James 5.

FLOURISH   Ask your tribe if you can all take things to the next level. Pray for healing. Seek freedom.

PRAY

Jesus,
I keep forgetting how free I am! Forgive me for keeping secrets, denying sins, and hiding my needs. I want to walk confidently, fearlessly, and freely. Lead me on. Amen.

Trials Prove Your Faith

These trials will show that your faith is genuine. It is being tested as fire tests and purifies gold—though your faith is far more precious than mere gold.

1 Peter 1:7

*E*very moment of our lives is packed with eternal potential. Hidden in every trial is an opportunity for faith. Every blessing comes with an invitation to be a generous steward. Every setback provides the chance to persevere and mature. We want relief. God wants to redeem our story. We want a break. God is after a breakthrough. Dudley Rutherford writes, "If there weren't a wall standing in your way today, how would you be able to give glory to God for the victory He wants to give you in the future? How would you be able to praise God in the sight of your friends and neighbors for providing for you, healing you, forgiving you, giving you grace, or coming through for you in the nick of time? Unless we had trials to defeat, what other opportunity would we have to cultivate our character and increase our faith?"* The Bible says that when your faith remains strong through your trials, your amazing faith will be acknowledged and honored *before the whole world* when Jesus is revealed as the King of Kings. Don't waste your trials. God tempers the storms so they will not destroy you. He allows enough hardship to refine you. And He provides ample opportunity for your faith to reward you.

LEARN Read 1 Peter 1.

FLOURISH By faith, look past your trial and see the eternal potential. Press on, in Jesus' name.

PRAY

Father,
You've given me everything I need to overcome. Help me to stand in faith today. Amen.

*Dudley Rutherford, *Walls Fall Down* (Nashville: Thomas Nelson, 2014), 24.

Be Tenderhearted and Humble

Finally, all of you should be of one mind. Sympathize with each other. Love each other as brothers and sisters. Be tenderhearted, and keep a humble attitude.

1 Peter 3:8

I saw an online poll today. The question? Is the media fair to our current president? The media is not fair in any way. Whichever way you slant, you'll find a news outlet that justifies your side and villainizes the other side. We fall into their trap when we believe everything they say. As Christians, we're called to maintain a heart of compassion and tenderness, of empathy and kindness *toward everyone*. But that doesn't just happen on its own. We must steward our perspective and be careful about which inputs we allow to shape our perspective. Since we belong to Jesus and He paid a high price for our freedom, we must identify more with Him than we do with our political persuasions. Not to say we don't have opinions, convictions, and positions on important issues. But as I've repeatedly said to my sons, if you have to let go of love to hang on to your cause, you've lost your way. Peter charges us to be tender and humble and full of empathy. He writes, "Don't retaliate with insults when people insult you. Instead, pay them back with a blessing" (v. 9). We don't have it in us to return a blessing when we're cursed, unless we allow Jesus to change us from the inside out. Jesus can only redeem communities through redeemed souls.

LEARN Read 1 Peter 3.

FLOURISH Take a break from the news and immerse yourself in the Word.

PRAY

Lord,
I need a kingdom perspective. Show me what You see. Help me to live accordingly. Amen.

Use Your Gifts!

God has given each of you a gift from his great variety of spiritual gifts. Use them well to serve one another.

1 Peter 4:10

*W*hen God gave me the desire to work in radio, a number of people told me that it would kill my "career" as a writer. First of all, I see what I do as more of a ministry than a career. And second, I follow the peace of God even when it makes no sense to me. They reasoned that if I spent all my time promoting everyone else's books, my books would never sell. But then one day a wise friend said, "Susie, you're not an author; that's something you *do*. You're a deeper-life woman and you thrive on rich, deep conversations. To me, you doing radio keeps you under the 'tent' of your calling; you're just holding a different pole." That made so much sense to me. Surprisingly, I became a better writer once I started my work in radio. It's important not to limit yourself by thinking only one way about your gifts. God is creative and loves to provide ample opportunity for you to thrive in your gifting. However, be sure to discern the difference between the endless opportunities before you and your God-given assignment. The need doesn't always dictate the call. And sometimes He'll call you to an assignment that seems small and insignificant at first, but hidden within is the chance for you to spread your wings and watch God raise you up beyond your wildest dreams.

LEARN Read 1 Peter 4.

FLOURISH Don't minimize your gifts. Embrace them. And steward them valiantly.

PRAY

Lord,
Forgive me for thinking I have substandard gifts. I love how You made me. Help me to serve boldly and gladly! Amen.

Humble Yourself

So humble yourselves under the mighty power of God, and at the right time he will lift you up in honor. Give all your worries and cares to God, for he cares about you.

1 Peter 5:6–7

Charlotte Gambill tells the story about a time when her family went on a ski trip. They were all skiers except for her. She took lessons on the small hill and then launched out when she thought she was ready. She picked up speed and soon found herself unable to slow down. As she hurtled toward a group of little children taking lessons, she noticed a tree close by. She thought, *I have to make a choice here. Personal pain or collateral damage.* She chose personal pain. She hit the tree, got a bit banged up, but never hurt the children. There will be times in our lives when we're faced with a similar choice. Absorb some pain or raise a ruckus because of how we're treated. We may have enough credibility to cause quite a bit of collateral damage. But what if we humbled ourselves instead? What if we entrusted our heartbreak to God, who misses nothing and deals meticulously with every situation? Scripture says that whenever we humble ourselves under God's mighty power, He will lift us up in honor, which translates this way: "to exalt; to raise to dignity, honor and happiness."* God cares when you're mistreated, dismissed, or overlooked. It's beneath you to start a riot. Go to God with every bit of your angst. Watch Him intervene in ways that establish and vindicate you.

LEARN Read 1 Peter 5.

FLOURISH Humble yourself before God today. Entrust every care to Him.

PRAY

Father,
You don't miss a thing. I trust You. Intervene by Your power and authority. Amen.

---

*Strong's Interlinear Bible Search, StudyLight.org, 1 Peter 5:6.

Power to Change

By his divine power, God has given us everything we need for living a godly life.

2 Peter 1:3

*G*uest speaker Pastor Jimmy Evans spoke at church today. He shared how he started smoking as a young teen. Though he became a Christian in his early twenties, he continued to smoke. He'd page through his Bible and tap the ashes off of his cigarette. One day the Lord spoke to him: "I want to use you in great ways, but you'll need to quit smoking." He tried and failed. Then one day he cried out to God, told Him he didn't have the willpower to quit smoking. The Lord affirmed that he was right. He couldn't do it on his own. But by the power of the Holy Spirit, he could. The Lord said to him, "Next time you're tempted to light up, just say out loud, 'I'm a nonsmoker.' And trust me to help you." It seemed so simple, but it worked. He realized that the flesh cannot be whipped into shape. There will always be a war between the flesh and the spirit within us. But when we walk by the Spirit, we will not gratify the desires of the flesh.* The power to change comes from the power of the living, breathing, activating power of the Holy Spirit at work within us. If you're tired of striving for change, try abiding instead. Pastor Jimmy charged us to pray daily, "Lord, give me righteous desires." Amen.

LEARN Read 2 Peter 1.

FLOURISH Ask the Holy Spirit to help you make the change you've longed to see. Trust Him more than you trust yourself.

PRAY

Father,
Remove every desire that weakens me. Awaken righteous desires so that I may thrive and live free. Amen.

*See Galatians 5:16.

You Just Never Know

Yes, Lot was a righteous man who was tormented in his soul by the wickedness he saw and heard day after day.

2 Peter 2:8

I was so surprised to read that Lot was considered a righteous man and that he was actually tormented in his soul over the wickedness that he saw and heard day after day. He did—after all—choose to camp among the ungodly. And when he warned his family about the coming judgment, they didn't take him seriously at first. Which makes me think he'd lost some credibility with them. But I love how God sees through our circumstances, past our appearances, and knows intimately what's going on in the heart. Interestingly, Peter uses much of this chapter to describe false teachers. Yet he mentions Lot as one of the righteous ones. A truly false teacher willingly departs from Scripture and teaches that which is contrary to the basic cores of Christianity. Unfortunately, this accusation gets unfairly hurled around a lot within Christian circles. We are all a work in progress. I've interviewed many guests who shared how in their past, as new believers, they still actively sinned yet passionately loved God. They were in process. If someone grabbed a snapshot of that moment of their life, they'd notice the disconnect and write them off. But not God. His patience in our process is breathtaking. He sees what's true, and He will not abandon His own, no matter how messy the story or how long the process.

LEARN Read 2 Peter 2.

FLOURISH Suspend all judgments and sincerely pray for those in whom you see a disconnect.

PRAY

Father,
We live in a snap-to-judgment world. But I want to live and perceive differently. Open my eyes to see what You see. Amen.

A Thousand Years

> But you must not forget this one thing, dear friends: A day is like a thousand years to the Lord, and a thousand years is like a day.
>
> 2 Peter 3:8

I interviewed Joni Eareckson Tada on my show. Most everyone knows her story—she broke her neck in a diving accident as a teenager. Joni shared how at first, those days in the hospital were a blur. She went from one therapy session to another. But once she left the hospital and moved in with her sister, the days slowed to a standstill. She felt depressed and hopeless. Then a friend came for a visit. He read her 2 Peter 3:8, and God met her in that moment. She reflected, "We've all heard that a day is like a thousand years. But it never occurred to me that a thousand years is like a day. That means I can bear a thousand years' worth of fruit in a single day. Though I'm limited by my wheelchair, I'm not limited in prayer. How might we live differently if we truly understood the eternal potential in every day God gives us?"* What if we lived like this was true? Would you pray with more passion? Speak with greater courage? Give generously with the assurance that God is storing up treasures in heaven *just for you*? Imagine if every kingdom investment you made today was multiplied a thousand times over. How might you live differently today?

LEARN Read 2 Peter 3.

FLOURISH Reframe your day. Seek His kingdom first. Believe Him for great things.

PRAY

> *Lord,*
> *Show me my God-given assignment today. Help me to live by faith, give by faith, and walk by faith, not by sight. Multiply my offering. Amen.*

*My paraphrase of my conversation with Joni.

Walking in the Light

> But if we are living in the light, as God is in the light, then we have fellowship
> with each other, and the blood of Jesus, his Son, cleanses us from all sin.
>
> 1 John 1:7

A couple of days ago, we explored how the process to holiness and maturity is messy for some, especially if there's a lot of heartache, brokenness, and dysfunction in their history. We need to be patient with the process of new believers because God has been patient with us. But here's the qualifier: Over time, there must be progress, evidence of fruit, growth in maturity. Some profess faith in Christ and go on their merry way and live no differently than they did before they said "the prayer." Jesus himself said that some who profess Him as Lord do not belong to Him. How do you know that you're saved? Did you sincerely repent of your sin when you first came to Christ? Are you bothered when you sin even now? Do you feel the conviction of the Holy Spirit when you step off of God's path for you? Do you love God's Word? Are you drawn to the light of God's redeeming power, or do you prefer to keep things hidden in the darkness? Is there fruit coming from your life? Someone once said, "God's not after perfection. Just progress." We're saved by grace, yes. But if there's no transformation, there's no fellowship with other believers. Two people cannot walk together if they're headed in different directions.

LEARN Read 1 John 1.

FLOURISH If you wonder about the salvation of another, ask God to overwhelm them with His saving power.

PRAY

> *Lord,*
> *Bring radical, transformative salvation to every person I wonder*
> *about! Amen.*

Christians and Shame

And now, dear children, remain in fellowship with Christ so that when he returns, you will be full of courage and not shrink back from him in shame.

1 John 2:28

Shame chokes the life right out of us. Consider what's true about some of the mindsets we embrace without even thinking about it: It's not humility that compels us to shy away from God and ask little of Him—it's shame. It's not integrity that keeps us from asking for God's help when we need it—it's pride, independence, or shame. It's not kindness that keeps us from "bothering" God with our persistent requests—it's either spiritual laziness or shame.* Jesus wants to deliver us from *all* of our shame. But here's a point we often miss. It's possible for genuine believers to shrink back in shame on that great day when we give account for our lives.† John's letter is to believers. He charges us to remain in Christ (abide, be held, kept continually) throughout our journey. God *wants* to reward a life lived in faith. Scripture charges us over and over again to stay the course. Still, some will ignore all warnings and live solely for themselves. And when they see all God has prepared for those who took Him at His word, they will feel ashamed, sober, and regretful. Still, they'll enjoy heaven forever with Jesus. But that day of reckoning is real.

LEARN Read 1 John 2.

FLOURISH Ask God to remove every shred of shame from your life. Live ready with joyful expectancy.

PRAY

Father,
You want to reward me! Thank You! Help me to live a life that pleases You. Amen.

---

*Adapted from Susie's book *Your Powerful Prayers*, 172.
†See 2 Corinthians 5:10.

We Shall Be Like Him

Dear friends, we are already God's children, but he has not yet shown us
what we will be like when Christ appears. But we do know that we will be like
him, for we will see him as he really is.

1 John 3:2

I've come so far in my faith journey. I don't at all resemble the person I once was. God has healed and delivered me from fear, anxiety, insecurity, and self-preservation. He's forgiven and delivered me from selfishness, striving, and jealousy. I cringe when I think of the person I used to be. But Jesus never cringes when He sees us. He pursues us with a heart full of compassion and love. I still have a long way to go in the ways of holiness. Yet I've noticed that when I focus on my frailties, that's all I see. John's letter reminds us that when we *hope in the Lord*, it actually *purifies us*. He's our life source. His oxygen energizes us. His blood cleanses us. His power redeems us. His life-giving power quickens our mortal bodies. Even though we're nowhere near the people we will one day be, Jesus treasures us *just as we are*. And when we finally see Jesus face to face, we'll become who we were always meant to be. Imagine! Your eyes will sparkle, your face will shine, and your heart will be healed and whole. That day *is* coming.

LEARN Read 1 John 3.

FLOURISH Spend less time thinking about how you fall down, and more time about how God continually holds you up.

PRAY

Father,
My hope is in You! I'm a work in progress, and one day I will be everything You dreamed I could be. Thank You, Lord. Amen.

He Loved You First

This is real love—not that we loved God, but that he loved us and sent his
Son as a sacrifice to take away our sins.

1 John 4:10

Before you were even born, God loved you first. Before you knew you
were capable of sin, He sent His only Son to save you, forgive you,
and totally redeem your story. Before you knew how others might hurt or
betray you, God promised to stay by your side. Before you knew that you'd
need divine direction during critical times in your life, God honored your
story and spoke peace to your soul, so you'd know which way to go. Before
you'd grasp the storms you'd have to endure, He offered His Holy Spirit to
guard and guide, comfort and provide. When you decided to strive for appearance's sake, He watched and waited and loved you through it. When
you got too big for your britches and thought too highly of yourself, He
gently and lovingly showed you what's true. When you tripped up and fell
down and friends scattered, He stayed close and loved you back to wholeness
again. He loves how He made you. He loves to think about you. He loves
to intervene on your behalf. And He loves what He's forming in you. He'll
never look away or forget about you. He'll never lose your address. And He'll
never be surprised by you. He knew who He was getting when He got you.
He absolutely, unequivocally loved you first.

LEARN Read 1 John 4.

FLOURISH Smile today as you ponder God's great, unfathomable love
for you.

PRAY

Father,
How can it be? Yet it's true! Help me to grasp Your affection for me. I
receive it and believe it. Amen.

Confident Prayer

And we are confident that he hears us whenever we ask for anything that pleases him. And since we know he hears us when we make our requests, we also know that he will give us what we ask for.

1 John 5:15

My husband was a workaholic. I missed him. And I wanted better for our family. He worked for a company that was life-draining, and it deeply impacted all of us. Still, he was a gentle giant of a man who loved God and his family. He just had this overdeveloped work ethic and couldn't seem to stop striving in a no-win situation. I believed with my whole heart that God had a better plan than the one we were living. I've written about this story in a couple of my books. Suffice to say, I went to the mat and prayed like I'd never prayed before. *Lord, I know You want more for our family. You said that if I pray Your will, I can know that I will have that which I ask for, so I'm thanking You now, ahead of time, for moving heaven and earth if You have to, to give my husband a new job and a new perspective on his work life. Do a mighty work in our family, Lord!* I prayed morning, noon, and night. God answered that prayer beyond anything I could have hoped for. God wants wholeness, redemption, and restoration in your story. If you don't have it, this promise gives you biblical grounds for passionate and confident prayer. What are you waiting for?

LEARN   Read 1 John 5.

FLOURISH   Pray this promise with humble, bold confidence and see what God will do.

PRAY

Lord,
You are a promise-maker and a promise-keeper. I trust You! Hear my prayer today. . . .

Your Full Reward

Watch out that you do not lose what we have worked so hard to achieve. Be diligent so that you receive your full reward.

2 John 1:8

Scripture charges us time and again to guard what has been entrusted to us. John encourages us to be diligent about our faith journey so that we will receive our *full reward*. The translation above reads, "Watch out that you do not lose what *we* have worked so hard to achieve," whereas others read, "what *you* have worked so hard to achieve." This passage shows how intermingled our lives really are. You've invested in other believers and they've invested in you. What they do with what's been entrusted to them will determine their reward on Judgment Day. What you do with what's been entrusted to you will determine your reward on Judgment Day. Not only does God reward you for the investments you make in others, for acts of faith, and for prayers of intercession, He rewards you for *guarding* all that He's sown into you for His kingdom's sake. Remember the parable of the soils?* Sometimes the Word lands on shallow, distracted, or unguarded hearts and the enemy snatches it away before it has a chance to sprout. That's a loss for the kingdom, and that's on us. If the devil can't have your soul, he'll do everything he can to destroy your influence and rob you of your future reward. May your relationship with Jesus be your highest aim and top priority.

LEARN Read 2 John.

FLOURISH Spend some extra time with Jesus today. Rely on His love. Listen for His voice.

PRAY

Lord,
You want me to finish strong. Show me how to better guard that which You've entrusted to me. Amen.

*See Matthew 13.

Healthy in Body, Strong in Spirit

Dear friend, I hope all is well with you and that you are as healthy in body as you are strong in spirit.

3 John 1:2

I spoke with a woman the other day who struggled with her weight. She shared about the judgmental, self-righteous atmosphere in which she was raised. She said, "And of course the Christian's acceptable sin is gluttony, so we always ate too much, and all of the wrong things, but we were sure righteous and spotted sinners a mile away." Have mercy. This dear woman shared how her soul had shriveled under such influence. If you've read my book *Fully Alive*, you've heard me say that *what happens in our soul, happens in our cells*. We will not flourish in mind, body, and spirit if we're out of whack in even one of these areas. Thankfully, Jesus stands before us with tender eyes and a kind heart and asks, "Do you want to be well?" If we answer yes, He will lead us into truth that sets us free. True flourishing comes when we care for our health, guard our mind, and feed our spirit on the things of God. He's wired us to thrive. Some of our wholeness we'll not know until we see Jesus, but far too many Christians settle for far less than they should because they don't want to make the necessary changes. Listen for Jesus' kind voice today and do what He says. He'll teach you how to flourish.

LEARN Read 3 John.

FLOURISH Ask the Lord for wisdom, and then implement a new discipline so you can flourish.

PRAY

Lord,
I want to flourish! Give me a heart for all that's good for me! Heal me, restore me, and strengthen me! Amen.

To the One
Who Will Keep You

Now all glory to God, who is able to keep you from falling away and will bring you with great joy into his glorious presence without a single fault. All glory to him who alone is God, our Savior through Jesus Christ our Lord.

Jude 24–25

I've seen quite a number of key leaders fall out of the race over the years. Each time, I'd shiver in my bones and think, *There but for the grace of God, go I.* So unsettling. I remember a season when I experienced unreasonable fear that I'd fall down and bring dishonor to my family. I wasn't secretly living in sin. I hadn't taken a doctrinal turn. And I wasn't all of a sudden breaking any laws. But the fear? Well, it made me constantly self-aware and insecure. But then I remembered this passage from Jude and my heart came alive. I began to pray it with boldness, thanksgiving, and conviction. The more I declared this promise, the more courage rose up within me. And interestingly, significant new doors of opportunity opened up after I prevailed through that battle. The devil doesn't know our future, but he sure sees our potential. If you're walking through a similar season and you second-guess yourself at every turn, remember who you are. Shut down the enemy's taunts and hang on to God's promises. God is likely getting you ready for a new place of promise. Your God-given call is a direct threat to the enemy's plan. God's got you. He'll keep you. Stay in step with Him.

LEARN Read Jude.

FLOURISH Pray this passage several times (out loud) and allow God's power to strengthen you from within.

PRAY

Jesus,
I cling to You! Thank You for Your faithfulness to me. Amen.

Don't Be Afraid!

When I saw him, I fell at his feet as if I were dead. But he laid his right hand on me and said, "Don't be afraid! I am the First and the Last."

Revelation 1:17

*J*ohn was worshiping in the Spirit when suddenly he heard a loud voice. He turned around and *saw Jesus*. He wore a long robe and a gold sash. His head and hair were white as snow. His eyes like flames of fire. His voice thundered like the ocean. John fell down like a dead man. We would too. We've grown so accustomed to a life without signs and wonders, so used to being present at church without a sense of God's tangible presence, that we cannot imagine anything else. But if Jesus were to visit us today in all of His glory, we would be perfectly undone. While John's face was in the dirt, Jesus touched his shoulder and said, "Don't be afraid! I am the First and the Last." The word *first* translates this way: "first in rank, influence and honor. The word *last* translates: last in rank, last man, lowest, last in time or place."* Jesus is the First. It all started with Him. And it'll end with Him. He's the Last. He humbled himself to the lowest place so we could reign with Him. He's at the front of the line leading us home, and at the back of the line, protecting us every step of the way. We have nothing to fear.

LEARN Read Revelation 1.

FLOURISH Consider the high rank of our Savior. No one is higher. Consider too how low He humbled himself for you.

PRAY

Jesus,
What You did for me is absolutely breathtaking. I worship You! Amen.

*Strong's Interlinear Bible Search, StudyLight.org, Revelation 1:17.

Your First Love

"However, I have this against you: you have abandoned your first love."

Revelation 2:4 VOICE

*T*he large, established church of Ephesus got a lot of things right. They worked hard and served tirelessly. They guarded their doctrine and refused to normalize sexual sin. But they lost their pulse. God's love no longer tenderized their hearts. Their love for others waned as well. Plenty of ministries today have the same problem. They appear put together from a distance, but a closer look reveals that they're overworked and completely under-joyed. They're no longer moved by acts of God, no longer undone by a sunset, a baby's birth, or a life restored. They move so fast that they've forgotten why they do what they do. Hard work has replaced passionate, grateful worship. Dr. Warren Wiersbe writes, "The Ephesian believers were so busy maintaining their separation that they were neglecting adoration. Labor is no substitute for love; neither is purity a substitute for passion. The church must have both if it is to please Him. The church that loses its love will soon lose its light, no matter how doctrinally sound it may be."* What was the Spirit's response? Look how far you've fallen. Repent. Or you will lose your influence. Return to your First Love. We're nothing but noise without His love.†

LEARN Read Revelation 2.

FLOURISH If hard work has replaced passionate, grateful worship, if doctrine has overshadowed love, repent and reconnect with the One your soul loves.

PRAY

Lord,
I can so often lose my way. Keep me close to You. I love You, Lord.
You're everything to me. Amen.

---

*Dr. Warren Wiersbe, *The Wiersbe Bible Commentary* (Colorado Springs: David C. Cook, 2007), 1041.
†See 1 Corinthians 13.

The Dead Church

"I know all the things you do, and that you have a reputation for being alive—but you are dead. Wake up! Strengthen what little remains, for even what is left is almost dead."

Revelation 3:1–2

The church of Sardis was all show and no go. They *appeared* successful but they were dead. They no longer cared about the lost or the hurting or the broken. "The church was also told to wake up. Their wealth and comfort had lulled them to sleep. Their self-satisfaction caused them to die spiritually."* "Sardis was a church of lifeless profession. It had a reputation as a Christian assembly, but for the most part, it simply went through a formal, dull routine. It did not overflow with spiritual life. It did not sparkle with the supernatural."† It's interesting that the Spirit had nothing good to say about this church save for the small remnant of believers who kept themselves pure and alive and awake to the things of God. Most every church has a remnant of fiery believers who accomplish more from their hidden place of prayer than the world could ever know. If you're a part of a lifeless church, seek the Lord. He'll either call you to hold your ground and intercede, or He'll release you to find a life-giving body of believers.

LEARN Read Revelation 3:1–13.

FLOURISH Stay awake. Stay engaged. Seek current experiences with God. Tend to the things He cares about.

PRAY

Lord,
How easy it is to rely on past laurels and ride the wave of past experiences. I earnestly look to You today. Awaken me! Amen.

Life Application Study Bible, 2846.
†*Believer's Bible Commentary*, 2358.

The Lukewarm Church

"I know all the things you do, that you are neither hot nor cold. I wish that you were one or the other!"

Revelation 3:15

*T*hey say that anger is not the most destructive emotion in a relationship. Apathy is. I once knew a woman who "fell out of love" with her husband and children. She broke their hearts and didn't care. She didn't move out because she wanted the benefits of her husband's provision but not the responsibility of being his wife. Her husband wept bitter tears, begged and pleaded for some kind of response from her. She shrugged her shoulders and simply disengaged. The church of Laodicea had a similar problem. Self-absorbed and impotent, they simply didn't care. "By neglecting to do anything for Christ, the church had become hardened and self-satisfied, and it was destroying itself."* The worst thing about the church of Laodicea was how blind and naked they were. They were rich so they thought they were fine. They'd so blended with the world, they no longer influenced culture. Their gatherings lacked substance, power, and life-change. They shrugged their shoulders over injustice, looked away from the lost, and enjoyed their wealth and comfort. Because of their spiritual impotence, *nothing happened in the spiritual realm.* Jesus gave everything to bring us into His family. He saved us from sin and death. He wants a bride that loves Him, serves Him, and enjoys life with Him. Why *wouldn't* we respond?

LEARN Read Revelation 3:14–22.

FLOURISH Ask God if you've become lukewarm about *anything* that's important to Him.

PRAY

Father,
Ignite my heart once again! I am Yours and You are mine. Your banner over me is love. Amen.

*Life Application Study Bible, 2847.

The Throne of God

From the throne came flashes of lightning and the rumble of thunder. And in front of the throne were seven torches with burning flames. This is the sevenfold Spirit of God. In front of the throne was a shiny sea of glass, sparkling like crystal.

Revelation 4:5–6

God opened John's eyes to the heavenly realm and showed him the very throne of God. One day our eyes will behold Him and we'll be changed in an instant. We will enter into the most powerful, pure worship we've ever experienced—worship that's in motion even now. No matter how vast our imagination, we're not at all prepared for what we will one day see and experience. Still, God invites us to worship Him now, by faith, because He is greater than our minds can conceive. He who spoke the galaxies into reality without lifting a finger, delights in you. He loves you. He even likes you. Grasping His love will heal your soul. And yet some have become so chummy with God, they've forgotten about His holiness and the sheer power that emanates from His throne. Even now, today, whenever the living beings give glory and honor and thanks to the One on the throne—the One who lives forever and ever—the twenty-four elders *fall down and worship* Him. They lay their crowns before Him and say, "You are worthy to receive glory and honor and power." Seek God daily. Run to Him gladly. But always remember who it is you're speaking to when you approach His throne.

LEARN Read Revelation 4.

FLOURISH Look for some new worship music that ignites powerful, humble, heartfelt worship.

PRAY

> *God in heaven,*
> *You deserve all of the power, glory, and honor! You are God Most High! Amen.*

The Lion of Judah

"Stop weeping! Look, the Lion of the tribe of Judah, the heir to David's throne, has won the victory. He is worthy to open the scroll and its seven seals."

Revelation 5:5

*J*ohn saw a scroll that would reveal God's ultimate plan to destroy evil and to redeem those who trust in Christ Jesus. No one was worthy to open the scroll. John wept bitterly. He longed to see God's plan unfold and be put in motion. Imagine that jarring moment when the angel told John that the Lion of Judah, Jesus our Lord, was the only One worthy to open the scroll. He's the only One who left heaven and entered into humanity's plight. The only One who died our death. The only One who faced off with the devil himself and dismantled his power over us. He did all of this with a pure heart and a victorious spirit. He is King. He has no rival. And He will finish what He started. Once the seals open up, terrible judgments will be unleashed on the earth. There are varying and equally respected views on whether or not the Church will be raptured (taken up) when all of this takes place. But one thing we know for sure: God's purposes will prevail. No one and nothing can snatch us out of His hand. What we suffer now is nothing compared to the glory that awaits us at the culmination of time. Our Lion roars a holy roar and He is coming for His Church.

LEARN Read Revelation 5.

FLOURISH Live ready for Jesus' soon return. Your faith may cost you. But God will redeem it all.

PRAY

Lion of Judah,
*   Help me to live ready for Your soon return. My soul waits for You.*
Amen.

They Overcame

"And they have defeated him by the blood of the Lamb
   and by their testimony.
And they did not love their lives so much
   that they were afraid to die."

Revelation 12:11

*J*esus intends for us to overcome because He overcame. The blood of Jesus forgives and cleanses us and secures our eternity for us. The word of our testimony activates the spiritual realm and adds momentum to the kingdom story God is writing on the earth today. The *blood* saves us. Our *testimony* activates us. And when we *love* Jesus more than our very lives, when we see our eternity as so precious that we'd give our earthly lives in whatever way He asks of us, there's nothing that the enemy can do to us. We render him powerless. We become overcomers. It's fear that keeps us under his thumb. It's self-preservation and love of comfort that render us powerless against him. But when we truly see that we are more spiritual than physical, more found than lost, more equipped than vulnerable, we will dare to follow Jesus wherever He leads us. Amazingly, if you ask persecuted Christians how you might pray for them, you'll never hear them say, "Pray for an easier life. Pray I can move to a safer country." They say, "Pray I will have the courage to endure for the cause of Christ." You may not have to die for your faith, but Jesus may ask you to stand up in a way that costs you. And He does ask us to *pray regularly* for our persecuted brothers and sisters.

LEARN ▶ Read Revelation 12.

FLOURISH ▶ Add the persecuted church to your regular prayer list.

PRAY ▶

Father,
   Awaken courage and boldness within me! I will overcome when I fully trust You! Amen.

The Great Divide
Has Already Begun

"Fear God," he shouted. "Give glory to him. For the time has come when he will sit as judge. Worship him who made the heavens, the earth, the sea, and all the springs of water."

Revelation 14:7

During the great tribulation, the enemy will seem to have free rein. God will give him authority to unleash evil for forty-two months. Sinfulness will abound. People will blaspheme our precious Lord in the most abhorrent of ways. Godly Christians will suffer. Those who love the world and reject God will be easily deceived when they see how the Beast's fatal head wound miraculously heals. God charges His own to endure persecution patiently and to remain faithful. Because suddenly, there will be a turn of the tide. John saw a vision of the Lamb standing on Mount Zion with the 144,000 who bear the Lord's name on their foreheads. *Sounds from heaven* will *thunder over the earth*. A great choir will sing a *new* song before the throne of God. John witnessed a glassy sea mixed with fire. Seven plagues will be unleashed upon the earth. This will bring to completion God's wrath against wickedness. Even now, the earth is shaking, and the divide is evident between those who fear God and those who revile Him. God is purifying His Bride, getting her ready for that great day. Know that every past trial has trained you to stand in this day as we speed toward that day.

LEARN Read Revelation 14.

FLOURISH Rid your life of needless distractions. Pursue God earnestly. Love Him wholeheartedly.

PRAY

Father,
I fear I'm not strong enough to stand in such days, but I know You are good and care deeply for me. Fill me with conviction, courage, and clarity. Amen.

No Middle Ground

"Who will not fear you, Lord,
   and glorify your name?
   For you alone are holy.
All nations will come and worship before you,
   for your righteous deeds have been revealed."

Revelation 15:4

*I*n another vision, John saw that the temple in heaven was thrown wide open. The seven angels who were holding the seven plagues came out of the temple. They wore white, spotless linen with gold sashes across their chests. They were given authority to pour out God's final wrath on the earth. The temple was filled with smoke from God's glory and power. No one could enter the temple until the seven angels had completed pouring out the seven plagues. "The fact that no one can enter the temple till these seven plagues are completed may mean that no priestly intercession can now delay God's wrath."* Throughout history, God has made sure that anyone who truly wants to know Him will find Him. During the great tribulation, there will be no middle ground. All people will be marked, either with the Lord's name or with the mark of the Beast. Some will sacrifice all to follow Jesus. Others will sacrifice nothing and lose everything. God's been patient with mankind. He wants none to perish. Ultimately, everyone will get what they choose: life forever with Christ, or life forever without Him. Things may get worse before they get better for us as Christians. But a *glorious eternity* awaits us.

LEARN   Read Revelation 15.

FLOURISH   Send your roots down into the soil of God's marvelous love. You're totally secure in Him.

PRAY

Jesus,
   Be glorified in my life. I need You every hour. Amen.

Believer's Bible Commentary, 2373.

King of All Kings

On his robe at his thigh was written this title: King of all kings and Lord of all lords.

Revelation 19:16

*J*esus stepped off His throne and entered our world by crawling into the womb of a teenage girl. He was born into poverty. Lived a humble life. He subjected himself to our trials, our temptations, and our troubles. He stayed out of the public eye but grew up under God's watchful eye. He first entered public ministry by going into the waters of baptism. Baptism was for sinners who longed to be forgiven and cleansed. He never sinned, yet in every way, entered into our plight with us. He put up with relentless harassment and disrespect. He didn't back down from religious bullies. He willingly associated with the lowliest of sinners. He noticed the ones the rest of the world missed. He died a criminal's death. It *appeared* as though the world shook Him like a ragdoll when He bled out on that cross. Yet in all of it, He was still God, still King, still the Savior of the world. People had and they still have varying opinions about who He was, who He is. But a day is coming . . . He will ride His white horse with fire in His eyes and many crowns on His head. Everyone both dead and alive will ultimately acknowledge Him as King of the world. *Holy, holy, holy is the Lord Almighty, who was and is and is to come!*

LEARN Read Revelation 19.

FLOURISH Spend some extra time in the gospels and acquaint yourself afresh with Jesus' heart.

PRAY

Jesus,
 You stayed the course, all the way to the cross, all for love. You deserve my highest praise and my heartfelt worship. I love You, Lord. Amen.

The Books Will Open

I saw the dead, both great and small, standing before God's throne. And the books were opened, including the Book of Life. And the dead were judged according to what they had done, as recorded in the books.

Revelation 20:12

Over the centuries, people have held God to a double standard. They've blamed Him for the evil in the world *and* have dismissed Him for having a wrathful side. People want a passive, gooey God that allows them to do anything they want. And they want a God that deals with anyone and everyone who would dare infringe upon their idea of what life should look like. God's ways are far higher than our ways. He is a God of love and a God of justice. His involvement is purposeful and His timing, meticulous. And He keeps good records. The pedophile who rejected Christ will have more hell to pay than the guy who cheated on his taxes. Just as there are levels of reward in heaven, there are levels of punishment in hell.* Those who have decided to live their life the way they want will face the great white throne of judgment. They'll face God's wrath with no one to advocate for them. Eternal punishment awaits them. Christians will go before the judgment seat. God's forgiven our sin, but He's recorded our deeds, not for punishment but for reward. No one is exempt from Judgment Day. Don't waste a minute of your life. Steward your gifts with passion and purpose. God cares deeply about what you do and why you do it.

LEARN Read Revelation 20.

FLOURISH Think eternity. Today. Tomorrow. And the next day.

PRAY

Lord,
I want every minute of my life to count for You! Draw me closer still!
Amen.

*See Matthew 11:20–24.

The New Jerusalem

And I saw the holy city, the new Jerusalem, coming down from God out of heaven like a bride beautifully dressed for her husband.

Revelation 21:2

After God deals a final death blow to the enemy of our souls, we'll behold the holy city, the new Jerusalem, as it descends from heaven, dressed like a glorious bride prepared for her husband. "The new Jerusalem is where God lives among His people. Instead of our going up to meet Him, He comes down to be with us, just as God became man in Jesus Christ and lived among us (John 1:14). Wherever God reigns, there is peace, security, and love."* In his vision, John witnessed the rise of Satan, the suffering of the saints, the wrath of God. Finally, he gets to see God's glorious plan for His people. God himself will wipe away every tear from our eyes. There'll be no more death or sorrow or crying or pain. Gone *forever*. God will make all things new. *Brand new*. We will drink freely from the springs of life. Every ounce of us will be satisfied. Our joy, uncontainable. Our hearts, healed. We'll experience a sensory explosion. We'll inhale scents that take our breath away. We cannot fathom the beautiful future that awaits us. But we can look forward to it with great expectation. God does not lie. Jesus is getting ready, preparing a place for us. Heaven awaits us.

LEARN Read Revelation 21.

FLOURISH Look forward to heaven. Jesus is right now preparing a place for you.

PRAY

Jesus,
I know that when I see You, I'll be undone. Thank You for preparing a place for me. You have my heart forever. Amen.

*Life Application Study Bible, 2881.

Jesus Is Coming Soon

"Look, I am coming soon, bringing my reward with me to repay all people according to their deeds. I am the Alpha and the Omega, the First and the Last, the Beginning and the End."

Revelation 22:12–13

*H*e put the galaxies in place. Told the land where to stop and the water where to begin. Created birds to fly and fish to swim. He instituted the dawn of each new day. He loves His creation. He especially loves us, for we bear His image. The Bible is God's grand love story to a sinful, wayward, broken people. All of the Old Testament points to the coming of the Messiah, our Savior. All of the New Testament testifies to His life, His death, and His resurrection. Jesus teaches us how to live, how to love. God's love story culminates with this epic declaration: *I am coming soon.* Here's the beautiful truth: *You* are a part of this supernatural story. The living, breathing Word of God has a way of sinking deep into your soul and transforming your life. God's plans for you are found in the pages of His Book. We've walked through the Bible together and it's quite clear: God wants an intimate, thriving relationship with you. His Spirit is alive in you. So steward your story well. Love people but keep your hope in God. Keep your faith alive. Keep your heart engaged. Live for the One who gave it all for you. The King is coming again.

LEARN   Read Revelation 22.

FLOURISH   Live for Jesus like He's coming back tomorrow.

PRAY

King of Kings,
   Help me live as one who is spoken for. Give me boldness, courage, conviction, and love. Work miracles in and through me. I'll be waiting for You. Amen.

Acknowledgments

To my husband, Kev . . .
Thank you for your patient, persistent encouragement.
Without you, I may very well have wrapped this
book up in Leviticus! Love you, honey.

To my Facebook friends and intercessors . . .
Thank you for praying for me when my arms got tired.
I'm forever grateful for your encouragement and intercession!

To Andy McGuire and Jeff Braun and the whole Bethany House team . . .
I just love you! I'm honored by and grateful
for our friendship. Appreciate you so much.

To my sons, daughters-in-law, and grandchildren . . .
You are my heart, more than you'll ever know. You bear God's image
and you bear our name. May you always live loved,
because that's what you are. And may God's Word be life
and breath to you every moment of every day.

To Jesus . . .
I was too big of a sissy to take on such a project. Yet You lovingly
invited me to try, and patiently endured as I struggled and persevered.
What an absolute honor it is to belong to You and to partner with You,
especially when You call us to attempt the impossible. I'll love You forever.

Susie Larson is a popular talk radio host, national speaker, and author of sixteen books. Susie has twice been voted a top-ten finalist for the John C. Maxwell Transformational Leadership Award. This award recognizes people who go beyond themselves to make a positive impact in the lives of others. Some of her previous books include *Fully Alive, Your Beautiful Purpose, Your Powerful Prayers, Your Sacred Yes, Blessings for the Morning, Growing Grateful Kids*, and *The Uncommon Woman*. Susie has been married to her dear husband, Kevin, since 1985, and together they have three wonderful sons, three beautiful daughters-in-law, two precious grandchildren, and one adorable pit bull named Memphis. Susie's passion is to see people everywhere awakened to the value of their soul, the depth of God's love, and the height of their calling in Christ Jesus.

More from Susie Larson!

Visit susielarson.com for more information.

In this eye-opening book, Susie Larson shows how intertwined our emotional, spiritual, and physical health is. For true healing to occur, it must happen holistically—mind, body, and spirit. Providing a fresh vision of what a flourishing life is, Susie shares practical, biblical ways to walk the path of healing and wholeness in every area of life.

Fully Alive

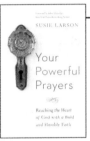

Through personal stories and biblical insights, Susie Larson shares the secrets to effective prayer in this warm and wise book. You'll be amazed at what your prayers can do when you combine reverence, expectation, and a tenacious hold on God's promises. Discover how to pray specifically and persistently with faith and joy!

Your Powerful Prayers

It's so easy to give away our time to things not appointed by God. In this practical and liberating book, Susie invites you to say *no* to over commitment and *yes* to the life of joy, passion, and significance God has for you.

Your Sacred Yes

You May Also Like . . .

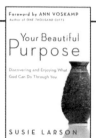

Respond today to that nudge in your spirit—that desire to use your gifts and passions more fully in God's work—and discover God's beautiful purpose for your life.

Your Beautiful Purpose

Give Jesus your worries and obligations, and let Him nourish your heart, comfort your soul, and show you wisdom from His Word. This collection of blessings abounds with inspiring Scriptures and exquisite floral artwork, and will be treasured by anyone seeking peace and encouragement.

Blessings for the Soul

Start and end each day with an uplifting reminder of God's promises, love, and purpose for you. Instead of focusing on your worries and concerns, replace them with these daily doses of encouragement rooted in God's Word.

Blessings for the Morning and Evening

BETHANYHOUSE